"This book is invigorating, sometimes infuriating, always interesting, often moving, and consistently well informed—not a surprise given the author's background but a huge bonus for literary readers when Groves discusses psychoanalysis. It is a surprise as well as a bonus when he discusses not just *Hamlet* but also its critical tradition, including the textual arguments: he's far better informed than you would expect, better informed than most professional Shakespeareans. This book will focus and refocus people's thinking about the play on the psychological aspects of its characters, so central to its greatness, and which have been so neglected in recent sociological and historicizing criticism. Groves brings Shakespeare back to the psychological terrain which is his home, to the advantage of playwright and analyst alike. The writing is wonderful, full at once of style, brio, wit, and earnestness, a tough combo to pull off. Groves has learned much from his psychoanalytic heroes about caring for the experience of his interlocutor—in this case his readers—including their central experience of coming to understand. There's a lot to learn from this superb book; superb not least in the way it skillfully conveys its insights."

—**William Flesch**, *Professor of English and Comparative Literature, Brandeis University*

"In *Hamlet on the Couch*, James E. Groves succeeds at something unique and remarkable. He approaches Shakespeare and Freud as equal partners in the construction and understanding of human psychological life. Traditionally analysts have 'applied' psychoanalytic ideas and methods to the *Hamlet* play, approaching it as if it were a dream to be interpreted, whose hidden unconscious truths are revealed behind Shakespeare's symbols and complex rhetoric. But Groves eschews a one-sided application, as he seeks an interpretive balance, using Shakespeare as much to understand Freud as vice versa. For Groves, Shakespeare is not some accidental Freudian, a naïve genius who stumbled on truths to be explained later by Freud and his followers. On the contrary, Shakespeare is shown to be a peerless psychoanalyst, and Groves demonstrates how a close reading of *Hamlet* (on Shakespeare's own terms, albeit enriched by Freud) reveals insights of which even Freud was only dimly aware. It is one of the great joys of Groves' book that, rather than using Freud to better understand Shakespeare, he uses Shakespeare's art to better understand Freud's creativity and science. I can think of no better demonstration of the fruitful partnership of psychoanalysis and the arts."

—**George Hagman**, *Psychoanalyst and author of* The Artist's Mind: Creativity, Modern Art, and Modern Artists *(Routledge, 2010); Faculty, Westchester Center for the Study of Psychoanalysis and Psychotherapy; Faculty, Training and Research Institute for Intersubjective Self Psychology*

"*Hamlet on the Couch* reminds us how deeply satisfying it is to be in the hands of a literate, wise, and seasoned observer of human nature. Groves creates something dazzling in his synthesis of the works of two geniuses. Freudian psychology and Shakespearean storytelling are marvels to behold, but Groves shows us how each illuminates the other, so that the resulting whole is much richer than the sum of these iconic parts. This is an invigorating read that leaves us marveling at the complexity and timelessness of human experience."

—**Robert J. Waldinger**, *Professor of Psychiatry, Harvard Medical School, and psychoanalyst, Boston Psychoanalytic Society and Institute*

HAMLET ON THE COUCH

Hamlet on the Couch weaves a close reading of Shakespeare's *Hamlet* with a large variety of contemporary psychoanalytic and psychological theory, looking at the interplay of ideas between the two.

Hamlet can be read almost as a psychoanalytic case study and be used to understand and illustrate a range of core psychoanalytic concepts. Covering such basic psychoanalytic concepts as identity, transference and countertransference, the 'good-enough' mother, the compulsion to repeat and the death instinct, James E. Groves shows how *Hamlet* can shed new light on understanding psychoanalytic theory, and how psychoanalysis can in turn enrich our understanding of Shakespeare's work. Perhaps the most radical feature of psychoanalysis is its tradition of self-examination. Mirroring it, the book throughout uses an eclectic, subjective critical approach to study how the poetry of *Hamlet* creates its realistically flawed and believably complex characters.

Combining deep, insightful knowledge of Shakespeare and of psychoanalysis, *Hamlet on the Couch* will be of great interest to psychoanalysts and psychoanalytic psychotherapists, as well as literary scholars.

James E. Groves, MD, is a psychiatrist at Massachusetts General Hospital and Harvard Medical School. He practices psychotherapy, supervises psychiatry and psychology trainees on their psychodynamic cases, and offers tutorials in Literature and Psychiatry.

HAMLET ON THE COUCH

What Shakespeare Taught Freud

James E. Groves

Routledge
Taylor & Francis Group
LONDON AND NEW YORK

First published 2018
by Routledge
2 Park Square, Milton Park, Abingdon, Oxon OX14 4RN

and by Routledge
711 Third Avenue, New York, NY 10017

Routledge is an imprint of the Taylor & Francis Group, an informa business

British Library Cataloguing in Publication Data
A catalogue record for this book is available from the British Library

Library of Congress Cataloging in Publication Data
Names: Groves, James E., author.
Title: Hamlet on the couch : what Shakespeare taught Freud / James E. Groves.
Description: London ; New York: Routlege, 2017. | Includes bibliographical references and index. | Includes filmography.
Identifiers: LCCN 2017028741 (print) | LCCN 2017038700 (ebook) |
ISBN 9781315150055 (Master) | ISBN 9781351368698 (Web PDF) |
ISBN 9781351368681 (ePub) | ISBN 9781351368674 (Mobipocket/Kindle) |
ISBN 9781138556270
(hardback : alk. paper) | ISBN 9781138556294 (pbk. : alk. paper)
Subjects: LCSH: Shakespeare, William, 1564–1616. Hamlet. | Psychology and literature. | Psychotherapy and literature.
Classification: LCC PR2807 (ebook) | LCC PR2807 .G78 2017 (print) |
DDC 822.3/3 – dc23
LC record available at https://lccn.loc.gov/2017028741

ISBN: 978-1-138-55627-0 (hbk)
ISBN: 978-1-138-55629-4 (pbk)
ISBN: 978-1-315-15005-5 (ebk)

Typeset in Bembo and Stone Sans
by Florence Production Ltd, Stoodleigh, Devon, UK

CONTENTS

ACKNOWLEDGMENTS

First of all to Alyce Faye Eichelberger Cleese, MS, DPMC, thanks for vociferously promoting ShakespeareReadsFreud.com and co-teaching *Psychoanalyzing Hamlet.* Likewise to John B. Herman, MD, who supported the project as cultural pulse taker and helped make the book readable. William Flesch, PhD, was an early and enthusiastic critic. John M. Sansone, JD, MBA, provided late editorial rescue of the manuscript and tolerated with fine humor rejection of many of his suggestions. My yoga co-author Marlynn Wei, MD, JD, leveraged our other project to help save this one.

Daniel Debowy, MD, PhD, co-taught the Core Seminars; David Grelotti, MD, Brian Schulman, MD, and Cristina Cusin, MD, were mainstays of the electives, and Davin Quinn, MD, Daniel Zimmerman, MD, and Margot Phillips, MD, offered early criticism. Margaret Cramer, PhD, was a tireless advocate and supporter. John Denninger, MD, PhD, was indispensible for his knowledge of evolutionary psychology and philosophy of mind. Tristan Gorrindo, MD, gave advice on technology, the Internet, and virtual worlds. Robert Waldinger, MD, Martha Stark, MD, and Mark Goldblatt, MD, provided tutelage in psychoanalytic theory. Mark A. Blais, PsyD, scored the MGH Personality Disorders instruments for "patient H.P.D." and provided unique insight into the personality disorders.

Ms. Martha Stone and the Treadwell Library amassed hundreds of books and papers; and the Freud Museums in London and Vienna gave help on Freud's personal library.

Dr. Ramon Alonso and the late Anne Alonso, PhD, took care of me after a near-fatal 1991 taxicab wreck, and Anne, of course, lives on in our hearts, still mentoring and teaching. Jerrold F. Rosenbaum, MD, kept us afloat through that decade. Donald S. Gair, MD, Gary Owen Todd, JD, Muriel Florent, PhD, Jennifer Snyder, JD, Dan H. Buie, MD, Ms. Alyce Mann, and Richard Sylva, JD, kept us together and functioning.

Voices now stilled echo through this project: Ruben A. Brower, Master of Adams House, taught me the New Criticism. Professors Roger W. Brown and Albert Gilman, Harvard Psychology and Boston University English, inspired me through the 1980s with their love of Shakespeare. Leon Eisenberg, MD, Thomas P. Hackett, MD, Ned Cassem, MD, SJ, and George B. Murray, MD, SJ, ably steered MGH Psychiatry through the straits of change, circa 1970–2000.

Michael Jenike, MD, John A. Parrish, MD, and Jeffrey Gelfand, MD, were warriors in several battles. Mr. Tyler Robinson at pcimpressions.com kept four computers running remotely and flew in from Idaho once, for support. While everyone else slept, Mrs. Elaine Robinson patiently organized and catalogued more than a thousand chapters and papers for the book, after Mr. Peter Scrivanos spent months delving the stacks of Widener Library digging them out.

My brilliant cheerleader at Harvard, Maria Ascher, PhD, provided wisdom and renewable hope through every step of the process, along with kindness when it mattered most.

Nearer home, Frank V. Interrante handled questions of design, art, and aesthetics and rendered a thousand thousand kindnesses. Annette L. Robinson organized us through the years, making life possible. And John Daniel Groves provided daily ad hoc editing and was, of course, the reason for doing this book in the first place.

PROLOGUE

When he was 9 years old Sigmund Freud began to read Shakespeare in English. It became a passion that continued the rest of his life; *Hamlet* was his favorite and he mentions it dozens of times in his works. For him the play opened a window into the unconscious, exposing the foundations of psychoanalysis. It's no exaggeration to say *Hamlet* is the principal literary precursor of what became Freud's theories of human psychology and behavior. What Shakespeare illustrated through narrative drama and character development, Freud described as the underlying dynamics of human motivation. This book is about how Freud uncovered in *Hamlet* the heart of what became psychoanalysis.

It's also about how to approach the play itself through close reading and know it at a more intimate level than you imagined. Take Hamlet and the inevitable skull:

> Alas, poor Yorick—I knew him, Horatio: A fellow of infinite jest, of most excellent fancy. He hath borne me on his back a thousand times—and now how abhorred in my imagination it is, my gorge rises at it. Here hung those lips that I have kissed I know not how oft. Where be your jibes now. . . . your flashes of merriment that were wont to set the table on a roar? Not one now to mock your own grinning? . . . Get you to my lady's chamber and tell her: Let her paint an inch thick, to this favor she must come. Make her laugh at that.
>
> *V.i.184* TLN 3372–3382

Unlike some royals in Shakespeare, Hamlet has no jester, certainly not Horatio, and Yorick is some 20 years dead. Hamlet is his own jester. Looking into the vacant sockets, he jests at the jester, mirroring his insults—and affection. He recalls playing piggy-back and kissing him. We see their daily life, the little prince and an adult in the household, their routine. We learn the lonely little boy had Yorick all to himself in the jester's off hours. Hamlet grown resembles him as much as he does old King Hamlet. It's no coincidence he spends a third of the play in his "antic disposition." Here's also Hamlet's pervasive misogyny. Who is Milady that Yorick is sent to mock? Who's painting her face an inch thick with makeup, his mother Gertrude going off to a ball? Ophelia, that chaste flower he accuses of being a whore? Hamlet's image of any female is subtly distorted. Here's "transference" pure and simple, an axial concept in psychoanalysis, one of Freud's best ideas. Not only is the image of a parent transferred from the past to present, but also ego defenses. The coping mechanisms the child used in the past to deal with the parent distort the present. This elusive concept, its effects both good and bad, was something Shakespeare intuited well before Freud: Hamlet with the skull of Yorick is using mockery to defend himself against pain, a mysterious sadness connected with women.

William Shakespeare is often called the world's greatest psychologist, so this, his most iconic and psychological play, ought to be perfect for understanding psychoanalysis. Fifty years before Freud, poet and scholar Samuel Taylor Coleridge coined the term "psycho-analytic" in connection with Shakespeare's dramatic characters. The early nineteenth century critic William Hazlitt discerned in the works of Shakespeare the presence of durable personality types, mixed motivations, ego defenses, overdetermination, and unconscious conflicts—much of the equipage of psychoanalysis, though he didn't call them by those names.

Since this book is about how psychoanalysis and *Hamlet* dramatize each other, it might be good to imagine yourself as the director of a performance. As director or actor, you would have scores of dramatic possibilities and dozens of interpretive decisions. Why does Hamlet hesitate—or does he? How can the Ghost's cry for revenge emanate from a Christian Purgatory? Why can't Gertrude see the Ghost in her closet when Hamlet can? How is she able to describe Ophelia's drowning when she wasn't there? It's possible to bring psychoanalytic theory to these questions, but we can find answers in the play itself. Prompted by Freud we ask, how does "transference" work? What is "narcissism" and is it always bad? Does Hamlet have an Oedipus complex? Did Gertrude neglect the infant Hamlet? And what do Hamlet's soliloquies tell us about *conscience*, a word he uses to mean both consciousness and moral scruples?

Books on psychology and literature mostly develop their main idea in chapters marching direct to a conclusion. The argument here meanders along the narrative arc of *Hamlet*. A plot directed synthesis of playable readings from *all three conflicting texts* of the play solves many problems of critical interpretation debated for centuries. Tracking the play, Freud's ideas are foreshadowed and unfold scene by scene, linking Shakespeare's craft to the unconscious transformative machinery of the psychoanalytic relationship. Though Freud no longer holds a preeminent place in modern psychology, psychoanalysis resonates with an instinctive truth, for all its ambiguity and subjectivity. What can't be denied is the continuing hold of analytic theory on our collective consciousness as a frame for viewing and understanding the human drama, much as Hamlet provides a deathless archetype of humanity readily understood by all who encounter him. Most of what you need to know about psychoanalysis you can get from *Hamlet.*

Many feel Freud has no place in modern psychiatry, but psychoanalysis is a milestone in the history of ideas. Rarely today is there intensive treatment of the recumbent patient on the traditional analytic couch. But as a philosophy of mind, psychoanalysis is all around us; it's become a school of popular criticism and cultural history so pervasive we barely notice it. One of the more distinctive contributions of psychoanalysis is its reinterpretation of classical traditions of skepticism. The history of psychoanalysis is the history of an art that yearned to be a science. Freud's detractors say it's full of neurotic analysts, tribal feuds, boundary violations, shameful secrets, quasi-religious fundamentalism, and intransigent scientific claims. Freud himself bequeathed many of these problems. Yet from the beginning, psychoanalysis tried to understand its own flaws and grapple with its own narcissism.

Perhaps the most radical feature of psychoanalysis is its tradition of self examination. Throughout the book, mirroring it, we use an eclectic subjective critical approach to study how the poetry of *Hamlet* creates its realistically flawed and believably complex characters. Particularly the analyst's study of countertransference—the barely glimpsed and initially disowned emotional reaction to the patient—is a thing *sui generis*, a brave and self skeptical fact checking unlike anything else in medicine. Backed by this tradition of facing its own darkness, psychoanalysis is now less a therapy than a conceptual thread running unbroken through the humanities. It endures as one of the dominant modes of social explanation of our day. You may love Shakespeare and revere Freud—generations have—but this book is equally for the person who's hated productions of Shakespeare or had an unsuccessful psychotherapy. It's about reading *Hamlet* with Freud—and reading Freud with *Hamlet*—to understand human nature.

1

WHO'S THERE?

A Question of Identity

It all begins in the dark. On the guard platform at Elsinore it is windy and cold. As the bell tolling midnight fades, Barnardo comes on duty. "Who's there?" he cries, but he's the one challenged: "Nay. Stand and unfold yourself." Confused—then sheepish—Barnardo gives the watchword, "Long live the King." The departing soldier greets Marcellus and Horatio who've come to hold the watch and look for "this thing" that has disturbed sentries two nights running.

T.S. Eliot called *Hamlet* an "artistic failure" but still thought the opening scene the finest in all drama. Jumpy sentinels, the changing of the guard. Footsteps. "Who's there?" From the first line it asks what's true, what's *there*? Horatio is a philosopher, a seeker of truth, but he's trusted by the military men, who address him by name several times. He's embarrassed he's come. They believe a figure resembling King Hamlet has appeared, silently walking up and down. "Tush, tush," Horatio scoffs.

Enter the Ghost. Horatio flings up his arms, "What art thou that usurp'st this time of night?" Just as suddenly it turns and leaves. Shaking, Horatio wonders whether—because the late king's image is in armor—this portends something for Denmark. Horatio's name is a Latin pun—*h* plus *oratio*—and unlike the soldiers, Horatio has Latin. Demons must be addressed in the language of scholars. He lectures his anxious friends, recalling Rome and Julius Caesar, and another throne usurped. Again, Horatio mentions usurpation. Again, he's interrupted.

Horatio But soft—behold. Lo—where it comes again.
I'll cross it* though it blast me: Stay, Illusion!
If thou hast any sound or use of voice,
Speak to me. If there be any good thing to be done . . .
Speak to me.

I.i.126 TLN 126–130

* head it off

Horatio spreads his arms, perhaps warding off the Ghost. Or he might be begging it not to leave. *Stay, Illusion*! The apparition lifts its head to speak but dawn is coming, the cock crows, and the figure slinks away. Pagan notions of the supernatural now blend with the narrative of Christianity. The men's thoughts turn to Advent, and Horatio is skeptical. *I do in part believe it.* But he has an intuition, *the Illusion will speak to Hamlet.*

Time stands still. A few dozen lines are spoken between "midnight" and "dawn," yet for the audience hours pass. A world is created whose version of time is the one we accept. Characters are differentiated in two dozen lines, all with such economy we feel this is real. The scene ends with Horatio's character established, a renaissance man living the examined life. *Hamlet* is set in medieval Denmark, not the English Renaissance, but Shakespeare delights in anachronism. He was "wonderfully careless on matters of time and space."[1]

Something is rotten in Denmark—and, indeed, had been in England until around the time of Shakespeare's birth. Elizabeth Tudor was not only religious herself but a brilliant practical theologian. The reign of her half sister, Mary, had reestablished Catholicism with a vengeance, and scores of heretics were burnt. But Queen Elizabeth prevented religious war with an ingenious strategy. Although she didn't believe in such doctrines as Purgatory, she still allowed some rituals of the Church of Rome. To the dismay of Puritans, she removed from the Prayer Book passages offensive to Catholics, earning their grudging support. Her policy has been ironically summed up as, "Believe what you want—but pray from this book!" She allowed freedom of conscience within limits permitted by a sometimes treasonous Counter-Reformation.[2]

For Shakespeare's audience royal England in the sixteenth century was about the legitimacy of the crown. History had taught that usurpation always lurks somewhere in the background. The culmination of the Tudor era was Elizabeth's long and peaceable reign (1558–1603). Because of the lack of male heirs that plagued the Tudors, the succession was problematic, and inconvenient pretenders were beheaded. Audiences would know about Lady Jane Grey and Mary Stuart, Queen of the Scots. Early performances of *Hamlet* overlapped another "public entertainment," the ongoing treason and eventual execution of the Earl of Essex in 1601. These events may have enhanced the play's popularity and accelerated publication of the First Quarto of *Hamlet* in 1603, which appears to have been pirated and rushed into print.[3]

Elizabeth Tudor was among the most educated people of her time, and one of the most capable rulers England ever had. Her choice of advisors was almost flawless. She prevented religious war by her own religious tolerance. With financier Thomas Gresham and First Secretary Sir William Cecil, she had purified the coinage of its brass (it had been repeatedly debased by her father, Henry VIII), stopped inflation, and brought her realm into unrivalled prosperity. Her thrift and dislike of bloodshed had spared the country from the rest of Europe's continual religious wars. When Elizabeth did at last fight, against the Armada, she crushed Spain and became the most respected prince in Europe. She never married of course—except, as she said, to her kingdom and her own people. And she cannily refused to name a successor. So while they were watching *Hamlet*, those early audiences, the question was, who will succeed? Who's there? The play is full of questions. Scholars tote up the times the word *question* is used (seventeen, more than any other play) or the number of question marks (seventy in the Graveyard scene). This seems odd but the contest of true and false beliefs running through *Hamlet* is a prime source of suspense and a major preoccupation of its hero.[4]

Truth is what psychoanalysis is about too. What's out there in the dark, dangerous and indistinct? Is it behind us? Or inside? We might call psychoanalysis *applied epistemology*. Historically where psychoanalysis couldn't effect a cure, it could at least question itself: *What do we know and how do we know we know it*? Freud toward the end of his life became more pessimistic—or realistic—and he called psychoanalysis one of those "impossible professions" like teaching, in which one can always be sure of disappointing results.

All of us are epistemologists, always deciding "is" versus "seems," judgments so automatic we forget survival depends on them. Freud read Darwin with the aim of making the truth of psychoanalysis jibe with the truth of natural selection. But there's a paradox: Perfectly truthful information can endanger survival if it's disconnected from emotion. It would be easier if we only had to know facts, but there's a trade off between raw data and emotionally processed meanings. Emotion evolved to sit in the middle of the brain, exaggerating one thing, minimizing another, diluting the heady liquor of concentrated fact. The intricate patterning of the social emotions shows that control of shame, guilt, anxiety, and vengefulness is crucial for survival, and it's done through emotional distortion. Especially key to survival is accepting paradox and bearing uncertainty, which depends on self deception. And that is what in fact Hamlet is doing when we first meet him—fooling himself.

What diagnostic use do we make of Hamlet's peevish behavior in the Council scene? Is his true nature exposed, or is his off putting behavior a defense, a regression?

In council, Claudius, the new Danish king, holds up a demand letter from Fortinbras, nephew to the Norwegian king: Prince Fortinbras, taking advantage of his old uncle's infirmity, is raising an army in the far reaches of Norway to take back disputed territory between them. Claudius cleverly dispatches an ambassador to Old Norway reporting Fortinbras's secret treasonous army. Then he turns to Laertes, son of chief minister Polonius, whose counsel he lavishly praises. Likewise fulsomely, he grants Laertes's request to return to France.

Claudius now turns to Hamlet. But the heir apparent is downcast, in deep mourning. Claudius chides him, saying his "son" is beclouded. The Prince parries with a brilliant multilayered pun: He's "*too much* in the sun," adroitly deflecting "son" and undermining Claudius's claim as stepfather. The Queen nips in to placate Hamlet.

Gertrude Good Hamlet,
. . . let thine eye look like a friend on Denmark.

	Do not forever with thy veiled lids
	Seek for thy noble father in the dust:
	Thou know'st 'tis common, all that lives must die,
	Passing through nature to eternity.
Hamlet	Aye, Madam, it is "common."
Gertrude	If it be, why seems it so particular with thee?
Hamlet	Seems, Madam, nay it is. I know not "seems."
	'Tis not alone my inky cloak, good Mother . . .
	No, nor the fruitful river in the eye
	Together with all forms, moods, shows of grief
	That can denote me truly. These indeed *seem*
	For they are actions that a man might play.
	But I have that within which passes show,
	These, but the trappings and the suits of woe.

I.ii.68 TLN 248–267

Gertrude is an intelligent, complex woman. Her problem is that she must balance a relationship with her new husband, the demands of a state threatened by invasion, and her job as exemplar of breeding and manners. These she must maintain during a sudden and very public tantrum of her adult son.[5]

"All that lives must die/ Passing through nature to eternity" is as fine as any poetry in the play, and Gertrude spends it wisely. She knows the difference between being and seeming, as maternal figure for the whole empire. And her tactic works, she draws Hamlet's fire, engages his intellect, and—very important—she lets him win. Once Hamlet's into his lecture, his anger starts to cool and undergoes sublimation into poetry. He ends with intellectual defenses shored up and his ego neatly tied up, like the rhyming couplet that caps off the speech. Claudius, with smarmy solicitude, chides Hamlet to drop this "unmanly grief" and abruptly turns to the court to proclaim Hamlet his chosen heir. In a quick aside, he forbids the Prince's return to school in Wittenberg. Gertrude seconds this as a mother's plea. Flanked, Hamlet hangs back as the court sweeps out to a loud, drunken celebration.

Of the early scenes, this seems to give directors and actors the greatest latitude for interpretation—and error. In available *Hamlet* films there are corrections that beg to be made: This is a plenary council, not a wedding, the queen is not in white, there is no confetti. This is not the private quarters of the royal family, there is no lolling, sauntering, or pacing. Hamlet does not weep, here or anywhere in the play (with two possible exceptions and, if then, only continently). Hamlet wouldn't sit in the King's presence if he had broken legs; he will respect the throne in case he ever wears the crown and always keep the courtly high ground; he never turns his back to the King. Hamlet doesn't have an antic disposition yet, he hasn't seen the Ghost, he doesn't cackle, giggle, or shout. He may imply disrespect with puns of sufficient subtlety ("Too much in the sun") but anything over the line must be an aside ("More than kin and less than kind"). No one knows etiquette—

or English—better than Hamlet. He always addresses Claudius and Gertrude with the formal pronoun.[6]

And the conversation between Hamlet and Gertrude is private. Openly asking him to "look like a friend on Denmark" would publicly acknowledge the family fracture. Claudius's reproach about dead fathers is between him and Hamlet. Some productions have all this out in the open, but this scene is a mix of public announcements, two-person whispers, three-person *sotto voce* conversations, and private thoughts muttered under one's breath. Such errors obscure the point of the scene. Hamlet is fighting to know the truth about himself and, simultaneously, trying to disown it.

Freud's "dual instinct theory" positing libido and aggression as prime human motivators suffered from the limitations that always occur when concrete metaphors fail to capture the complexity of real life. Worse, Freud's "pleasure principle" lacks traction in the clinical setting: It's the masochistic departures from direct pleasure seeking that are interesting.[7]

But it is his closely observed clinical papers that are most fascinating. Freud disliked a certain self-deceiving personality type, one who knows the truth of what happened but avoids facing the moral weakness it engenders. In "The 'Exceptions' " he depicts individuals with a deformation of character rooted in real suffering—earlier loss, accident, illness—something in their past he calls a *circumstance of congenital disadvantage* that leaves them with a characteristic stance toward the world, an attitude of entitlement.

> Their neuroses were connected with some experience or suffering to which they had been subjected in their earliest childhood, one in respect of which they knew themselves to be guiltless, and which they could look upon as an unjust disadvantage imposed upon them. The privileges that they claimed as a result of this injustice, and the rebelliousness it engendered [make them refuse to] submit to a necessity which applies to everyone. "Nature has done me a grievous wrong. . . . Life owes me reparation for this, and I will see that I get it. I have a right to be an exception, to disregard the scruples by which others let themselves be held back."[8]

Life owes me. This is what psychiatry calls "narcissistic personality disorder," people who are selfish, grandiose, ruthless, unempathic, and aggrieved. There's a distinctive flavor to the Exceptions. They seem to disgust Freud. They dwell on how unfair the world is and how unjustly they've been treated, yet they're unfair to those they exploit. And under their thick skin, entitled narcissists have the most sensitive nerves where shame is concerned. That's why Gertrude lets Hamlet win the argument, to salve his raw self-esteem.

Is Hamlet one of Freud's Exceptions? Though entitled, they're clever, focused, determined, creative, persuasive, and successful. Suppose we ask whether Hamlet's fighting for psychological survival. We avoid the issue of which behaviors are more pathological and which are less but ask only how effective any feature is for coping. We could call "narcissistic" any psychic operation that acts to preserve the integrity of the self image: *Narcissistic ego defenses protect the coherence, temporal stability, and positive emotional coloration of the picture of the self.* Each of us needs a solid mental image, one that's resistant to fragmentation under stress. It must be durable and consistent over time. And it should reflect back a positive picture of the self under most conditions. This is health as much as it is "narcissism."[9]

But does Hamlet have pathological "entitlement"? He's petulant, insensitive, grandiose, and petty. There's a righteous tone with "seems, Madam," beyond normal adolescence. How do we understand our feelings? Hamlet's self-pity undermines our sympathies and will do so even more in Soliloquy 1. Our wary visceral response makes us wonder whether he's trading on a long ago "circumstance of congenital disadvantage." Or is he asking for justice? Certainly, as a prince he has legitimate claims, but they seem remote, he seems to have gone backwards. Perhaps what we see isn't his best self. In the nineteenth century William Hazlitt wrote,

> The character of Hamlet stands quite by itself. It is not a character marked by strength of will or even of passion, but by refinement of thought and sentiment. . . . He seems incapable of deliberate action, and is only hurried into extremities on the spur of the occasion, when he has no time to reflect. . . . Shakespeare was thoroughly a master of the mixed motives of human character [so he] has been accused of inconsistency in this and other characters, only because he has kept up the distinction which there is in nature, between the understandings and the moral habits of men, between the absurdity of their ideas and the absurdity of their motives.[10]

Mixed motives. Hazlitt spots dead-on the gap between the thinking of human beings and their behaviors, between surface rationalizations and hidden desires. These run as deep in Hamlet as in any of us, reflecting *the distinction which there is in nature.* Hamlet is inconsistent like us, that is why we love him. Hazlitt, like a psychoanalyst, is talking about rationalization of behaviors and unconscious conflicts—about the dynamic unconscious—a century before Freud.

On September 21, 1897, Freud writes a confession to his great friend Wilhelm Fliess. He admits he cannot distinguish which of the patient's free associations are *facts* and which are *inventions* of the patient's unconscious. He had discovered mistakes in his "trauma theory" of hysteria, he had been wrong to connect hysteria to molestation—usually by the father—because there was so much hysteria and little evidence of incest, which would have to be "immeasurably more frequent" than was realistic. Also, there was the "discovery that there are no indications of reality in the unconscious, so that one cannot distinguish between the truth and fiction" of events that are emotionally charged, so that "sexual phantasy invariably seizes upon the theme of the parents." The emotion invested in the parent makes the patient take the incestuous wish as a real fact—so we can't count on "the unconscious being completely tamed by the conscious."[11]

The unconscious can lie without the conscious knowing it. The epistemological burden is heavier than Freud thought. For the question, *What do we know about the mind and how do we know it*? Freud found the answer harder than he thought. And for the question, *How can we be sure*? Freud was forced to conclude regarding the unconscious, we can never be certain. And it's our shifting uncertainty about Hamlet's unconscious that makes him so human.

The play's begun, posing questions of illusion and identity. Hamlet is forbidden to go back to school lest he foment treason against a king the court has elected. Claudius is king by a process similar to acclimation—legitimate no matter how the throne came vacant. And several times through the play Hamlet's speeches show he expected to succeed his father. He mentions the election twice, not objecting to the process, it's the order of succession he resents. And the haste.

Freud held that it's pleasure that drives us, that the pleasure of libido is the payoff for helping the species survive. But a moment's reflection on the historical fact of masses of soldiers charging from the safety of cover into certain death tells us that *meaning* is the most important force driving us, stronger than direct pleasure from libido, stronger than a fear of death. Seeking honor and avoiding shame are enough to die for.

Hamlet O that this too too solid flesh would melt,
Thaw and resolve itself into a dew,
Or that the Everlasting had not fixed
His canon 'gainst self-slaughter. O God, God!
How weary, stale, flat, and unprofitable
Seem to me all the uses of this world.
Fie on't, ah fie, 'tis an unweeded garden
That grows to seed. . . . That it should come to this!
But two months dead, nay not so much, not two —
Why she would hang on him
As if increase of appetite had grown
By what it fed on and yet within a month —
Frailty, thy name is woman!—a little month,
why she. . . . married with my uncle. Within a month
Ere yet the salt of most unrighteous tears
Had left the flushing of her galled eyes
She married. O most wicked speed to post*
With such dexterity to incestuous sheets!
It is not, nor it cannot come to good —
But break my heart—for I *must* hold my tongue.

I.ii.129 TLN 313–343

* gallop

Hamlet is—and is not—"suicidal," it's *both and*, not *either or.* He'd "rather be dead" than feel the shame, but there's no possibility. Surrender and righteous indignation can alternate, but they can't coexist. His shame is deep and poisonous, and he's self-treating it by finding "reasons." Over the speech Hamlet collapses the interval between the death and the wedding from a month to weeks. In Tudor times, a month might elapse between a sovereign's death and the state funeral—and some time later, the coronation. But Shakespeare's audience wouldn't question the timing of the death, funeral, marriage, and accession. They would be focused on Hamlet's being skipped over. The play reflects a moment as complex as any in English history, the question of rightful succession. England is holding its breath, awaiting the passing of the old Queen. And that's where the play begins: *Who's there*?

The procession in which Gertrude followed King Hamlet's body, was it to the funeral or the interment? Hamlet says he saw his father laid in his crypt. The wedding came after the funeral, but how long could it take for the news to travel to Wittenberg? Even if Polonius engineered a delay, how could Hamlet's return take enough time to allow Claudius to court and marry Gertrude? To allow Polonius to lobby the nobility on Claudius's behalf? He must have arrived in Elsinore later. The chronology is always just out of reach, but audiences are never troubled—the play unfolds so naturally with suspense from every direction that we don't notice.

The soliloquy is hard to play right. When the reading's even a bit off, we see Hamlet as whiny. And if he's weak the audience sides with Claudius. The challenge is, how to be princely without arrogance, heroic without bombast. But Shakespeare has written into the character sufficient intelligence, insight, irony—and heart—to make this a very interior performance. Look at films of the speech by Burton, Hawke, Olivier, and Williamson. In Olivier's film, the scene is shot in tight close up, the speech in voice-over with an occasional spoken outburst—*nay not so much, not two*! Sometimes Hamlet talks inside his own head, sometimes out loud. *Frailty, thy name is woman*! Sometimes he just mutters.

Different directors and actors, but the words are the same. Kline, Doran, Brook, and Bennett all have imagined a Hamlet on the edge of hysteria—or over the line. Zeffirelli has cut half the speech and avoids the difficulty of getting a convincing reading from Mel Gibson of the near-impossible "break my heart" couplet at the end. Branagh is more contained but still not as persuasive as Burton, Williamson, and Hawke. These three are understated, poetry does the work and despair builds. Burton and Hawke do the speech without external contact and, exactly opposite, Williamson does it maintaining eye contact with the audience. He gives a completely natural reading of "It . . . cannot come to good/ So break my heart" as he bites the lines like a terrier killing a rat and then—very intimately to the audience confides through clenched teeth—"I *must* hold my tongue." Hamlet comes across as a late adolescent and, as with many patients early in treatment, it's not possible to know exactly what's going on. He reminds us of the Exceptions but he's actually entitled, not so-called "entitled." He could be the rightful king.

What's the attitude he gives off? Do we suspect Freud's *circumstance of congenital disadvantage*? He's clearly suffering, but he doesn't make demands on it. Despite cringing at his self-pity, we feel for him if the soliloquy is done right. We don't have the nausea toward him Freud seems to feel for his Exceptions. If Hamlet were a patient, these reactions would be *countertransference*, musings going on in the therapist's head. Shakespeare had this ability to write lines playable in numerous contradictory ways. They can be read to mean almost anything. And, the more you know your patient—in some ways—the less certain you are at various points in treatment. At times in the middle of it, you're completely in the dark.[12]

Freud said, "Everywhere I go I find a poet has been there before me." That would be Shakespeare. When he read and reread *Hamlet*, it gave him a mental laboratory for his studies of human nature. But more, it offered him a pre-existing plot line about mental causation already three centuries old, a foundation concept, taken for granted by the audience he hoped to persuade: *The clash of contending forces in the dynamic unconscious explains much of the self defeating inconsistency we see in human behavior.* The index to the *Standard Edition* lists thirty-four entries for *Hamlet*, exceeded only by the Bible and *Faust*. Freud loved the play but it scared him. He was grateful for authors he found comfortable, like a good friend, but towering works of art like *Hamlet* elicited "timid reverence, the feeling of one's own smallness."[13]

Discussion of the Shakespearean subtext of psychoanalysis begins almost with the birth of Freudian theories, finding its most extended arguments in the work of Harold Bloom. He says Shakespeare invented our modern concept of the human, in his portrayal of interiority, our individuated sense of a personal self. It's as if Shakespeare had foreknowledge, in some sense, of later Freudian theory. Two of Bloom's ideas, "the anxiety of influence" and "the invention of the human", depend on his way of thinking backwards. In both, Bloom creates a whole new idea by reversing cause and effect. He noticed something new about *influence*, the "misreading" of one writer by another. He then intuited that every strong poet had to misread her predecessor poet (or had to "commit poetic misprision" in his terms) in order to become mentally free to create a distinctive style. So we'll be on the lookout for whether Freud committed literary "misprision," whether he misread *Hamlet* and ended up creating something original of his own.[14]

Bloom famously called Hamlet "Freud's mentor." He implies for them a kind of reverse influence, a kind of preparation: Shakespeare so well understood psychology that his poems and plays prepared modern culture to see it. Psychoanalysis is sometimes called the subtext of literature, but it's the other way around: Literature is the unconscious of psychoanalysis. What psychoanalysis owes to Shakespeare is what the world owes both Shakespeare and Freud. Hamlet and *Hamlet* constitute a template without which we couldn't see the world as clearly (and darkly) as we do. Freud revises and updates that referent.[15]

Facing the Ghost, Horatio calls out, "Stay, Illusion!" Does he bid it to stop approaching—or to not leave? This ambivalent rejection and holding on is like clinging to illusion even when we suspect it's not real ("denial"). The opposite is "repression." In a later scene comes the Vicious Mole of Nature speech, on responsibility and evil character, a condensed complete version of Hamlet's philosophy of determinism versus free will. This is what psychotherapists do every day, wonder with the patient what one is responsible for, what can one actually change?

Shakespeare and Freud are embedded in western civilization, icons like the skull of Yorick or Freud's cigar. Reminders of *Hamlet* and Freud reflect the merger of psychoanalysis as a philosophy of mind with the humanities' treasure house of culture. Even if you know it, imagine you never read Soliloquy 4. Try to hear the speech new, as if it were the first time.

> To be or not to be? That is the question:
> Whether 'tis nobler in the mind to suffer
> The slings and arrows of outrageous fortune
> Or to take arms against a sea of troubles
> And, by opposing, end them. To die, to sleep —
> No more—and by a sleep to say we end
> The heartache and the thousand natural shocks
> That flesh is heir to? 'Tis a consummation
> Devoutly to be wished: To die, to sleep —
> To sleep perchance to dream. . . .
>
> *III.i.55* TLN 1709–1719[16]

Around this speech burns a debate consuming forests of paper: Is Hamlet "suicidal," does he *want* to kill himself—*could* he kill himself? Absolutely not, say partisans in one camp (Bloom, most recently), he's just meditating on death itself. Well, say others (Bradley, most conspicuously), he *says* he is—just as in Soliloquy 1—and now he's formulating how he would do it. What more evidence do we need? Let the text speak to you.

Consider *flesh.* Flesh lives, flesh dies. Flesh sleeps, flesh wishes. Flesh (or the soul therein) dreams. Flesh has heartache, it is not just a mental thing (as surely your own body knows). It hurts from a thousand natural shocks. Life battles death; body and soul clash on the battleground of the flesh, *Death, where is thy sting? Hell, where is thy victory?* And look at the idea of *mind*: The mind suffers, as well as the flesh. Mind appreciates honor, it has to decide, it must consider either this *or* that. Mind knows what a dangerous thing a *question* is, what a weapon, like slings and arrows. Mind is prayerful, it wishes devoutly. Behind this soliloquy you hear echoes of Saint Paul writing to the people of Corinth, you see Homer's seas and spears and battles in your mind's eye.

So—mind and body, spirit and flesh—is he suicidal or not? You probably see where this argument is headed—to be or not to be? Based on the complexity and natural contradictions that make these lines impossible to pin down, it must be that both are true at the same time, both the thing and its opposite. Given the deceptive transparency of the language, all its contradictions suggest Hamlet is both contemplating suicide *and* determined to live. Suicidal or not? The answer is *both and*—not *either or.*

But can an individual actor or director have it both ways? If you get the chance, watch this speech in several video clips. Most of them do choose one interpretation or the other. Try to look at the performance of Ethan Hawke under the direction of Almereyda, of Laurence Olivier, of Gibson directed by Zeffirelli, of Kenneth Branagh, of Kevin Kline, and of Williamson directed by Richardson. Each is brilliant in its way. Versions run from insane intensity (Gibson), to world-weary irony (Hawke), from indecipherable grief (Kline, tears running down his cheeks, why we don't know) to dry-eyed realism (Branagh). And there is Williamson's flirtatious Hamlet, holding intimate eye contact, seducing the audience.

To illustrate *both and* versus *either or*, look at Richard Burton directed by John Gielgud (a great Hamlet himself hundreds of times). Actor and director struggled over whether Burton would have eye contact with the audience, his choice, or soliloquize to himself alone, which Gielgud insisted on. Perhaps it has to do with the actor-director conflict, but this particular version captures Hamlet's interior debate. Perhaps Burton's constant fight to keep himself from making eye contact with the audience ballasts it, perhaps Burton's tendency to mostly be Burton and allow his character only a little say in it makes this version watchable ten, twenty, thirty times. You don't habituate. It's different every time. This is a specimen performance of Shakespeare's ability to write lines that say one thing and its opposite simultaneously. It is the apotheosis of negative capability in the hands of Burton and Gielgud.[17]

How can a truth and its opposite coexist in a poem? We get help from Keats in a letter in which he defines Shakespeare as having the greatest *negative capability* of any poet. This is hard, Negative Capability; it refers to Shakespeare's capacity to contain so many conflicting ideas, yet hold them harmoniously—a term Keats coins just for this attribute. He was a great poet himself, and when he wrote to his brothers, he knew as a consumptive that he had not long to live. Keats of course made it forever impossible to forget that truth is beauty. But the opposite of a truth in art is not ugly. The thing and its opposite are *both* true *and* both beautiful. This is the dual nature of the unconscious, and it needs explaining—especially since it's here that Freud and Shakespeare have much in common. Each of them owned unsurpassed familiarity with this unseen. Each had an uncanny sense of what it's like on the dark side of the moon.

Shakespeare is to the written word what Newton was to physics, so why shouldn't he also have laws named after him? *If there's one perfect way to say something, Shakespeare will have found it.* We could call this The First Law of Shakespeare. It might be useful when we analyze "O that this too too solid flesh would melt." The Second Law might be *Any problem in Shakespeare's text or dramaturgy can ultimately be traced to a universal problem of humankind.* This enabling fiction holds that problems in the poetry exist because they mirror problems in us. This could be helpful when we use *Hamlet* to fathom self-defeating behaviors arising from conflict in the dynamic unconscious and when we study symptom formation.

And for understanding the unconscious that Shakespeare and Freud both knew so well, we could discover a Third Law: *Whatever is a Truth in Shakespeare will be found to have an opposite—and that opposite will also be true.* This finds its proof in great art and letters, as well as philosophy. Freud had his own version even if sometimes he chose not to see a particular truth. He used several examples to show the unconscious doesn't have the word *no* in its vocabulary. This is easily refuted, he's able to find "no" in the unconscious when he needs it. Perhaps it's just his figure of speech, but whatever is true in a dream, its opposite is also true. Whatever is wished in a dream is also unwished. If the unconscious seems unable to say *no* it's because it's also saying *yes*. The study of the deep structures of "yes" and "no" is a good way to discover the psychotic nature of the unconscious. There, any wish or any fear may glimpse its twin in the dark mirror.

Freud said that in creating *Hamlet* (the play) the unconscious of Shakespeare well understood the unconscious of Hamlet (the man). But he sounds a little smug, and we have reason to believe Shakespeare had an unconscious at least as spacious as Freud's. We also have to wonder whether his view of Shakespeare's unconscious is anxiously influenced. Is Freud inventing psychoanalysis by misreading Shakespeare? For instance, does Hamlet have "an Oedipus complex"? If he doesn't, might this be an example of anxious influence on Freud's part?

Freud deserves credit for sharing with Shakespeare a fully developed negative capability: *A masochist is also at the same time a sadist*, he said. And, *The goal of all life is death*. But why did Freud say there was no "no" in the unconscious? It can't be strictly true that the unconscious can only depict "yes." It's certainly not true for my patients: The night after a day trying to decide whether to kill yourself, *You dream that your dead father comes to you at sundown, talking and gesturing. He points to the horizon in the east, nods. He points to the horizon in the west, shakes his head emphatically*. This is clear, your father's saying, *Do not go toward the sunset*. But what misled Freud? He says the unconscious is only attracted to something, not repelled; he says that "in analysis we never discover a 'no' in the unconscious and that recognition of the unconscious on the part of the ego is expressed in a negative formula." He means it's up to the ego to defensively translate "yes" into "no."[18]

Which goes to show that genius is original, catalytic—and often wrong. Approach and avoidance are hard wired into the deepest level of the organism, humans all the way to protozoa. There must be avoidance as well as approach deep in the mind. So what is it that threw Freud off? Later when we look at the *Dora* case, we see deeper into how Freud's mind works. One thing that becomes clearer as Dora's analysis progresses is how determined Freud is to win—he crows in triumph time after time when she says, "No," something isn't true, and then he finds out it is and compels her to admit it. As the case goes on, he won't take no for an answer. Perhaps his seeing only "yes" in the unconscious started here, in his determination to break Dora's will, to make her say *yes* to him whenever she tried to say *no*.[19]

But you can never know reality. Truth hides behind illusion. This is embodied in Freud's concept of *screen memories*: Recollections from the past may "screen" other more conflicted memories. Memories of events occurring from about age three to eight are often remembered as sharp, isolated dreamlike vignettes, usually of quite mundane occurrences. *Why would I remember such a trivial thing*? we think. The content is ordinary, the memory is vivid. These images turn out to reveal, in coded form, the content of even earlier deeper buried material. They can be decrypted the same as dreams. In fact, patients in recalling the screen memory often make the slip of calling it "a dream—I mean, the memory." Freud tended to see dreams and screen memories as unidirectional concealment. But the information also wants to be remembered, to come out. The "screen" is a two-way filter. Dreams work to conceal conflicted forbidden wishes, but they also yearn to speak forth and symbolically gratify those wishes through narrative.[20]

Slips, screen memories, jokes, dreams, and symptoms all conceal and reveal information. But information actually endangers survival when it's disconnected from meaning. There's a trade off between raw factual data and usefully processed meanings. And there's emotion sitting in the middle of all this machinery, exaggerating one thing, minimizing another. It seems one of the functions of emotion is to smooth the edges of facts to make them fit better the mosaic of mental processes. Routine affective distortions serve adaptation and promote survival.[21]

Human beings form false ideas about themselves and others—but not randomly—there are standard, patterned biases in perception and information processing that evolved because they were adaptive. If we already believe a proposition to be so, we're more likely to notice data confirming the proposition. These preprogrammed errors suggest that, while natural selection is capable of making us better truth and fact detectors, it's chosen not to. Nature has built in several types of error on purpose. Overestimating one's value in many circumstances is more adaptive than realistic self-appraisal. In other circumstances, a falsely devalued self-image may provide an adaptive advantage, retreating and living to fight another day.

What we call "meaning" is this emotional commitment to the ideas we hold: Altruism and honor, God and country, tribe and family. This emotional investment is inextricable from our use of symbols. Symbols gather meanings together, but meanings also generate symbols. The importance of symbol formation can't be overstated. It may be the most characteristic of all human capacities, the infrastructure of art and language. For Freud, symbols and meanings were always intertwined and mutually enriching. His oedipal theory of Hamlet's "hesitation," as first told to Fliess, relies on a symbolic conversion of Hamlet's rivalry with King Hamlet into its opposite. Hamlet as hysteric first appears here, and incestuous impulses are not distinctly seen but only indirectly revealed by the inhibitions they cause.[22]

Psychoanalysis is in part the process of creating the self through storytelling. And through deep listening. Freud instructed beginning psychoanalysts on how to listen. His technique was the "evenly hovering attention" of the analyst, and it mirrored what was going on in the patient's free associations. To give a bit of the flavor of this intuitive process, consider a textual question from Soliloquy 1: Does Hamlet want his *solid* flesh to melt, or his *sullied* flesh? This *solid* versus *sullied* is a big deal in Shakespeare studies. Until the twentieth century, everyone accepted the First Folio text's "O that this too too solid flesh would melt/ Thaw and resolve itself into a dew." But after a letter to the *Times* by John Dover Wilson, there came another candidate, *sullied*. Astonishingly *sullied* came out of nowhere; there was no textual support for it at all. Just on the strength of Wilson's reputation and impassioned arguments, *sullied* flashed into vogue. And for decades now in academia, the almost unanimous choice is *sullied*. In performance it's still always *solid*.

To free associate to it, a major idea in this speech is *undoing*—Hamlet rejects the fleshy bond between his mother and Claudius. Perhaps by vicarious shame his own flesh repels him. So *sullied* makes some sense. But it seems more visceral than that: Hamlet wants to excoriate his flesh, not just give it a bath. Shame makes you feel dirty, yes—but a more primal aspect is that shame makes you want to disappear, to *melt*. It's a very dense matrix of meaningful poetic relationships if *solid* is the word. If there's one perfect way to say something, Shakespeare will have found it. Had Shakespeare preferred *sullied*, there ought to be more internal evidence in the poetry. What does *sullied* have to do with thawing and melting and evaporating and re-condensing into a dew? With transformations from solids to liquids to vapors? Nothing. But *solid* does. So don't let experts do your thinking for you.[23]

You may not be convinced that close analysis of disputed texts is practice for thinking psychoanalytically, but perhaps you can accept that Freud's skills were honed reading *Hamlet*. Today the optimal training of an analytic therapist is still a subject of debate. In its heyday, therapy was taught by weekly one-on-one supervision of the new therapist, working alone with the patient and taking responsibility. From the beginning, psychoanalysis understood you can't teach experience—you can only experience experience—so a senior analyst went over detailed notes of sessions with the trainee, criticizing therapeutic technique and interpreting transference problems in the doctor-patient relationship.

Also, psychoanalytic therapy was taught by observed clinical experience. A class of trainees and a teacher, all behind a one-way mirror, watched a senior therapist doing therapy with a patient. After the session, the patient was excused and the therapist, the observing teacher behind the mirror, and the class all came together to critique the process. What happened over and over was the sharp disagreement of observers viewing the same thing at the same time. Trainees eventually came to realize that "reality" on one side of the mirror was different from "reality" on the other. In psychotherapy *the reality is in the experience.* Again and again the class, the teacher, and the therapist would disagree what had "actually happened" in the session. It's this type of paradox that makes us ready to embrace the *both and* rather than the *either or.*

Whenever a new patient comes to my office and sits down for the first time, I ask, *How can I help, what is it you come for?* Whatever the answer—and I have heard hundreds—under it is a deeper answer: *I want to be loved, I am here looking for a way to be lovable, I need your help on love.* It's not just a good feeling in the body, love, or a good thought in the brain, it's the glue that holds the self together. *I need you to help me find my real self,* the patient's saying, *help me find my loveable true self.*

> I have of late, but wherefore* I know not, lost all my mirth, forgone all custom of exercise and, indeed, it goes so heavily with my disposition that this goodly frame the earth seems to me a sterile promontory, this most excellent canopy, the air—look you—this brave o'erhanging firmament, this majestical roof fretted with golden fire—why, it appears no other thing to me than a foul and pestilent congregation of vapors.
>
> *II.ii.292* TLN 1342–1350
>
> * why

Some think Hamlet is gulling the schoolfellows with disinformation on his true state. (They point to the inconsistency between his not exercising here and later when he tells Horatio he's been fencing every day.) But if he's deceiving Rosencrantz and Guildenstern, it's to test them by being utterly truthful: He seems both to hate the world and his life in it *and* to love it and relish living. Hamlet's multitudinous personal identity is intact, and he knows who he is—in the moment. When we come to look at *transference* and *narcissism* the idea of individual identity will never be far from the investigation. Many indicators of mental illness and health hinge on the presence or absence of distinctive personal selfhood. The play embodies two contrasting modes—the medieval self, seen in speeches of Polonius, and early modern concepts of selfhood, seen in Hamlet's soliloquies. Both *selfs* have characteristic voices and each has its own rules, but to become a true self, the ego has to tolerate the *both and* rather than forced choice *either or*.[24]

Bloom says Shakespeare invented the modern personality by creating characters that grow and change, not just with respect to God and their fellows, but also with respect to themselves. He finds passages in which Shakespeare's people find their identity by listening to what they themselves say. Such characters become human by eavesdropping on their own speeches. They become human by dint of "overhearing" themselves, by psychoanalyzing themselves. As a proposition we'll develop later, the character of Hamlet proves the power of the imagination to narrate the self into existence.

Questions of reality in psychoanalysis revolve around *transference*. Projection of past experience onto the present distorts what we think we know right now. It's a defense and a resistance in therapy, but it's also an ego function trying to bring back the past. Transference is shaped by many factors in the individual personality and development that we'll approach from several directions. And in the next chapter, we continue with the almost inseparable concept of narcissism, which will engage us because of its popping up in almost every scene of *Hamlet*.

Notes

1. Harold Bloom, *Hamlet: Poem Unlimited* (New York: Riverhead Books, 2003).
2. David Starkey, *Elizabeth: The Struggle for the Throne* (New York: HarperCollins, 2001). J.E. Neale, *Queen Elizabeth* (New York: Harcourt, Brace and Company, 1934).
3. James Shapiro, *A Year in the Life of William Shakespeare: 1599* (New York: HarperCollins Publishers, 2005).

4. Harry Levin, *The Question of Hamlet* (New York: Viking Press, 1959).
5. Carolyn Heilbrun, "The Character of Hamlet's Mother," *Shakespeare Quarterly* 8 (1957): 201–206.
6. Roger Brown and Albert Gilman, "The Pronouns of Power and Solidarity," in Roger Brown, *Psycholinguistics: Selected Papers* (New York: The Free Press, 1960/1970), 302–335. Grammatical rules reflect and shape power and belonging. A psycholinguist and a Shakespeare scholar track the intimate pronoun across centuries and several languages, including Elizabethan English.
7. Allan D. Rosenblatt and James T. Thickstun, "Energy, Information, and Motivation: A Revision of Psychoanalytic Theory," *Journal of the American Psychoanalytic Association* 25 (1977): 537–558.
8. Sigmund Freud, "The 'Exceptions'," in *The Standard Edition of the Complete Psychological Works of Sigmund Freud*, vol. 14, James Strachey, Ed. and trans. (London: The Hogarth Press, 1916/1957), 311–315.
9. Robert D. Stolorow, "Psychosexuality and the Representational World," *International Journal of Psycho-Analysis* 60 (1979): 39–45.
10. William Hazlitt, "Hamlet," *Characters of Shakespeare's Plays* (1817; reprint, New York: Chelsea House, 1983), 73–81.
11. Sigmund Freud, "Letter 69, to Wilhelm Fliess, 21 September 1897," in *The Standard Edition of the Complete Psychological Works of Sigmund Freud*, vol. 1, James Strachey, Ed. and trans. (London: The Hogarth Press, 1966), 259–260.
12. Strictly speaking, all transference, even countertransference, is unconscious. But through linguistic drift, subjective responses to the patient have all come to be called countertransference.
13. Sigmund Freud, "Contribution to a Questionnaire on Reading," in *The Standard Edition of the Complete Psychological Works of Sigmund Freud*, vol. 9, James Strachey, Ed. and trans. (London: The Hogarth Press, 1907/1959), 245–247.
14. Harold Bloom, *Shakespeare: The Invention of the Human* (New York: Riverhead Books, 1998).
    Harold Bloom, *The Anxiety of Influence: A Theory of Poetry*, ed. 2 (New York: Oxford University Press, 1973/1997).
15. Shoshana Felman, "The Case of Poe: Applications/Implications of Psychoanalysis," in *Essential Papers on Psychoanalysis and Literature*, Emanuel Berman, ed. (New York: New York University Press, 1987/1993), 300–322.
16. The punctuation here follows George Bernard Shaw in a review of *Hamlet* in *The Saturday Review* of December 18, 1897:

    > Mr. Forbes Robertson, his lightness of heart all gone, wandered into another play at the words *Sleep? No more!* which he delivered as "Sleep no more." Fortunately, before he could add "Macbeth does murder sleep," he relapsed into Hamlet and saved the situation.

    For Shaw, "Tis a consummation devoutly to be wished" is the answer to the question, "To die, to sleep?" And by extension, "To be or not to be?" needs a question mark.
17. Richard L. Sterne, *John Gielgud Directs Richard Burton in Hamlet: A Journal of Rehearsals* (New York: Random House, 1967).
18. Sigmund Freud, "Negation," in *The Standard Edition of the Complete Psychological Works of Sigmund Freud*, vol. 24, James Strachey, Ed. and trans. (London: The Hogarth Press, 1925/1961), 235–239.
19. Sigmund Freud, "Fragment of an Analysis of a Case of Hysteria," in *The Standard Edition of the Complete Psychological Works of Sigmund Freud*, vol. 7, James Strachey, Ed. and trans. (London: The Hogarth Press, 1905/1953), 18–122.
20. Alvin Frank, "History and Screen Memories," *International Journal of Psycho-Analysis* 65 (1984): 85–88.
21. Malcolm Owen Slavin and Daniel Kriegman, *The Adaptive Design of the Human Psyche: Psychoanalysis, Evolutionary Biology, and the Therapeutic Process* (New York: Guilford Press, 1992).

22. Sigmund Freud, "Letter 71, to Wilhelm Fliess, 15 October 1897," in *The Standard Edition of the Complete Psychological Works of Sigmund Freud*, vol. 1, James Strachey, Ed. and trans. (London: The Hogarth Press, 1966), 265–266.
23. John Dover Wilson, "Letter to the Editor," *Times Literary Supplement*, July 25, 1918 p. 349, cols. b, c.
    Quentin Skinner and Christopher Ricks, "Up for Interpretation *or* What Is This Thing that Hearsay Is Not?" *Literary Imagination* 14 (2012): 125–142.
    But once you've read Dover Wilson's argument, it's impossible to hear "too, too solid" without also hearing "too, too sullied."
24. Judith H. Anderson, *The Growth of a Personal Voice: Piers Ploughman and The Faerie Queen* (New Haven: Yale University Press, 1976).

2

THE GHOST'S COMMANDMENT

Revenge My Shame

Enter the Ghost. It may be "a spirit of health or goblin damned." Hamlet doesn't know whether it brings "airs from heaven or blasts from hell." But it does bring shame and a lust for revenge. Emotion emanates as a signal carrying social information to motivate those receiving it. "Mark me," the Ghost says, and displays the six "primary negative emotions," *rage*, *sadness*, *fear*, *shame*, *disgust*, and *contempt*. In addition, the Ghost displays vengefulness and jealousy, which are basic emotions mixed with desires, beliefs, and intentions. Emotions and their facial expression are human universals, innate, hard wired, and similar from culture to culture.[1]

Picture a man in the grip of shame. He averts his eyes. His face pulls away from his accuser. He flushes. He drops his head; his mouth pulls down at the corners. He seems to shrink, he turns pale. Then picture someone filled with contempt. He stands tall, he cocks his head back, looks down his nose; he stares out from under half lowered lids and purses his lips. He turns his head a bit away from the object of scorn. One of his nostrils dilates (the nostril closer to the target of contempt) and his upper lip on that side curls up, exposing a single canine tooth.[2]

Contempt is shame projected outward; the two faces mirror blame and apology. If you made images of their expressions and shopped them around the world to various tribes and ethnic groups, they would elicit in the native languages the local names of the two emotions. From the remotest hunter gatherers to the most highly industrialized modern cultures, these are identifiable as shame and contempt, essences of the Ghost.

Breaking free of his friends, Hamlet pursues the Ghost. The Ghost tells him the hour is approaching when it must return to the flames of the afterlife to burn away its earthly sins. It claims to be the spirit of his father and, if Hamlet loved him, he must "Revenge his foul and most unnatural murder." His father did not die, the Ghost says, from being bitten by a serpent in his orchard as had been given out.

Ghost But know, thou noble youth,
The serpent that did sting thy father's life
Now wears his crown.
Hamlet O my prophetic soul! Mine uncle?
Ghost Aye, that incestuous, that adulterate beast
With witchcraft of his wits . . . won to his shameful lust
The will of my most seeming-virtuous Queen.
O Hamlet, what a falling off was there
From me . . . to decline
Upon a wretch whose natural gifts were poor
To those of mine.

I.v.138 TLN 725–739

It's the hasty happy marriage of Claudius and Gertrude more than anything that suggests adultery. If any would know, the Ghost should, if it is in fact the old king's spirit. The interest in her current sexual life is creepy, and you wonder whether it's spying on the newlyweds. The term "adulterate beast" means lustful; Shakespeare uses *adulterate* as an adjective six times and it means "filthy," but for those wanting to see Gertrude as unfaithful, this is a quibble.

The Ghost radiates hatred. It affirms Hamlet's loathing for his uncle and adds murder to the list. Tellingly, it's repelled by its very self, a *sine qua non* of shame. The Ghost's speech moves from fear to contempt, from contempt to shame, and from shame to self pity.

Ghost Brief let me be: Sleeping within my orchard
Upon my secure hour thy uncle stole
With juice of cursed Hebona in a vial
And in the porches of my ears did pour
The leprous distilment whose effect
Holds such an enmity with blood of man
That swift as quicksilver it courses through the body
And with a sudden vigor it doth . . . curdle
The thin and wholesome blood. So did it mine,
And a most instant tetter barked about
Most lazar-like with vile and loathsome crust
All my smooth body.

I.v.59 TLN 744–758

By now the audience has completely suspended disbelief. Nobody notices the utter medical impossibility of poisoning a healthy sleeping man through his ears. But Hamlet's horrified reaction brings the audience in. The serpent has come into Eden, a garden gone rank and disgusting. He pictures his father's blood curdling and skin oozing and flaking like leprosy and scaling like tree bark. "O horrible, O horrible. Most horrible." What is rotten in the state of Denmark is the crown.

The Ghost orders Hamlet to avenge the family honor (leaving the means unclear) and, in so doing, issues a fateful command concerning the Queen.

Ghost But howsoever thou pursues this act
Taint not thy mind nor let thy soul contrive
Against thy mother aught. Leave her to heaven
And to those thorns that in her bosom lodge
To prick and sting her.

I.v.84 TLN 769–773

Eden corrupted, gone to seed: The dying king covered with bark, like the trees in his orchard; the faithless queen growing brambles in her own breast, heaven's punishment fitting her crime, *prick* meaning penis, then as now. Out of this decay the Ghost gives the order *Leave her to heaven.* Is this Christian forgiveness and proof that the Ghost is Hamlet's father? If so, can it still be demonic? (Problems in the plot of *Hamlet* caused by the implication of a Catholic Purgatory will preoccupy us later.)[3]

The devil can quote scripture too, as Hamlet remembers. The speech is ambiguous, but Hamlet interprets it according to his needs. As the play unfolds from this point, he begins to veer away from the Ghost's actual words. As he becomes more obsessed with his mother's sexuality, Hamlet seems to reinterpret his mandate not so much leave her to heaven as *lead* her to heaven. And does *Taint not thy mind* refer to Hamlet's killing Claudius for reasons of state, with virtuous intent? Is the Ghost ordering justified *public* revenge with mind untainted? Or does it refer only to the Queen and the un-Christian act of *private* revenge? It's unknowable, yet Hamlet is supposed to memorialize his father by carrying out the ambiguous commands.

The Ghost—if it is Hamlet's father—doesn't take a second to inquire how Hamlet is, nor does it have any other agenda than its own, to punish Claudius and interfere with the happy couple. And undo King Hamlet's cuckold's horns. The Ghost is ashamed, jealous, possessive, controlling, and unable to perceive objects as real people through the haze of hatred. The Ghost exemplifies one kind of shame, the kind that's conscious: Narcissistic injury—shame is felt but immediately projected outward. In every culture there's a concept for this transformation, a word for doing terrible things. In Hamlet's world it's the word *honor.*

While he was reading and rereading Shakespeare Freud also read Darwin. Although he didn't understand the full implications of natural selection (he thought learned traits were inherited by offspring), he did frame parts of psychoanalytic theory in light of survival of the fittest. He cites Darwin's *Expression of Emotions* that emotional displays echo archaic defenses, such as disgust closing off the nostrils to prevent inspiration of toxins, or rage unsheathing the teeth before battle. But Freud didn't further delve the survival value of emotions and their physiological aspects—the gooseflesh of the uncanny, the tears of grief, and the involuntary blush of shame. He bypassed other questions too. Why did shame and contempt evolve?

What was the value in their expression by one person to another? And especially—what clues do the social emotions give about transference and narcissism, two ideas that run all through *Hamlet*?

Freud struggled with the concept of narcissism all through his career and never really settled it. He was captive to his own hydraulic metaphor and unable to get past the notion of libido (or love, speaking loosely) as a fluid under pressure. He stuck to the idea that the more love one had for oneself, the less was left for the object of desire. When Freud made mistakes, they were the mistakes of genius—big—since a teenaged boy can tell you that the more the object is loved, the more the lover loves the world and all its creatures, himself included.

But in addition to the narcissism of the Ghost, the fragile self and its conscious shame, there's another kind. Viewed from one angle, Hamlet has this second kind. Given how the Ghost treats him, he fits what analyst Alice Miller calls a *prisoner of childhood*. She describes the perfect child grown up, having everything necessary for a good life but, all the same, feeling not fully alive inside. This kind of shame isn't conscious; it begins before language so there's no name the growing child can give it. It's aware and unaware at the same time. Unlike a child that was neglected—and unlike a child that was unconditionally loved—the child doesn't grow up with an accurate memory of the parents but a myth. They say how good their parents were and blame themselves. They say, how odd it is that they, given so much, should feel so little.

> It is one of the turning points in analysis when the patient achieves the emotional insight that all the love which he captured with so much effort and self-denial was not meant for him as he really was; that the admiration for his beauty and achievements was aimed at his beauty and these achievements and not the child himself. In the analysis the small, lonely child hidden behind his achievements wakes up and asks: "What would have happened if I had appeared before you, bad, ugly, angry, jealous, lazy, dirty, smelly? Where would your love have been then? . . . Does this mean that it was not really me whom you loved, but only what I pretended to be? The well-behaved, reliable, empathic, understanding and convenient child, who in fact was never a child at all? What became of my childhood?"[4]

When he describes his father the plot is moving fast, emotion is high, and the audience takes Hamlet at his word. His father was a god. But there's something general and excessive in it. And the Ghost, if it is his father, treats him the way a child is treated who's a foil of the parent, the "convenient child" of Miller's description. To be used as a need-satisfying tool—to be loved for what one stands for rather than loved for oneself—is to be what self psychology calls a *selfobject*. Their fate is to grow up feeling always unknown, with a subtle self-disgust the more potent for its namelessness. But when it finally gets a name, the word is *shame*.

Freud uses *guilt* hundreds of times, but *shame* barely two dozen. He sees it as a rule of civilization and a warning signal against breaking that rule. And an aversive stimulus, like anxiety and pain. Shame is a social enforcer arousing defenses like repression, normally a good thing. But it's pathologically absent in the perversions, which as their sexual object seek something most people are disgusted by. Freud also takes shame to mean a subjective experience, a near involuntary, almost animal, response to public exposure of a physical flaw, public urination, or public nakedness; and it's accompanied by involuntary physiologic responses of blushing or sweating. It's a signal that an unconscious wish is exposed. This, he says, is an almost universal reaction to being caught in a slip of the tongue.

So Freud was struck by the lack of shame in the perversions. And he was impressed by the presence of an atavistic nervous system response to the revelation of hidden sexual impulses. But he veered away to investigate guilt because it seemed a more advanced emotion and because guilt was supposedly the penalty for oedipal urges. This led to theories about the resolution of the Oedipus complex as the basis for the grown up conscience. And after Freud's interest turned more toward guilt, shame became increasingly confused as mainstream psychoanalytic theory drifted further from the emotions as they actually appeared in clinical practice. Common sense definitions (as used by actual patients) better matched clinical practice than did psychoanalytic theory. This one was a telephone lineman. His words speak for themselves: "What I mean by shame and what I mean by guilt? That's easy, Doc, everybody knows that. Guilt's a bad feeling about something you've done. Shame's an awful feeling about something you *are*."[5]

Despite scanting shame, Freud got its essence, two ideas of opposite valence. The positive, socially necessary type of shame and the self-degrading emotion of filth and ugliness. Both meanings come from a common ancestry in ancient languages; the word comes from *to conceal*. It's about covering something up. Aristotle held shame was useful in the education of children, but he believed negative aspects of shame were inappropriate in adults and its inhibitions indicated a lack of self control. Philosophy, theology, and psychoanalysis all recognize shame in its two socializing aspects.

Evolutionary psychology arrived at the same bifurcation: Shame as a warning signal of impending transgression. And, shame as punishment for the transgression, "an awful feeling about something you *are*." As social beings we strive for two goals, group membership and mating success, *belonging* and *love* (romantic and parental). Evolutionary "inclusive fitness" depends on an individual's pushing forward genetic material into the next generation, not only through children but also nieces, nephews, and cousins' children. We're preprogrammed to altruistically help even remote kin who carry our genes.

For successful membership and mating, a human being has to reach a certain level of success in conformity, altruism, social status, and sexual behavior. An optimal experience of both the warning and punitive aspects of shame is key—not too much, not too little—and the right kind for the situation. Evolutionary success depends on optimal "signal shame" and optimal "shame responsiveness." Individuals with too much anticipatory shame may be inhibited in seeking status and competing for mates. Individuals with too little shame responsiveness are the ones to whom society says, "Have you no shame!" Low shame responsiveness correlates with antisocial personality, destructive narcissism, addictions and perversions. Hypersensitivity to signal shame is linked to depression, social phobia, and avoidant personality.[6]

This duality of shame helps explain the paradox of the thick-skinned/thin-skinned narcissist—social imperviousness plus extreme vulnerability to narcissistic injury. Narcissistic individuals have low signal shame, so they routinely transgress social norms. But they have extreme shame responsiveness when their pride is punctured. When they feel it, it's so toxic they'll do anything to escape it, from suicide to murder. Standard narcissistic defenses include *shame projected outward* as contempt and compensatory grandiosity.

The Ghost's speech shows creation of "sliding meanings" of reality. The individual slides meanings to evade personal responsibility. This leads to insensitive reactions to others and exaggeration of importance of the self. Such people take things personally. And there's manipulation of the syntax of propositions to displace responsibility, the scoundrel's excuse: "Mistakes were made."[7]

Ghost Thus was I sleeping, by a brother's hand,
Of life, of crown, of queen at once dispatched,
Cut off even in the blossoms of my sin,
No reckoning made but sent to my account
With all my imperfections on my head.

I.v.74 TLN 759–764

It's Claudius's fault there wasn't time for confession and penance. But "blossoms of my sins" puts a pretty smell on King Hamlet's transgressions, and the "imperfections" were grave enough to warrant being burnt and purged away. And of course, the heart of the matter: He had opportunity to be shriven at any point before his nap.

One of the more astonishing discoveries of evolutionary psychology is the intimate (and biologically hard wired) relationship between revenge and altruism. Like it or not, we have genes that are busily and unsentimentally trying to replicate themselves by manipulating our behaviors to increase our evolutionary fitness. Hidden among these ruthless genes are a few genes that—paradoxically—evolved to selfishly advance their cause by promoting "unselfishness." These are genes that perpetuate themselves by simulating *altruism* in their human pack mules (who naively believe in their own generosity). But the irony is that these genes lie functionally close to the genes that incite revenge.[8]

Hundreds of experiments in game theory tend to show how generous any tribe or group is likely to be, even to strangers. In a significant number of specific instances, altruism is the human default setting; people are more giving than you might expect. But if generosity is exploited, even generous people lust for revenge. People will pay enormous personal cost in effort and money to avenge themselves. These results point to the existence of something evolved in us called "strong reciprocity." This is a disposition to cooperate *and* punish those who violate social norms—to collaborate and to punish rule breakers at a personal cost even if the expense will never be recouped ("expensive" punishment). And strong reciprocity is more the rule than the exception.[9]

In the ancestral environment there would be an evolutionary advantage for groups containing vengeful individuals who punish social defectors and chronic free-riders. Groups that don't have individuals carrying genes for altruism *plus* revenge don't cooperate well and are easily defeated by groups where there are punishments for non-cooperation. Cheaters infiltrate these "nice" groups. But where does altruism come from—and how is it connected with shame? Its evolution would start with parental empathy for offspring and family and then extend to more distant kin. An altruistic act toward kin increases the individual's evolutionary fitness even if never reciprocated because the act preserves at least part of that individual's shared family genes. Over evolutionary time, the mechanisms for kin altruism would generalize to unrelated but familiar others in the group. "Prosocial reciprocity" would utilize the same cognitive and motivational systems that evolved for kin altruism.

But the evolution of brain and behavior from kin altruism to successful trading of altruistic acts with biologically unrelated others is a big step, and it requires shame. Early humans who were able to use shame "to control their sexual and aggressive behavior were able to attract altruistic actions toward themselves. Potential altruists were developing the ability to discern reciprocal altruists from cheaters. The cheaters could be identified . . . by their selfish instinctual behavior" and by their apparent lack of empathy. Shame "developed along with other sources of motivation toward trading altruistic acts and functioned as a signal."[10]

Cheaters don't show shame. The individual carrying the genes for altruism would need to be able to recognize other altruists. The theory is that shame evolved as a manifest of cooperation. You can imagine scenarios for the evolution of complex social emotions: As a part of the cognitive capacities for living in groups, there might evolve more subtle deception capacities (self-deception included) and better cheater detection. Group dynamics might select for strong signal shame and shame responsiveness. Responsiveness is balanced perhaps by "ego mechanisms of defense" so that shame defensively projected outward becomes contempt. Contempt, then hitch-hiking on the expensive punishment mechanisms evolved for strong reciprocity, combines with rage to make up the complex emotion of revenge.[11]

Emotion is a fundamental organizer of behavior but, beyond that, our emotions still detect the threats and opportunities of the ancestral environment, not present realities of industrialized society. Emotions act "as if" certain things are true in the present moment, rightly or wrongly, simply because they were true in our ancestral past. We think we do things for a reason. We love our children, die for our country, despise those without honor, kill if somebody is trying to take our mate. A pre-programmed behavior flashes outward to the external world, responding to *what is meaningful for evolutionary fitness* of the individual. The "meaning" of an act seems persuasive, but it is a surface emotional "reason" layered over an evolved reflexive survival behavior.

We've come full circle to "strong reciprocity," or altruism *plus* punishment of cheaters. Punishment of non-cooperators—added to reciprocity—probably enhances the survival of a group. This suggests a relation among the *intensity* of shame, the *capacity* for altruism, and the *appetite* for revenge. If, indeed, the Ghost is the spirit of King Hamlet, should we allow the possibility that his huge lust for revenge was coupled with a commensurately large capacity for giving back to the community? It's tempting to dismiss this notion, that great generosity coevolved with intense vengefulness. But remember, the Ghost's narcissism aside, King Hamlet risked his life in single combat with the King of Norway to save his army the horrors of battle. How ever imperfect as a father, this was no small man.

And Hamlet's not just a prisoner of childhood. After the Ghost leaves, Soliloquy 2 shows him coping despite severe narcissistic injuries. His ego has resources—symbol formation, intelligence, a nimble memory, and the conviction that written language is key.

Hamlet O all you host of heaven—O earth—what else?
And shall I couple hell? O fie—hold—hold my heart!
And you, my sinews, grow not instant old
But bear me stiffly up. Remember thee!
Yea, from the table of my memory
I'll wipe away all trivial fond records . . .
And thy commandment all alone shall live
Within the book and volume of my brain
Unmixed with baser matter. O most pernicious woman!
O villain, villain—smiling damned villain!
My tables—my tables—meet it is I set it down
That one may smile and smile and be a villain —
So, Uncle, there you are. Now to my word.
It is "Adieu, adieu—remember me."

I.v.92 TLN 777–796

The "baser matter" that Hamlet is cleansing from the Ghost's commandment is his base Mater. Hamlet's rage at Gertrude, and his contempt, raise the question of what happened between them back in the supposedly golden days of his childhood. This question will receive an answer in a discussion of the Closet scene later. We'll see laid bare Hamlet's unspeakable shame over his mother's "lust." But she has in fact no lines that are lustful anywhere in the play.

There's an interlude before the Ghost scenes, before the cold darkness and terror, which shows a very different family. Polonius and his children are not haunted. Polonius doesn't use his children primarily as selfobjects for his own needs. For all their humanness there is no evidence of malignant narcissistic sensitivity in any of the three when we first meet them, and nobody seems to have been a prisoner of childhood. But those very pathologies in Hamlet's family, transmitted through Hamlet, will eventually destroy Polonius and his children.

Notes

1. Paul Ekman, "Basic Emotions," in *Handbook of Cognition and Emotion*, Tim Dalgleish and Mick J. Power, Eds. (New York: John Wiley & Sons, 1999), 45–60.
   Charles Darwin, *The Expression of the Emotions in Man and Animals*, ed. 3, Paul Ekman, ed., "Introduction, Afterword, and Commentary," (1872; reprint, New York: Oxford University Press, 1998).
2. Erving Goffman, "Embarrassment and Social Organization," *American Journal of Sociology* 62 (1956): 264–271.
   Corine Dijk, Peter J. de Jong, and Madelon L. Peters, "The Remedial Value of Blushing in the Context of Transgressions and Mishaps," *Emotion* 9 (2009): 287–291.
3. Stephen Greenblatt, *Hamlet in Purgatory* (Princeton: Princeton University Press, 2001).
4. Alice Miller, "Prisoners of Childhood," *International Journal of Psycho-Analysis* 60 (1979): 47–58, 51.
5. Exactly echoing Helen Block Lewis.
   Helen Block Lewis, *Shame and Guilt in Neurosis* (New York: International Universities Press, 1971).
6. David W. Harder and Deborah F. Greenwald, "The Psychotherapy of Shame-Related Pathology from an Evolutionary Perspective," in *Genes on the Couch: Explorations in Evolutionary Psychotherapy*, Paul Gilbert and Kent G. Bailey, Eds. (Hove, East Sussex: Brunner-Routledge, 2000), 304–329.
7. Mardi J. Horowitz, "Sliding Meanings: A Defense Against Threat in Narcissistic Personalities," *International Journal of Psychoanalytic Psychotherapy* 4 (1975): 167–180.
8. William Flesch, *Comeuppance: Costly Signaling, Altruistic Punishment, and Other Biological Correlates of Fiction* (Cambridge: Harvard University Press, 2007).
   By "biological correlates of fiction" he means storytelling as an evolved human universal growing out of reciprocal altruism, costly punishment, involuntary signaling, dissimulation strategies, and the evolution of culture. We're hard wired to recognize and respond involuntarily to transactions among an *exploiter*, an *innocent*, and a *rescuer*. Our responses to this universal triangle are reflexive and emotional. These essential character elements of *all human narratives* provide a template for processing reciprocity versus cheating and for responding with either enhanced bonding or a subsequent lust for revenge ("comeuppance"). This is a persuasive account of how humankind evolved literature and how literature shaped modern humans.
9. Herbert Gintis, Samuel Bowles, Robert Boyd, and Ernst Fehr, "Explaining Altruistic Behavior in Humans," in *Oxford Handbook of Evolutionary Psychology*, R.I.M. Dunbar and Louise Barrett, Eds. (Oxford: Oxford University Press, 2006), 605–619.
10. Malcolm Owen Slavin and Daniel Kriegman, *The Adaptive Design of the Human Psyche: Psychoanalysis, Evolutionary Biology, and the Therapeutic Process* (New York: Guilford Press, 1992), 299–300.
11. Conscious or not, for shame to be experienced, there must be an *offending* self and an *offended* internal image of the parents or culture. If somebody is alone in the jungle and sees a snake, there will be fear on the individual's face. But how is it a social signal? Well, like all signals, emotions can be sent without being received. Emotions evolved to be broadcast, to the individual and the tribe. A fear of snakes is instinctive in primate species, but to activate this fear, the young must *see* the mother's reactions. This kind of evolved biological preparedness to "learn" a "reflex" is especially relevant to shame. A human infant is born with a greater or lesser *potential* for shame. Whatever this innate capacity is, it accumulates, from the parents and the culture, habitual responses to both anticipatory shame as a signal and responsiveness to shame as punishment.

3

FREUD'S "FAMILY ROMANCES"

Power and Belonging

Freud says "the whole progress of society rests upon the opposition between successive generations." Family conflict is desirable. Without repulsion and attraction in balance, the child can't grow up. This conflict is seen in the typical daydreams of children in which the parents are "replaced by others of better birth." Boys especially will picture themselves as the consort of the mother. A boy who feels slighted and in the shadow of the father or older siblings "tends to picture to himself in erotic situations which bring his mother . . . into secret love-affairs." Plus which, the motive of revenge makes him attribute "to his mother as many fictitious love-affairs as he himself has competitors . . . his brothers and sisters are eliminated by being bastardized."[1]

But if you're already a prince, what kind of people of better birth do you substitute for parents? Do we believe Hamlet's idealized picture of his father? Is the usurper Claudius as bad as he claims? How does the progress of Denmark rest upon the opposition between generations? Does Hamlet's contempt for Claudius help him grow up? Does his rage at his mother help him separate? (No and yes, respectively, as we see later.)

Beneath the surface of "Family Romances" are themes of the child's disillusionment with previously idealized parents and formation of the "ego ideal" as a standard within the conscience. This adds a nice layer of explanation to the question of *Hamlet's* durability and popular fascination: When we meet Hamlet, he is already in the midst of an inverted family romance; we are predisposed by our own family romances to identify with someone adopted by a king. In Hamlet's case it's not a bigger, better father but a degraded, disgusting one. And the theme of the mother's infidelity is strong and bitter from the start. Disowned—and more compelling because it resonates with hidden desire in the audience—is a longing for paradisal fusion with infantile pleasures lost but not quite forgot.

Early scenes in *Hamlet* plot the tension between power and belonging. The Council scene shows Hamlet starting to push back against Claudius's order not to return to Wittenberg, but he submits when prevailed upon by his mother. Often the King is played as a drunkard, but it is a mistake to overdo it. He's persuasive, charming, holding forth in the elevated register of courtly discourse. Claudius deftly outflanks young Fortinbras, the immediate threat to Denmark, and then handily contains Hamlet. He's leapt over young Hamlet in the succession by means of the "better wisdoms" of the court and his marriage to Gertrude. Hamlet, Laertes, and Fortinbras all are only sons of powerful fathers, and the three have much in common. For all of them, the price of belonging is submission in the present to be exchanged for power in the future.

Polonius adores his children and they reciprocate even when they roll their eyes. Laertes, departing for France, gives his sister advice that may be too late; he warns Ophelia not to give her love to Hamlet. Here, women are a store of value and medium of exchange. Laws, manners, and language define the hierarchy from highest to lowest. The individual is nested in the family as the family is in the tribe, a concentric arrangement that gives stability as structures at the family level reinforce those at the tribal level (father as king, mother as queen, and so on).

The talk of Polonius's children is frankly erotic. The darling buds of spring are prey to rosewom and blight. Tender buttons wetted with dew and wafting perfume have their contours assailed by the weapons of young men. Ophelia, that rose of May, is to keep her tender buttons away from the perimeter of lust, guarded behind the watchman of her heart by a shield of fear.

Laertes For Hamlet and the trifling of his favors —
Hold it a violet . . . sweet, not lasting,
The perfume of a minute, no more —
Perhaps he loves you now but you must fear!
His greatness weighed, his will is not his own. . . .
Then weigh what loss your honor may sustain
If with too credent ear you list his songs
Or lose your heart—or your chaste treasure open.
Ophelia I shall the effect of this good lesson keep
As watchman to my heart. But good my brother,
Do not as some ungracious pastors do,
Show me the steep and thorny way to heaven
Whilst like a puffed and reckless libertine
Himself the primrose path of dalliance treads
And recks not his own rede.*

I.iii.5 TLN 467–514
* heeds not his own rules

Her father tells her not to believe the Prince's vows or she'll be got with child: Passion can make a young man persuasive. Polonius's own fiery youth comes suddenly back, and when he doesn't get an obedient response, he forbids Ophelia letting Hamlet near her—from now on.

Polonius 'Tis told me . . . you yourself
Have of your audience been most free and bounteous.
Ophelia He hath, my lord, of late made many tenders
Of his affection to me . . . he hath importuned me with love
In honorable fashion . . . with almost all the holy vows of heaven.
Polonius When the blood burns, how prodigal the soul! Daughter,
I would not in plain terms, from this time forth,
Have you . . . give words or talk with the lord Hamlet.
Look to it, I charge you. Come your ways.
Ophelia I shall obey, my lord.

I.iii.91 TLN 557–602

Almost all the holy vows. Some modern productions omit her promise to obey, but it sacrifices a note of irony: Ophelia is warned not to yield her virtue to Hamlet—so what if she already has?

"Family Romances" was written 3 years after a case which is less a romance than a tragedy. *Dora* showcases Freud's brilliance, but in some ways he felt her psychoanalysis was a failure. This is his most tendentious narrative, the case of the girl Freud called "Dora."[2]

In the autumn of 1900 Dora's father dragged his pretty and bookish 17-year-old daughter up the stairs to Freud's second floor office at Berggasse 19, Vienna. "Please try and bring her to reason," he said. Dora was "in the first bloom of youth—a girl of intelligent and engaging looks." To Freud's eye, she was "unmistakably neurotic," this "girl of nearly nineteen." Precocious too, as Freud writing up the case always put her age a year or two older than she actually was.

Dora had a history of symptoms ranging from a barking cough to a limp and pressure in her chest. The girl had of late written a suicide note she "hid" in her writing desk. And although her father didn't think she would kill herself, he was shaken. You know, he told Freud, "she inherits my obstinacy." He well understood Dora's threat as part of a campaign to break up the sexual triangle he had had with Herr and Frau K, "intimate friends" of the family since Dora was twelve. It was an open secret Dora's father and Frau K were lovers despite his telling Freud they were just friends. "The poor woman is most unhappy with her husband, of whom, by the by, I have no very high opinion." Besides, Dora's father told Freud, "You know already that I get nothing out of my own wife," a strange, unhappy woman utterly obsessed with housecleaning. And on his part, the cuckold Herr K was content to turn an unseeing eye to the affair of his wife with Dora's father and busied himself trying to seduce teenaged girls. This idyll was ripped apart when Dora accused Herr K of sexually forcing himself upon her 2 years back when the families were on vacation in the Alps. She and Herr K were alone up at the lakeside when Herr K began, "You know, I get nothing out of my wife—" and Dora slapped him and stormed off.[3]

Herr K angrily countercharged that Dora was obsessed with sex because of the suggestive material in books she was always reading. Herr K assured Dora's father that Dora had imagined the whole thing. Dora's father inquired no further because Frau K, up to now Dora's trusted confidante, sided with the other adults. Worse, Frau K, "whom she used positively to worship," was the source of the calumnies on Dora's racy reading habits. This was especially bitter because she and Frau K had often giggled and enjoyed together the pseudoscientific and titillating popular books on sex brought out for the reading public. Betrayed on all sides, Dora grew more symptomatic, depressed, and fatigued.[4]

Freud had already heard the family history some years earlier from Dora's father. Freud treated him with mercury injections during a flare up of neurosyphilis and probably saved his sanity. He was wealthy and powerful and Freud makes much of his intelligence and character. Dora, Freud writes, was "most tenderly attached" to him and therefore her critical powers were all the more offended, for she "had no doubt that what bound her father to this young and beautiful woman was a common love-affair."

Freud had seen Dora the previous year but she refused to come for treatment. His diagnosis was *petit hystérie* from the history of unexplained physical complaints—abdominal pains, bedwetting, breathlessness, and facial numbness. But symptoms aside, the real trigger was Dora's assault on her father's adultery. Nonsense, said her father; he was just grateful to Frau K for nursing him through bouts of his illness, a denial Freud didn't believe for a second. From the first he suspected a sexual triangle that involved Dora, and he intuited that it was causing her chest pressure and shortness of breath.

For years Freud had tried to cure hysteria. Its symptoms were many and varied, mysterious and infuriating, and impossible to ignore because they often mimicked "real" disease and had to be presumed somatic until shown to be psychogenic. But typically the clinical presentation of the patient—usually female—made no medical sense. So Freud had long thought such symptoms were symbolic expressions of unconscious conflict. The conflict was always sexual and it always stemmed from some trauma of a sexual nature.

To explain the kaleidoscope of hysterical symptoms, Freud posited for the unconscious mind a fundamental feature, *overdetermination*, the simultaneous existence of more than one psychological cause: Symptoms, like dreams, like all psychological "structures" have within them several unconscious meanings. A symptom could have one meaning viewed one way and another seen from a different vantage. Dreams, symptoms, slips of the tongue, and jokes all emerge from the same symbolic dream machine. A symptom might appear briefly after its first provoking cause, or sexual trauma, and lie dormant for years until a later trauma produced it again. There were, of course, other behaviors Freud's nineteenth century mind considered pathogenic. Dora masturbated, she admitted, and Freud felt she was bringing her vaginal discharge upon herself. Masturbation dammed up normal libido and was the source of physical and mental ills. Hysteria was to Freud an illness of thwarted sexuality. And, Freud was convinced, Dora was frigid.

Several years earlier, when Dora was thirteen, Herr K got her alone upstairs in his second floor office, cornered her, grabbed her, and began kissing her and rubbing his body against her. (Freud told her bluntly that she must have felt Herr K's erect penis through his trousers.) She broke free and ran from Herr K's office down the stairs into the street, making her escape. She recalled a "violent feeling of disgust." For Freud this was symptomatic. "This was surely just the situation to call up a distinct feeling of sexual excitement in a girl of fourteen who had never before been approached." Dora was not aroused—therefore she was frigid. Besides, Freud added, he himself knew Herr K, who "was still quite young and of prepossessing appearance."[5]

Freud has been criticized for his view of female sexuality and for going easy on Herr K. But to his credit Freud had taken Dora more seriously than anyone else. At least Freud's needs, so far as he could make them conscious, were medical and directly expressed, in contrast to Herr K and Frau K; they showered gifts and affection on Dora as they involved her in their sexual triangle with Dora's father as they all were using her as a pawn in their game. At first Freud was impressed with Dora's father, "a man of rather unusual activity and talents" and with Herr K's looks and charm. Also, the fee for Dora's case was not insignificant. But Freud refused to be bought. He trusted his own powers of analysis over the clubby camaraderie of the father, who wanted Freud to stop the girl making a fuss about his affair with Frau K and to discredit Dora's story of Herr K assaulting her. Freud immediately spotted the tacit deal in which everyone would look the other way. Herr K would

> send Dora flowers every day for a whole year while he was in the neighbourhood . . . take every opportunity of giving her valuable presents [and] spend all his spare time in her company, without her parents noticing anything in his behavior that was characteristic of love-making.[6]

Flowers every day. But what has *Dora* to do with family romances? Where are the daydreams that replace parents with others of higher birth? Dora had no such fantasies, but she did have a rich fantasy life enacted as somatic displays narrating conflict. Her symptoms were projected onto the screen of her body and served a self defining function. They helped her differentiate by substituting for the child role the sick role—providing Freud's "opposition between successive generations" necessary to individuation of the growing child. But her symptoms tied Dora to her father through identification with him as an ill person. Thus she had

> even at the age of eight begun to develop neurotic symptoms. She became subject at that time to chronic dyspnoea [breathlessness]. . . .unilateral headaches. . . .attacks of nervous coughing, . . .complete loss of voice. It was in such circumstances as these that the child had developed into a mature young woman of very independent judgment, who had grown accustomed to laugh at the efforts of doctors.[7]

Doctors, laughed at or not, played a major part in Dora's family life. Dora's father had infected her mother with gonorrhea (which the woman took to be syphilis), causing her chronic abdominal discomfort and vaginal discharge. The father had tuberculosis as well, and at some point Dora's mother spent time in a sanitarium. Any part her venereal infection by her husband played in her cleaning mania is mentioned only in passing. Unexplained—and unquestioned—is her shunning her husband's bedside. Freud, insatiably curious otherwise, doesn't explore these connections except to note that Dora took her mother's place nursing her father.

From her eighth through her twelfth year, Dora must have lived in a dream world of her father's various illnesses. Nowhere does Dora as patient say what the feelings and fantasies were of a girl nursing her father while the mother obsessively cleaned house. But a central determinant of life for the family was sickness, from the detached retina that threatened her father's one good eye (likely syphilis related) to the tuberculosis spa where the family summered. Dora was his devoted nurse until Frau K displaced her at the bedside. Dora then resumed being merely the daughter, a role not about doing, but waiting—for a husband to come along.

Freud's tale of this nubile teenager validates anthropology's theories of the incest taboo. In exchanges between kinship groups, a virgin was the most precious object of all and commanded the highest bridegift. The incest taboo is not only about father-daughter sexual relations but traces to a more ancient prohibition against trading damaged goods. Freud never acknowledged one of the determinants of the pseudonym he gave his patient, but anthropologists remind us "Dora" means "gift" in Greek.[8]

While Dora is slighted in her father's attentions, she does accept gifts from Herr K, including an expensive *jewel case*—in German, slang for intact and *inviolate female genitalia*. Freud notes the inappropriateness of these tokens, but he hammers away at the theme of Dora's incestuous wishes for her father. Though critics blame Freud for pushing Dora toward Herr K, we can understand the taboos Freud was bound by when her father "handed her over" to Freud; he had an obligation to see that Dora gave her "gift" not to her father but to another man. Both agreed the proper object of her maiden gift was Herr K.

But Dora felt used and took revenge by getting sicker. Freud tells us

> she was a source of heavy trials for her parents. . . . She tried to avoid social intercourse, and employed herself—so far as she was allowed to by the fatigue and lack of concentration of which she complained—with attending lectures for women and with carrying on more or less serious studies.[9]

More or less serious studies. Dora lost her place as substitute wife. With it, she lost her meaning in life. She then fell back on the educational make-work of the other young women in her world. Feminist critics wonder why Freud was so dismissive of Dora's intellectual life given the dozens of acts of reading and writing in *Dora*. Her analysis is triggered by her father's discovery of her "suicide note" and "breaks off with Freud's interpretation of a dream that ended as she 'began reading a big book that lay on her writing-table.' " In the analysis she mentions "letters from her uncle, Herr K, her governess, her aunt, her grandmother, her mother, and Frau K, and recollects reading books with her governess and Frau K."[10]

Freud misread Dora while Dora was reading Freud correctly. Such readings and misreadings are a way of understanding the transference distortions that aborted Dora's analysis. Besides getting her well, Freud had competing aims in writing her case, his demonstration of dream analysis and the pathogenesis of hysteria. These critics remind us how exclusionary Freud's narratives are, especially of the mother, establishing more secrets than they disclose.

> All narrative has this double function: to proclaim and conceal. . . . Freud sought the origin of Dora's narrative, and so to an important degree neglected its purpose. He pondered the purpose of his own narrative, and so to some extent neglected its origin. This double neglect, which conceals double desire, is figured in Freud's disregard of the mother and her role in Dora's history.[11]

To proclaim and conceal. So this underscores the greatest puzzle—Freud's straying further and further from the issue of the mother-child relationship as the case proceeds. But is it such a puzzle after all? As transference increases over the relationship, so does countertransference—*double neglect concealing double desire.* When Freud was just starting the case he saw the psychodynamics more clearly than during the case, or after. In a letter to Fleiss on October 13, 1900, the beginning of the analysis, he said that he had just begun working with an 18-year-old girl. The case, he told his friend, was simply one of

> hysteria with *tussis nervosa* and aphonia, [cough and loss of voice] which can be traced back to pronounced sucking tendencies, and the chief issue in the conflicting mental processes is the opposition between an inclination towards men and towards women.[12]

Pronounced sucking tendencies and an inclination towards both men and women. Freud saw the case more clearly early on. The deeper he got, the less he perceived Dora herself.[13]

Thus for daughters—it's different for sons. Polonius's advice to Laertes was a declamation piece for centuries so it's tired; but with a naive audience it gets the sympathy of parents who know how it feels when a child leaves home. Generations of English speaking schoolboys had to memorize it and hated it—perhaps only to recall it wistfully in later years.

Polonius . . . my blessing with thee
And these few precepts in thy memory:
Be thou familiar, but by no means vulgar.
The friends thou hast, and their adoption tried,
Grapple them to thy soul with hoops of steel,

But do not dull thy palm with entertainment
Of each new hatched comrade. Beware
Of entrance to a quarrel but, being in,
Bear it that the opposed may beware of thee.
Give every man thine ear but few thy voice:
Take each man's censure, but reserve thy judgment.*
Costly thy habit as thy purse can buy,
But not expressed in fancy; rich not gaudy,
For the apparel oft proclaims the man. . . .
Neither a borrower nor a lender be,
For loan oft loses both itself and friend,
And borrowing dulls the edge of husbandry.
This above all: To thine own self be true
And it must follow as the night the day
Thou canst not then be false to any man.

I.iii.57 TLN 522–545

* listen to each man's advice but think for yourself

Polonius's mind is medieval. He's no student of "conscience" or self consciousness. By "being true to yourself," Hamlet would mean, *Honestly know yourself, then you will be honest in all respects.* Polonius uses the word *self* to mean something less distinctive, more archetypal, *Follow the codes and rules you grew up with, in the cultural niche defining you.* There's a curiosity about the self missing in Polonius; his mind, though nimble, is prescriptive and descriptive, not reflective. He bores Hamlet to death.

The political side of his parenting shows as he and his man put final touches on a mission to Paris for replenishing Laertes's purse and the purpose of spying on him, for his own good.

Polonius Enquire me first what Danskers are in Paris. Take you,
as 'twere, some distant knowledge of him and there
put on him what forgeries you please. . . . drinking,
fencing, swearing. Quarrelling. Drabbing*—you may go
so far. . . .breathe his faults so quaintly
That they may seem the taints of liberty,
The flash and outbreak of a fiery mind.

II.i.7 TLN 898–925

* whoring

The relationship with his servant is key to Polonius's character. If you're directing *Hamlet*, you have to decide whether to make him a fool. But if you don't play it for laughs, Polonius is a mentor, passing along lessons of statecraft from years of service to Denmark.

Polonius	You laying these slight sullies on my son —
	As it were a thing a little soiled in the working —
	. . . your party in converse . . . closes with you thus:
	I know the gentleman, I saw him yesterday . . .
	There was he gaming. . . . I saw him enter a brothel. . . .
	Your bait of falsehood takes this carp of truth,
	And thus do we . . . by indirections find directions out.
	II.i.39 TLN 932–958

A tragic Polonius is a high-risk concept because the more sympathetic he is, the harder for Hamlet not to seem petty. However Polonius is tilted, his family has its own internal politics. If you accept that it's moral for Polonius to protect his son, then spying on him is not lubricious, it's mercantile. Polonius cares about his children, and he can change his mind—even apologize. As the servant exits, Ophelia rushes in telling her father she is "so affrighted." The lord Hamlet came into her room disheveled, pale, shaking, with a look on his face as if "he had been loosed out of hell/ To speak of horrors." He held her wrist and stared at her face and then, his head turned back over his shoulder, he drifted from the room without looking where he was going.

Polonius	This is the very ecstasy of love —
	Have you given him any hard words of late?
Ophelia	No but . . . I did repel his letters and denied his access. . . .
Polonius	That hath made him mad.
	I am sorry. . . . I feared he did but trifle
	And meant to wrack thee! But beshrew my jealousy —
	Come—go we to the King. This must be known!
	II.i.99 TLN 999–1016

Ophelia is Dora's age, and it's difficult to decide who's more controlled—Ophelia by her brother, her father, her lover—or Dora by her father, her would-be seducer, or her doctor. Yet they are loved. Freud made Dora recount her dreams so he could treat her, and we can read her dream associations in light of the cryptic language of power. And as Ophelia drifts into utter powerlessness, her language falls apart according to the laws of the unconscious. Then, as we see, it re-forms itself into the ravishing poetry Shakespeare uses to depict madness.

Freud identifies with Polonius. He explicitly compares his techniques to Polonius's. The mission is to get the patient to remember repressed memories and find out what's under the repression by means of the clues left behind, "to *construct* it." An interpretation applies "to something that one does to some single element of the material" such as a slip of the tongue. But "it is a 'construction' when one lays before the subject of the analysis a piece of his early history that he has forgotten. . . ."

No damage is done if the patient is given a wrong construction. If it happens, there's little emotional reaction from the patient, which shows "that we have made a mistake and we shall admit as much to the patient. . . ." In suggesting constructions to the patient, subsequent work allows the analyst to correct errors and "we often get an impression as though, to borrow the words of Polonius, that our bait of falsehood had taken a carp of truth." Freud-as-Polonius notes the signs of a truthful report—there's less reaction if it's off target, but if the analyst has hit the mark, the patient "reacts to it with an unmistakable aggravation of his symptoms and his general condition." After describing certain dazed waking states identical to Ophelia's mad scenes, Freud turns to the nature of a delusion, which is like a waking dream of wish fulfillment in which there is not only a method in madness "but also a fragment of *historical truth*; and . . . the compulsive belief attaching to delusions derives its strength precisely from infantile sources of this kind." So it's futile to try to convince the patient of the error of the delusion. On the contrary, "the recognition of its kernel of truth would afford common ground upon which the therapeutic work could develop."[14]

Freud prescribes teasing out the fragment of historical truth from its attachments to the present and leading it back to the point in the past where it started. He's setting out a commonsense and humane way of approaching a delusional system—as a symbolic version of a truth. Freud has Ophelia in mind. She isn't supposed to know Hamlet killed her father, but her poetry says she knows all too well.

> The delusions of patients appear to me to be . . . attempts at explanation and cure, though it is true that these, under the conditions of a psychosis, can do no more than replace the fragment of reality that is being disavowed in the present by another fragment that had already been disavowed in the remote past. . . . Just as our construction is only effective because it recovers a fragment of lost experience, so the delusion owes its convincing power to the element of historical truth which it inserts in place of the rejected reality.

"Family Romances" shows personal identity is shaped by two forces—belonging and distinctiveness. Dora and Ophelia must belong, but each wants mental freedom; each reflects the values of the family and the culture. Neither can escape her role. Family dysfunction causes—and is caused by—distortions in roles, communication, and boundaries. Rigid, poorly fitting *roles* constrain members, so one's place in the family is determined by power more than fit. Distorted *communication* uses language to get and maintain power by shaming and secrecy rather than to convey information. And porous, fuzzy, personal, and social *boundaries* blur differentiation between self and others. There's a lot of reading into the motives of others, shaming, guilt-inducing, re-labeling and misremembering of history—all in service of control. And there's little respect for healthy privacy but deliberate confusion of privacy with secrecy.

Role rigidity creates niches within the family that shape differences between generations and siblings. Freud is right that the progress of society depends upon the opposition between generations, but this progress comes at a high cost to some. By the end of the play two whole families are wiped out, and only Horatio survives—a man entirely without a family.

Notes

1. Sigmund Freud, "Family Romances," in *The Standard Edition of the Complete Psychological Works of Sigmund Freud*, vol. 9, James Strachey, Ed. and trans. (London: The Hogarth Press, 1908/1959), 236–241.
2. Sigmund Freud, "Fragment of an Analysis of a Case of Hysteria," in *The Standard Edition of the Complete Psychological Works of Sigmund Freud*, vol. 7, James Strachey, Ed. and trans. (London: The Hogarth Press, 1905/1953), 18–122.
3. Ibid, 19, 51.
4. Ibid, 98, 26, 32.
5. Ibid, 26, 29.
6. Ibid, 34–35.
7. Ibid, 21–22.
8. Caroline G. Banks, "A Dream of the Incest Taboo, Exchange of Women, and Seduction: A Reinterpretation of Freud's Dora," *Psychoanalysis and Contemporary Thought* 14 (1991): 251–269.
9. Freud, "Fragment," 23.
10. Sara van den Berg, "Reading and Writing Dora: Preoedipal Conflict in Freud's 'Fragment of an Analysis,'" *Psychoanalysis and Contemporary Thought* 10 (1987): 45–67.
11. Sara van den Berg, "Reading Dora Reading: Freud's 'Fragment of an Analysis,'" in *In Dora's Case: Freud—Hysteria—Feminism*, ed. 2, Charles Bernheimer and Claire Kahane, Eds. (New York: Columbia University Press, 1990), 294–304.
12. Sigmund Freud, "Letters 139–141," in *The Origins of Psychoanalysis: Letters, Drafts and Notes to Wilhelm Fliess, 1887–1902* (New York: Basic Books, 1954), 327.
13. Neil Hertz, "Dora's Secrets, Freud's Techniques," in *In Dora's Case: Freud—Hysteria—Feminism*, ed. 2, Charles Bernheimer and Claire Kahane, eds. (New York: Columbia University Press, 1990), 221–242.
14. Sigmund Freud, "Constructions in Analysis," in *The Standard Edition of the Complete Psychological Works of Sigmund Freud*, vol. 23, James Strachey, Ed. and trans. (London: The Hogarth Press, 1937/1964), 257–269.

4

"SOME VICIOUS MOLE OF NATURE"

Bad—or Just Unlucky?

It is night. The only sound is the crashing of waves on rocks at the base of the castle. Passing clouds part and moonlight shows three figures ascending the sentry platform. Hamlet and Marcellus are armed with cold steel and pumped for action. Horatio thinks it's nearly midnight, but Marcellus has heard the stroke of twelve. Horatio says, "Then it draws near the season/ Wherein the spirit held his wont to walk." From down below, they hear the noise of a drunken celebration and the sudden thunder of cannon. The explosion startles Horatio. "What does this mean, my lord?"

Hamlet says that although he is Danish and "to the manner born," this custom of revelry is "more honored in the breach than the observance." Drink has ruined the country's reputation, Denmark is now known abroad as a land of drunken swine. Hamlet has a point. Earlier at the plenary council meeting, after forbidding Hamlet's return to Wittenberg, the King gloated over the Prince's grudging assent to stay in Denmark.

King Why 'tis a loving and a fair reply —
Be as ourself—in Denmark. Madam, come.
This gentle and unforced accord of Hamlet
Sits smiling to my heart—in grace whereof
No jocund health that Denmark drinks today
But the great cannon to the clouds shall tell,
And the King's carouse the heavens shall bruit* again,
Respeaking earthly thunder.

I.ii.121 TLN 304–311

* sound

Every toast I drink shall make the heavens thunder. It was humiliating, and Claudius styles himself as Jupiter, mocking whatever "freedom" Hamlet had on earth to be *as ourself*—the royal we—in Denmark. The Prince is not to leave the country.

The three wait in the dark. The court's noisy demonstration of bad character is a cue for Hamlet to expound on a "vicious mole of nature." He's not talking about a mere birthmark but depravity in the person who wears it—*vicious* is from *vice*—worsened by causes exacerbating each other (the "vicious cycle"). It isn't just a stain, there's an association with the devil. (Later, Hamlet will call the Ghost "old mole" as it demonically tunnels the earth beneath their feet.)

Hamlet So oft it chances in particular men
That, for some vicious mole of nature in them,
As in their birth wherein they are not guilty
(Since nature cannot choose his origin)
By their o'er-growth of some complexion
Often breaking down the pales and forts of reason,
Or by some habit that too much o'er-leavens
The form of plausive manners,* that these men
Carrying, I say, the stamp of one defect
(Being Nature's livery or Fortune's star),
His virtues else—be they as pure as grace,
As infinite as man may undergo —
Shall in the general censure take corruption
From that particular fault: The dram of evil
Doth all the noble substance o'er-daub
To his own scandal.

I.iv.23 TLN 621+7–22[1]
* civility

It's astonishing—Hamlet thinks men with the vicious mole are *not guilty*. This foul blemish is part of their nature, just bad chance. Given that flaw, they can't do otherwise. It may be the extreme of some personality trait or some habit that's got out of control. But no matter how virtuous otherwise, the man's whole reputation is spoilt. Hamlet's thoughts on Claudius have a certain dramatic irony. Laurence Olivier clipped out the speech to use as a prologue to his 1948 *Hamlet*. The film begins with a shot of Elsinore Castle in the background and Olivier's voice reading the speech over the actual Vicious Mole text in antique lettering in the foreground. Olivier's point is that the Prince is unwittingly talking about himself. "This," intones Olivier after the fade, "is the tragedy of a man who could not make up his mind." He doesn't underestimate his audience and assumes their ability to grasp the Elizabethan audience's notion of tragic flaw leading to a hero's downfall. The idea of Hamlet's flaw being procrastination is of course not a unanimous opinion. Some commentators see Hamlet as moving as fast as he realistically can without tipping his hand to Claudius.

Olivier's *Hamlet* was praised for making Shakespeare accessible to the general public, but it was attacked by critics and scholars of Shakespeare as "too Freudian." In the film Hamlet has an attachment to his mother that is overtly sexual. Olivier's interpretation is indeed Freudian insofar as his Hamlet is conflicted and some of the conflict is repressed, the essence of Freud's dynamic unconscious. The problem is, not only is it unconscious in Hamlet, it's inaccessible to the audience. Olivier leaves it to us to surmise Hamlet's procrastination comes from some muddy combination of melancholy and idealism—and, somewhere in the mix, a vaguely unwholesome relationship with Gertrude.

But Freud's Hamlet has a distinct Oedipus complex: He hesitates to avenge his father because of an identification with Claudius. He would be killing a part of himself. For Freud, the hesitation is proof of Hamlet's unconscious ambivalence toward his own father. (Never mind the fact that Hamlet, when he thinks it's Claudius behind the arras in Gertrude's closet, stabs him without any hesitation whatsoever.) His procrastination is the manifestation of a deeper guilt over an unconscious wish to supplant the father and have his mother to himself. This is the classic oedipal triangle, and Freud did seem to find it almost any time he looked—the triangle of mother, son, and father.

Olivier's Hamlet has a passionate relationship with his mother that resembles Sophocles's Oedipus more than Freud's Hamlet. Olivier depicts one side of the oedipal triangle, Hamlet and his mother. He omits the other, Hamlet's unconscious competition with his father, much harder to dramatize. Olivier's *Hamlet* sprouted from a misreading of Freud, but still it was a monument. Each director and each Hamlet since Olivier had the problem of deciding how—or whether—to link Hamlet's attachment to his mother to a supposed hesitation in revenge.[2]

The Vicious Mole speech comes in response to another cannon volley. Hamlet looks back at the castle, ablaze in revelry, and philosophizes. The speech is also a dramatic lull before the intensity that follows. *Look, my lord, it comes*! Horatio, true to his function as stage prop, is first to spot the Ghost, and Hamlet says he'll speak to it since it comes in the shape of his father. It beckons Hamlet to come away.

Only four characters ever see the Ghost—two soldiers, Horatio, and Hamlet—and there's no explanation as to why it materializes to them and not to others. One belief about spirits in Tudor England was that the ghost of the murdered person might return to loved ones to accuse the murderer or warn the next victim, in this case Hamlet, along with the soldiers to fetch him. We never know the factors that determine to whom the Ghost shows itself and, indeed, the audience never asks. Horatio and Marcellus try to stop Hamlet's following after, warning it could be a devil in disguise. It might drive him mad or lead him off the cliffs to his death below. But Hamlet says he doesn't have any fear for his body, and as for his soul, "what can it do to that/ Being a thing immortal as itself?" (This is not the last time he'll mention his soul.) He fends off his companions with his sword and charges after the Ghost. Horatio thinks Hamlet is losing his reason, and Marcellus agrees. "Something is rotten in the state of Denmark."

Three questions in the background of the play come forward in the Vicious Mole speech: What does temperament contribute to an evil act? What part is played by natural forces and what part random chance? And, how does culture react to a character flaw? Hamlet ponders them: First, addictions are linked to extremes of personality traits, as habits grown too much. Second, natural innate forces in a person are balanced against accidental external forces acting on the person. And, third, an individual's vicious mole—despite all virtues—elicits the censure of the tribe.

Hamlet is a prince of the Renaissance. He lays out his theory of causation in the universe, something he's apparently given a good deal of thought. Consider the powerlessness of humankind against Nature, in the first instance, and against Fortune, in the other. Then, note that a person doesn't choose to be born to a lower status (one's external givens) nor does anyone choose to possess maladaptive extremes of personality or temperament (one's internal givens). To these, add the fact that these innate unchosen traits may exceed a person's ability to control the impulses that "break down the pales and forts of reason." Therefore the individual is not "guilty"— Hamlet's word—laying out the modern insanity defense in sixteen lines of blank verse. There are a couple of towering ironies here, and Hamlet is the supreme ironist, so he may realize one of them: He could as easily be talking about himself as about Claudius. And—perhaps unwittingly—he's just made the case that Claudius's vicious mole is not his own fault.

How important did Shakespeare regard the speech dramatically? It's omitted from the First Folio, so it was considered inessential by fellow actors John Heminges and Henry Condell. Omissions from playing scripts of the King's Men likely reflect its absence in their performances after Shakespeare's death. Yet it tends to slip back into *Hamlet*. Many productions are unable to drop it entirely. It seems essential to Hamlet's thinking, and a clue to the mind of his creator. Shakespeare is the soul of the English Renaissance, so what he read and thought is endlessly debated. And entered as evidence in questions of correct readings of the texts. *Hamlet* scholars have wondered, did he read another Renaissance genius, Michel de Montaigne? Questions still persist about the extent of the French philosopher's influence.[3]

Notions common to Shakespeare's works and Montaigne's *Essais* may simply derive from the spirit of the Renaissance circulating among thoughtful individuals at the time. But parts of the Fourth and Seventh Soliloquies, Hamlet's relativist comments to the schoolfellows, his hymn to the "quintessence of dust" that is humanity—these seem to bear the distinctive stamp of Montaigne's thought. Hamlet's meditations on free will versus social and biological necessity echo the Essays: How much is an individual truly able to choose? How much are choices mere illusion? What is morality, what is law? And not trivially, what about Shakespeare's astonishing familiarity with the law—did he clerk for a lawyer—was he a copyist and scribe for the courts? No one knows despite tantalizing suggestions and disputes over legal references all through his work, as well as a sample of his supposed law clerk handwriting.[4]

But Michel Montaigne's career in the law is a given; until the age of thirty-seven, he had an active public life and career as a magistrate. At thirty-eight Montaigne retired from being a judge to the relative seclusion of a tower in his chateau—and the vast library in it—to study and to write Hamlet-like investigations of his self. In so doing he was responding to changes in self consciousness that were abroad in the Renaissance, just as he was personifying those changes.[5]

Montaigne's biographers tend to draw a line between his time as public servant and his ascetic turning inward, but both stages show continuity of investment in human nature. In the first part of his life Montaigne judged others; in the second, he judged himself. The issue of a balance of bad character versus ill luck fascinated Shakespeare too, and ideas in the *Essays* are reminiscent of Hamlet's meditations. Montaigne's experience as judge thrust before him the excruciating dilemmas of humankind, so he must have asked the question we're asking. Is the prisoner cowering in the dock bad? Or just unlucky *in their birth, wherein they are not guilty*. By ancient precept, there is no crime if a person was forced to an act. Under God's law, there is no sin (except original sin) without free will. It hinges on whether, in performing the deed, one could have done otherwise, whether one acted "of necessity" independent of "free will."[6]

Modern diagnostic psychiatry calls a certain group of temperamental abnormalities "personality disorders," things like "dependent personality," or "histrionic personality," or "obsessive compulsive personality." Like Hamlet in the Vicious Mole speech, scientific psychiatry has tried to differentiate lifelong inborn temperamental *traits* in their extremes from reactive situational *states* mimicking character. Many debates in *Hamlet* scholarship boil down to this state versus trait distinction. Is a particular passage telling us about Hamlet's character? Or is this his freely chosen response to external realities impinging on him, for instance the constraints of the revenge plot? Hamlet swears Horatio and Marcellus never to talk about the Ghost; the two companions are to be secret should Hamlet ever put "an antic disposition on." How much the antic disposition is a biological trait he can't control and how much is state of mind he can decide to change is still up for critical debate.

"Personality" is the durable, distinctive, characteristic mode of an individual's relating to the social environment. And *style* or distinctiveness is a key concept in personality theory. What makes us human is our differences, our various styles. The word comes from *stylus*, writing implement. "Style" in the sense of individual distinctiveness comes from a realization by the ancients that the identity of a scribe could be recognized by handwriting and differentiated from that of others. The metaphor of writing in personality is further seen in *charassein* and *charakter*, words for engraving *tool* and the deeply graven *sign*, so it's not only the distinctiveness of personality or character that's signified but also its durability, carved into the individual.[7]

On the fundamental level, there are different styles of approach and avoidance. Approach-avoidance mechanisms, which evolved in most living things, undergird human personality disorders. When normal personality traits become so extreme that they breach *the pales and forts* of community standards, they then become personality disorders—an *overgrowth of some complexion* as Hamlet puts it. And considering our infinite human variety, a surprisingly small number of personality factors make up the universe of stylistic differences, psychological phenotypes or *nature's livery*. The consensus is five. *Agreeableness*, *Emotional Flexibility*, *Extroversion*, *Conscientiousness*, and *Openness* to new ideas. Extremes of these traits underlie discussions of malignant narcissism in a later chapter, but for now, suffice it to observe that different cultures have their own cut offs defining when a personality trait is too much or too little. Any trait is distributed in a continuum through the population (from weak to strong), so there will statistically always be a cohort of people, a subgroup at the extremes, that's seen as odd or different or high maintenance. Personality disordered people have temperamental set points that are significantly different from average. Since these five personality traits regulate the interface between people, extremes in their presentation disturb the social order. There's a folk saying that 10 percent of people cause 90 percent of the interpersonal problems in society—and, coincidence or not, that's approximately the world prevalence of "personality disordered" people as currently defined, 5 to 10 percent, those generally seen as "difficult."[8]

People are social animals and want to be a part of the tribe. Equally important, members don't want to be crushed or used, though submission is the price of membership. *As in their birth* individuals in the hierarchy of family and tribe are regulated not just by external punishments and rewards but by internal controls—guilt, an evolved internal punishment for wrongful acts, and shame, a feeling of self disgust that evolved as a lie detector for social trustworthiness. All these internal mechanisms of punishment and reward evolved in delicate balance. And what is balanced can tilt. Many aspects of the emotional control systems of the brain, what we call the "social emotions," can be overactive or under responsive. Emotions are momentary and reactive to events, but the trigger mechanisms—what we might call set points or dispositions—tend to be stable over time for a given personality. But *often it chances in particular men* that one of those personality default settings deviates markedly from the expectable range and causes what is defined as a personality disorder.[9]

So what about Hamlet? Soliloquy 1 raised questions about the Prince's narcissism; we wondered whether he were one of Freud's Exceptions (by which he meant a type of narcissist). Eventually we decided Hamlet's "entitlement" wasn't a core personality flaw that *over leavens plausive manners* but a result of regression from psychic trauma in a late adolescent. Distinctions between lifelong personality diagnoses and episodic disease-like mental illnesses are confounded by external events. How modern psychiatry might diagnose him is problematic. He probably misses the threshold for "narcissistic personality disorder," but barely. Psychiatrists would disagree whether Hamlet satisfies the official Diagnostic and Statistical Manual (DSM) criteria and *shows arrogant, haughty behaviors or attitudes* because on several occasions, he displays modesty and genuine humility. In other instances where he is arrogant, who is to say what's "normal" for the heir presumptive to the throne of Denmark? Hamlet diagnostically resembles some aspects of narcissistic personality—theatricality, need for an audience, and dismissive defenses. For many clinicians, Hamlet would seem narcissistic because of his intermittent lack of empathy for the feelings of others, his vengefulness, authority conflicts, feelings of being misunderstood, and tendency to feel victimized.[10]

But Hamlet's strengths are undeniable. He has openness to experience coupled with skepticism, keen curiosity, and sparkling imagination. For good or ill, he possesses strong sensitivity to the emotional tone of relationships. Within the frame of modern personality diagnosis, Hamlet would be seen as extroverted, energetic, and fun loving. To his credit are towering aspirations, phenomenal eloquence, daring, independence, and humor. The most likely DSM diagnosis is that he is a charming, brilliant "normal" personality in a tight spot, one with the types of defenses artists have.[11]

In imagining Hamlet, Shakespeare has so directly observed human nature responding to *fortune's star* that the character of the Prince in its entirety still remains unexplained and inexplicable after four centuries. The main argument against the diagnosis of a personality disorder in him is—obviously—that he's just been hit with massive psychic trauma. This is on top of a lifelong career in a royal role. It's impossible to know how much of Hamlet's narcissism is role assigned and how much is personality. Modern psychiatric diagnosis is too knife-edged and rigidly quantitative to do a good job on him: Small differences can swing the verdict drastically. Scientific psychiatry might call Hamlet an antisocial personality if his lack of remorse over his treatment of Ophelia and of the schoolfellows weren't balanced by two other instances of deeply felt guilt—his remorse for the death of Polonius and shame over his rage at Laertes. Two "antisocial" traits are present—impulsiveness and reckless disregard for others' safety—but they're the least vicious of antisocial descriptors. This would acquit him of "moral insanity," as sociopathy used to be called.

As for the official criteria for narcissistic personality disorder, Hamlet's *grandiosity* and *entitlement* are learned in part from his being groomed to be king and partly defensive against the trauma he's been through. Two other narcissistic traits, *exploitiveness* and *lack of empathy*, are also debatable. Are they character or are they some mix of trauma and training? And further, Hamlet doesn't have a *preoccupation with success*, one of the main narcissistic criteria; success he takes for granted, assuming it or even feeling it as a burden. Similarly for *feelings of specialness*, he appreciates how gifted he is, but he's bored with it. He has a sense of his smallness in the universe and of the accident of his birth. As for a *need for admiration*, Hamlet takes it for granted or shuns it. And of *enviousness*, there are two instances confounded by other issues: He envies Claudius the throne. And, according to Claudius, he envies Laertes his reputation as a swordsman.

There's an ironic parallel between how psychiatrists might diagnose Hamlet and how scholars and critics have seen him. In the first 200 years of *Hamlet* criticism, plot and genre predominated over notions of mind and interiority. It wasn't until the nineteenth century that something complex within Hamlet was supposed to cause his hesitation. The first half of its critical life, *Hamlet* was about what Hamlet did; it was never asked why he hesitated. But with modern notions of selfhood, it was inevitable that Hamlet would go on the couch and become a case study in personality theory.

Deep in the Vicious Mole speech lies the single most vexing question posed by personality and its disorders: Why are we so blind in ourselves to flaws others see perfectly clearly? Why have we such high regard for our own motives and so little doubt about the truth of our feelings? This is the paradox of personality. The more disordered it is, the more right it seems to us.[12]

Hamlet's meditation in this speech is a window on his theory of motivation, personal agency, and cause and effect. In its sixteen lines he moves from the plural to the singular, from the general to the particular. It spirals down from the cosmic (Nature, Fortune's star) to the little sip of individual evil soiling the whole. This flaw, is it the man's fault? Hamlet's answer: The man with the vicious mole is not guilty of it any more than of circumstances of birth, his station in life. It's rooted in a personality trait that's exaggerated and can diminish his reason. It may come from an appetite or addiction that contaminates normal behavior. It's innate, a part of his physical makeup. And it's his destiny ordained by his stars acting through his environment. The playwright seems eerily prescient of Newton's clockwork universe and the difficulty deterministic philosophies pose for "free will." Clearly, to "sin" one must be able to do otherwise. His vision and intellectual reach are astonishing. Anachronism can even project onto Shakespeare modern concepts like complexity theory, quantum probability, and chaos theory.[13]

Hamlet seems undecided whether the universe is deterministic like a clock or random like a dice game—but in practice he treats it as a mix of both. In questions of free will or determinism, and of nature or nurture, he moves from *either or* to *both and*. His spirituality evolves, mixing Christian elements with pagan ones. In Gielgud's film, on seeing the Ghost, Burton falls to his knees and blesses himself. Restrained from pursuit, Hamlet draws his sword and handily backs his companions off. Pursuing the Ghost, in some versions Hamlet carries the sword straight-armed out in front of him, hilt up like a crucifix. Although he defaults to classicism—referring to the Nemean lion, the first labor of Hercules—his spirituality is evolving. In the play, "soul" is sometimes synonymous with "mind," as psyche, a cognitive concept. But from his encounter with the Ghost, it takes on a spiritual meaning, and a quasi-religious one as when Hamlet says his soul lives beyond the life of his body. This is someone who's mainly inclined to pagan sensibilities. By the end of the play, he is alluding to the Sermon on the Mount—yet even then he hasn't entirely abandoned Wittenberg's skepticism.

If, as Freud said, neurosis is an inability to tolerate ambiguity, then Hamlet is becoming in one sense less neurotic. With a couple of disastrous exceptions, as he goes along he displays more and more negative capability. Freud saw this progression as emergence from neurosis, bringing with it development of the ability to love and work. But Freud never oversimplified the struggle, and he grew more and more skeptical about our ability to know—and our ability to freely choose. One of the coping mechanisms of the ego, Freud thought, is the illusion of freedom of choice, a self deception whereby the ego wants to imagine

> all the unfulfilled but possible futures to which we still like to cling in phantasy, all the strivings of the ego which adverse external circumstances have crushed, and all our suppressed acts of volition which nourish in us the illusion of Free Will.[14]

Freud and Hamlet are uneasy about whether free will exists, or whether it's just a necessary illusion. *Nature cannot choose its origin.* "Freud's mentor" brings the point sharply home in the Vicious Mole speech: When Hamlet hesitates, maybe it's because he's compelled to decide *as if* he had free will—when deep down he knows he doesn't.[15]

Notes

1. Barbara Everett, *Young Hamlet: Essays on Shakespeare's Tragedies* (Oxford: Oxford University Press, 1989).
   Presented here is her exegesis, but she prefers "o'er-cloud" to "o'er-daub" for Q2's "of a doubt," which everyone agrees is a transcription error.
2. Patrick J. Cook, *Cinematic Hamlet: The Films of Olivier, Zeffirelli, Branagh, and Almereyda* (Athens: University of Ohio, 2011).
3. Except for one undisputed instance in *The Tempest.*
4. W. Nicholas Knight, *Shakespeare's Hidden Life: Shakespeare at the Law 1585–1595* (New York: Mason & Lipscomb, 1973).
5. Katherine Almquist, "Writing Pluralist Biography of Montaigne's Legal Career," in *The New Biographical Criticism*, George Hoffman, ed., vol. 9 in *Studies in Early Modern France*, Anne L. Birberick and Russell Ganim, Eds. (Charlottesville: Rookwood Press, 2004), 58–76.
6. R. v. Dudley and Stephens, (1884) 14 Q.B.D. 273 (D.C.).
   This precedentary case on the "necessity" defense (starving castaways in a lifeboat murder and eat the cabin boy) is no more about cannibalism than Montaigne's essay "Of Cannibalism"; it's about human nature. The high court's ruling draws the finest legal line between freedom of the will and the compulsion of death. The decision is written by someone who seems to have read both Shakespeare and Montaigne, the Right Honorable John Duke, Lord Coleridge. His majestic prose balances on the knife edge between *did do* and *could have done otherwise.*

   > [I]t appears sufficiently that the prisoners were subject to terrible temptation, to sufferings which might break down the bodily power of the strongest man, and try the conscience of the best. . . . Though law and morality are not the same, and many things may be immoral which are not necessarily illegal, yet the absolute divorce of law from morality would be of fatal consequence. . . . To preserve one's life is generally speaking a duty, but it may be the plainest and the highest duty to sacrifice it. . . . it is not forgotten how terrible the temptation was; how awful the suffering; how hard in such trials to keep the judgment straight and the conduct pure. We are often compelled to set up standards we cannot reach ourselves, and to lay down rules which we could not ourselves satisfy. But a man has no right to declare temptation to be an excuse, though he might himself have yielded to it.

   He then proceeded to pass sentence of death upon Dudley and Stephens. Queen Victoria promptly commuted it.
7. Ruth F. Lax, "Introduction," in *Essential Papers on Character Neurosis and Treatment*, Ruth F. Lax, Ed. (New York: New York University Press, 1989), 1–21.
8. Mark A. Blais, Patrick Smallwood, James E. Groves, Rafael A. Rivas-Vazquez, and Christopher J. Hopwood, "Personality and Personality Disorders," in *Massachusetts General Hospital Comprehensive Clinical Psychiatry*, ed. 2. Theodore A. Stern, Maurizio Fava, Timothy A. Wilens, and Jerrold F. Rosenbaum, Eds. (New York: Elsevier, 2016), 433–444.
9. Nicholas B. Allen and Paul Gilbert, "Social Intelligence, Deception, and Psychopathology," in *Genes on the Couch: Explorations in Evolutionary Psychotherapy*, Paul Gilbert and Kent G. Bailey, Eds. (Hove, East Sussex: Brunner-Routledge, 2000), 151–175.

June Price Tangney, Jeffrey Stuewig, and Debra J. Mashek, "What's Moral About the Self-Conscious Emotions?" in *The Self-Conscious Emotions: Theory and Research*, Jessica L. Tracy, Richard W. Robins, and June Price Tangney, Eds. (New York: Guilford Press, 2007), 21–37.

Deception and self-deception are hard wired processes evolved to facilitate social inclusion, mating, and parenting: Submissive strategies in the face of likely defeat; self-assessment capacities for judging social value for mating and dominance; tactical self-deception enabling both "faking up" and "faking down" during negotiations; "cheater detection modules" for altruistic exchange; "mind reading" abilities by a "theory of mind" module computing others' desires, beliefs, and intentions; "mate retention strategies" for both sexes; involuntary emotional displays for intimidation and apology; "moral emotions" of shame and guilt for promoting trust in social exchange; and inducements for mutually beneficial relationships, such as gifts and gratuitously high initial offers.

10. Eric Russ, Jonathan Shedler, Rebekah Bradley, and Drew Westen, "Refining the Construct of Narcissistic Personality Disorder: Diagnostic Criteria and Subtypes," *American Journal of Psychiatry* 165 (2008): 1473–1481.
    Otto F. Kernberg, *Severe Personality Disorders* (New Haven: Yale University Press, 1984.)
11. Andrew E. Skodol, Leslie C. Morey, Donna S. Bender, and John M. Oldham, "The Alternative DSM-5 Model for Personality Disorders: A Clinical Application," *American Journal of Psychiatry* 172 (2015): 606–613.
    Eve Caligor, Kenneth N. Levy, Frank E. Yeomans, "Narcissistic Personality Disorder: Diagnostic and Clinical Challenges," *American Journal of Psychiatry* 172 (2015): 415–422.
12. This right-seemingness is called *ego syntonicity*. When psychoanalysis can't explain things at a fundamental level it at least tries to give them names. Symptoms and acts that are unwanted and seen as "not me" or not part of the self are called *ego alien*.
13. F. Elizabeth Hart, "Matter, System, and Early Modern Studies: Outline for a Materialist Linguistics," *Configurations* 6 (1998): 311–343.
14. Sigmund Freud, "The 'Uncanny,'" in *The Standard Edition of the Complete Psychological Works of Sigmund Freud*, vol. 17, James Strachey, Ed. and trans. (London: The Hogarth Press, 1919/1955), 219–252.
15. Daniel C. Dennett, *Freedom Evolves* (New York: Viking Penguin, 2003).
    Thomas McFarland, *Originality & Imagination* (Baltimore: The John Hopkins University Press 1985), ix.
    McFarland puts it this way:

    > Kant said, near the end of the *Critique of Pure Reason*, that human reason in its transcendental employment is directed toward three topics: the freedom of the will, the immortality of the soul, and the existence of God. It takes only a little reflection to realize that all three are a single collocation, and that if one exists, all must exist.

    That it takes *only a little* reflection is perhaps McFarland's attempt at humor.

5

MAD FOR THY LOVE

Infected by the Social Emotions

Hamlet's "madness" is both sword and shield. As deceivers, Claudius and Polonius are adept at lie detection, but Hamlet's antic disposition can hide the revenge he's planning. His "ecstasy" is a coping strategy; he can discharge pent up emotion without revealing feelings, even to himself. But sanity is balance, and the Ghost might drive Hamlet over the edge.

Horatio What if it tempt you toward the flood, my lord,
Or to the dreadful summit of the cliff
That beetles o'er its base* into the sea,
And there assume some other horrible form
Which might deprive your sovereignty of reason
And draw you into madness?

I.iv.69 TLN 658–663

* that frowns beetle-browed over its base

His interview with the Ghost is to change Hamlet forever. He'll remember its commandments even if he must erase everything he's learned and on the clean slate of his mind write one "can smile and smile and be a villain." He's thinking of Claudius but he's also preparing a different face for the world. Horatio and Marcellus burst on the scene to find him pale and shaking. He's about to tell them what the Ghost said but instead blurts out the first thing that comes to mind.

Hamlet There's never a villain
Dwelling in all Denmark —
But he's an arrant knave.

Horatio There needs no ghost, my lord, come from the grave
To tell us this.

I.v.123 TLN 814–818

They try to settle him down. They reach out, not quite touching him. After a frozen moment, Hamlet becomes less paranoid, but he's still incoherent.

Hamlet	I hold it fit that we shake hands and part — For every man hath business and desire — Look you—I'll go pray.
Horatio	These are but wild and whirling words, my lord.
Hamlet	I am sorry they offend you—heartily! And much offense too, touching this vision here: It is an honest Ghost—that let me tell you.

I.v.128 TLN 820–831

Hamlet sees Horatio's reaction to his infectious emotions, and this gives him an idea. He will feign madness to the King and court—but he needs their help.

Hamlet	How strange or odd so ever I bear myself (As I perchance hereafter shall think meet To put an antic disposition on*) That you at such times never shall . . . note That you know aught of me. This do swear not to do. Swear!

I.v.170 TLN 866–877
* to feign madness

His friends must play along. Although he'll later come to doubt it, Hamlet now assures them of the spirit's authenticity. There's shaking of the earth and noise from below. The Ghost is tunneling beneath the earth. Trying to placate the unquiet spirit, Hamlet calls it "truepenny" and insists Horatio and Marcellus take a vow. "Swear on his sword," the Ghost commands, and Hamlet nods, "Well said, old mole." They swear and the noise and shaking cease.

This brush with the supernatural has Hamlet doubting the academic skepticism they learned at university. Seeing Horatio's stunned disbelief, Hamlet says, "There are more things in heaven and earth, Horatio/ Than are dreamt of in our philosophy"—there's more than logic. Hamlet's rational world is upended, and after the oath, he bids the spirit "rest, rest." Insisting they all go back together, Hamlet promises Horatio and Marcellus his love and friendship—and his trust. "The time is out of joint," he confides, "O cursed spite/ That ever I was born to set it right."

A few weeks later the court of Denmark is tiptoeing around Hamlet. He told Horatio he was going to act crazy, and now they all think he is. Hamlet swings between normal and antic, and he talks about his mental state on and off through the play, right up to the end, Scene 20, when he will explain it—with breathtaking understatement—by saying he wasn't himself.

Yes and no. Imagine putting on a "false self" like a garment. Its inner surface shapes and colors the personality, the core of the self. Donald Winnicott—always alert to the adaptive aspects of mental symptoms—saw a maternal function in the false self. It could nurture and protect the true self until it matured enough to have a feeling life of its own. A similar idea was current in academia. Harry Levin said Hamlet "stands in need of a new *persona*, once the Ghost has excited his suspicions, not so much in order to feel his way as to speak his mind with impunity."[1]

His mental state is a major subplot, and critics have questioned the need for it, since he does nothing while acting mad he couldn't have done equally well acting sane. Aside from being a nuisance to Claudius, the antic disposition achieves little for plot development. But from a dramatic standpoint it does much. Hamlet has a strong identification with the jester Yorick, so it's natural to his character to act—pretend—play. Hamlet's simulated madness underscores his being a frustrated actor. Some say the madness theme is left over from the lost *Ur-Hamlet* that Shakespeare's play takes after, and that Hamlet's madness is inserted whole into the new play—and clumsily at that. But *Hamlet* wouldn't be *Hamlet*, Hamlet wouldn't be Hamlet, without the question of madness that runs from Scene 6 all the way through the middle of the final scene. The pivot of much of the poetry is violent changes in Hamlet's mental state. And Shakespeare doesn't just tell us the Prince is a poetic genius—he shows it in Hamlet's incomparable repartee. By now the observation is tired, but of all Shakespeare's hundreds of characters, only Hamlet is smart enough to have written a play by Shakespeare.

So critics are technically right about the non-necessity for madness in the plot, but texture is added, depth beyond the sum of parts, with the riddle. (And mirth: Oscar Wilde once asked whether in *Hamlet* scholarship the critics were actually mad—or only pretending to be.) Two deserving mention in this connection are W.W. Greg before the 1920s and Bernard Grebanier in the 1960s. Greg was struck as many have been by Claudius's non-reaction to the *Mousetrap* Dumb Show. His theory was that Claudius doesn't react to the poisoning of the Player King through the ears because Claudius hadn't poisoned King Hamlet: The Prince hadn't actually seen a ghost, he was hallucinating. Hamlet wasn't "mad in craft," he was mad in fact.[2]

Obviously this never pulled much weight, but it spurred John Dover Wilson to revisit the critical arguments. One theory has it that Claudius in the audience sees his murder of his brother depicted onstage, but it doesn't really register. It takes a moment to sink in, and by then Claudius has got hold of himself and overrides any reflex of surprise (Hamlet was looking for him to go pale). But Dover Wilson doesn't think Claudius overmasters his reaction to the depicted murder; he thinks Claudius *doesn't even see it*. He ties the King's non-reaction at the Dumb Show to Polonius's theory about "mad love." It pleases the vanity of the old counselor to think his daughter is the reason for the madness of a prince. So during the Dumb Show, Polonius has engaged Claudius in conversation over the "country matters" mentioned by Hamlet, and the King doesn't actually see his crime pantomimed onstage. And it is an interpretation that's used in some productions and seems to work.

But the most noted Hamlet-is-not-mad scholar is Dover Wilson's academic nemesis, Bernard Grebanier. Not only is Hamlet not mad, says Grebanier, he's not even *pretending*. This ignores the text where Hamlet several times alludes to feigned madness and the antic disposition. Given his lines in the script, a Hamlet not pretending madness would be illogical onstage. The whole court would be taking a normal-acting Hamlet as mad—presumably a kind of mass hysteria. But Grebanier is not totally unsupportable. Such is the social impact of psychosis in tight little groups. If someone in the right context claims to be crazy, others will believe it.[3]

If Hamlet is "Freud's mentor" then Polonius is Freud's alter ego. Both are keen on flows of information, the heft of influence, the levers of power. They're addicted to manipulation, eavesdropping, and gossip. Freud references the old counselor when he compares psychoanalytic "constructions," reconstructed patient histories, to psychotic delusions. Freud borrows Polonius's trope of a method in madness; a delusional story hides something deeper. Polonius is an amateur psychoanalyst, and as the play progresses, he spends more and more of his time pursuing the source of Hamlet's "ecstasy." It eventually costs him his life.

The "antic disposition" subplot starts several weeks after the council meeting where Hamlet was named heir apparent—after Horatio arrived, after Hamlet encountered the Ghost—so things should be back to normal at the castle. But much has happened. The audience is not shown Hamlet's early attempts at the antic disposition, but certainly the royal court of Denmark all see Hamlet as a madman now. This whole time Ophelia has kept Hamlet away. Now she runs to her father and tells of Hamlet's invading her chamber acting strangely.

Her description of his bizarre intrusion and his terror, as if he had just arrived from hell, comes for the audience only a few minutes after Hamlet was placating an underground demon.

Ophelia O my lord, my lord, I have been so affrighted —
. . . as I was sewing in my closet
Lord Hamlet, with his doublet all unbraced,
. . . his stockings fouled,
Ungartered and down-gyved to his ankle,*
Pale as his shirt, his knees knocking each other —
And with a look so piteous in purport
As if he had been loosed out of hell
To speak of horrors—he comes before me. . . .
He took me by the wrist and held me hard,
Then goes he to the length of all his arm
And with his other hand thus o'er his brow
He falls to such perusal of my face
As he would draw it. Long stayed he so.
At last, a little shaking of mine arm
And thrice his thus waving up and down,
He raised a sigh so piteous and profound
That it did seem to shatter all his bulk
And end his being. That done, he lets me go

And, with his head over his shoulder turned,
He seemed to find his way without his eyes,
For out of doors he went without their helps
And to the last bended their light on me.

II.i.72 TLN 971–997

* vest unlaced, his hose fallen down to his ankles

She bounces from present to past tense and back, then again to present, to past, and then again present tense. These time shifts are exactly like Hamlet's antic rant to Marcellus and Horatio when he's seen the Ghost. Her speech is at the center of some controversy. The relationship of Hamlet and Ophelia is by no means clear, and there's a range of opinion on what history they share. For some it's a question whether Hamlet's even able to love. Interwoven with these are two other questions—the cause of Hamlet's "madness," and what kind of person Ophelia actually is, since her lines allow a wider range of readings of character than anyone else in the play.

This is Ophelia's eyewitness testimony—best evidence—so it goes to the heart of the arguments. One school of criticism holds that Hamlet is so disillusioned by his mother that he can't trust Ophelia to keep the secret of his pseudo-madness. Granted, she does seem young and certainly not crafty, but he doesn't give her a chance. Also she has, on the manifest level, rejected him so—the argument goes—Hamlet feigns madness invading her chamber so she'll carry disinformation back to her father and Claudius. This puts into question Hamlet's love of Ophelia, it overstates the danger of his being found out to be sane, and it sentimentalizes her into one of Shakespeare's typical father-bound daughters. If Hamlet's coldly playing with Ophelia's heart, it poses a problem for his character: Over the course of the play, Hamlet does become more cynical, more ruthless; this early in the play though he still ought to have some idealism left over from student days. But it all depends on the production. Directors seem to get away with just about any convenient Ophelia they conceive, so fluid is her role.

A few critics think Ophelia is not only correctly reporting what she's just seen but that she's interpreting it accurately. This theory accepts that Hamlet is in the grip of horror and, indeed, her words have the ring of truth observed close up. Ophelia's description of Hamlet's eyes captures the spectral aspect of his sudden visitation, reminding us these eyes have literally seen a ghost. Hamlet's going pale is evidence of anguish on leaving her, his blanching vouches for the sincerity of his pain in this visit, his valediction to her as lover.[4]

Though Ophelia will seek reconciliation later, she's seen—and credibly reports—her lover's final adieu. He can't stop looking back as his unwilling body drags itself out the door. Polonius is right for once, Hamlet is mad for love. And this last visit is his farewell to love: Now he can concentrate on revenge. The Prince's next step will be to infect the court of Denmark.

A classic paper of psychoanalysis, "The Effort to Drive the Other Person Crazy" of Harold Searles, grew out of his experience trying to treat schizophrenic inpatients on the analytic couch. Although he probably didn't cure any, he must have been a comfort in their suffering. In the process Searles seems to have become a bit strange himself. But his having gone a bit native in the land of the insane renders his reports back indispensible.

There are, Searles says, unconscious reasons why parents may try to make their child crazy, or a child the parent, a patient the therapist—or even why a therapist may try to drive a patient mad. The human root of crazy-making is our innate ambivalence about people we love. And our disowning half that ambivalence. From birth to death, there is a constant struggle for any person to find the right emotional distance from another—not too close, not too far away—and except for rare moments of bliss, the ideal distance is never exactly the same for each person.

Trying to make someone crazy is an attempt to control the power relationship between two people. The psychosis between them is designed to increase their separateness, to prevent fusion and loss of a discrete sense of self. It's also an attempt to bridge the loneliness of being human—both distancing and fusion are going on simultaneously. Techniques of driving a person crazy we see demonstrated in Hamlet's mockery of Polonius, his irony with the schoolfellows, and his savaging the King. His mother and Ophelia are objects of scorn, but Hamlet doesn't try to make the women crazy. To the extent that he causes Ophelia's madness, it's unintentional.

Strategies for fostering conflict inside the other person include activation of areas of the other's personality which lie in opposition to each other—especially over stimulating the other person's sexual or aggressive desires on the nonverbal level while on the manifest level shaming those very impulses. And when one person tries to drive another crazy, Searles says there's a prior wish to murder that person, physically or mentally, along with an attempt to rid oneself of a deep-lying ambivalence—a psychotic split-mindedness, a craziness in the self that must be expelled into the other person. (Pioneers like Searles describe eerie moments in the treatment of schizophrenics when quite literally the hair stands up on the analyst's neck.) One way to make somebody crazy is relating on two disjointed affective levels at once, with sudden switches "from one emotional wavelength to another."

> In the course of an hour with a 24-year-old schizophrenic woman I became assailed with feelings of confusion and unreality, when she, a luxuriantly delusional person, was reading to me from an instruction book concerning the Japanese game of 'Go'. She appeared to find some hidden meaning in almost every word and even in almost every syllable, looking at me significantly, with a sarcastic smile, very frequently, as though convinced I was aware of the secret meanings.[5]

Luxuriantly delusional. The obverse of this tactic is sudden unexpected switching from one topic to another without any shift in feeling. The two work well in tandem.

> *Polonius* Do you know me, my lord?
> *Hamlet* Excellent well—you are a fishmonger.*

Polonius Not I, my lord.
Hamlet Then I would you were so honest a man.
Polonius Honest, my lord?
Hamlet Aye, sir, to be honest as this world goes
Is to be one man picked out of ten thousand —
Polonius That's very true, my lord —
Hamlet For if the sun breed maggots in a dead dog, being a
good kissing carrion—have you a daughter?
Let her not walk in the sun. Conception is a blessing,
But not as your daughter may conceive, friend—look to it.

II.ii.173 TLN 1210–1224

* a pimp

For us to evolve as social primates, emotion had to become an external signal as well as an internal regulator. The text makes us wonder how much of Hamlet's "madness" is the character he's playing and how much is who he is. The director must decide. To what extent Hamlet's contagious mania is conscious never gets resolved, an ambiguity that keeps the audience off balance, just as it does the elegantly mannered court of Denmark.

Freud carefully read the Greeks on character. Spelling out his theory of drama as sexual release, he traces ancient tragedy back to its function as a sacrificial offering. Drama entails conflict, an effort of will against a resistance, found in its original fulfillment in tragedy as "a struggle against divinity" he says. Later in the evolution of drama are the "tragedies of character," which must have two heroes struggling with each other to produce the excitement of an *agon*. A further stage in Freud's theory of the evolution of drama is "psychological tragedy." By Freud's definition it's fought out inside the hero's mind, a struggle between two *conscious* impulses.[6]

In any kind of drama, watching a play entails, first, identification with the hero, then "unquestionably the process of getting rid of one's own emotions by 'blowing off steam'" and "an accompanying sexual excitation." The culmination of drama's evolution is "psychopathological drama," *Hamlet* being the first such ever written. Freud sees the psychopathological protagonist's neurosis as a sympathetic mirror to the neurosis of the spectator. The nearly conscious conflict in the neurotic spectator is projected onto the neurotic stage hero, who contains it for them both and makes it infect the rest of the audience. Freud says that

> psychological drama turns into psychopathological drama when the source of the suffering in which we take part . . . is no longer a conflict between two almost equally conscious impulses but between a conscious impulse and a repressed one. Here the precondition of enjoyment is that the spectator should himself be a neurotic, for it is only such people who can derive pleasure instead of simple aversion from the revelation and the more or less conscious recognition of a repressed impulse.

He makes the startling claim that only neurotic individuals can relish psychopathological drama. He sees in the thrill of the spectator universal seeds of repression of childhood incestuous wishes—and not only that, but repression that was inadequate to the task of seamlessly hiding them.

Freud's theory of drama begins with *katharsis* in Aristotle's sense and proceeds all the way to its endpoint—sexual catharsis—climaxing in his discovery of incest in the Oedipus complex. In oedipal neurotics the repression is just barely working, so incestuous wishes are always on the edge of breaking through. There needs to be a constant renewal of the defense against recognition of the wishes, in this case projection of the conflict vicariously into the hero. There's a struggle between the defense and the incestuous wish becoming conscious which "can be made the subject of a drama; but even in them the dramatist will provoke not merely an *enjoyment* of the liberation but a *resistance* to it as well."

This adds extra suspense. The repressed impulse in *Hamlet* is one repressed in all of us, he says. In the beginning of the play Hamlet is not neurotic but becomes neurotic because of the task placed on him. It overtaxes his ego and breaks through his coping mechanisms. Hamlet's healthy repression (of incestuous wishes) that was once in place has been shaken by the Ghost's commands. Everyone has a breaking point says Freud. Moreover, in *Hamlet*,

> the impulse that is struggling into consciousness . . . is never given a definite name; so that the spectator to the process is carried through with his attention averted. . . . just as, in an analytic treatment, we find derivatives of the repressed material reaching consciousness while the repressed material itself is unable to do so. After all, the conflict in *Hamlet* is so effectively concealed that it was left to me to unearth it.[7]

After all, it was left to me to unearth it. Nowhere more than here is Freud infected with self regard. This is Freud-Polonius "mad for love," besotted with the Oedipus complex, his proudest claim. But what if Freud misread *Hamlet*, what if he was simply blind to the resolution of Hamlet's Oedipus complex after the second appearance of the Ghost in Gertrude's closet? Harold Bloom favors a Shakespearean reading of Freud over a Freudian reading of Shakespeare, and he says that Freud suffered from a Hamlet complex, "the true name of the Oedipus Complex."[8]

Freud's competitiveness with other men sometimes led him to over diagnose their oedipal problems. He seems smug about Shakespeare's unconscious motives in creating *Hamlet*. But what if anxiety about the poet's influence caused Freud to commit psychoanalytic "misprision," in Bloom's terms? In his *agon* with Shakespeare, did Freud fail to give the poet full credit? This question returns later, like the repressed, in different form.

Notes

1. Donald W. Winnicott, "On Transference," in *Essential Papers on Transference*, Aaron H. Esman, Ed. (New York: New York University Press, 1990), 246–251.

Sylvan Barnet, Ed., "Introduction," *The Tragedy of Hamlet*, ed. 2 (New York: Signet Classics, 1998).
Harry Levin, *The Question of Hamlet* (New York: Viking Press, 1959), 112.

2. John Dover Wilson, *What Happens in Hamlet* (Cambridge: Cambridge University Press, 1935/ 1951).
Bernard Grebanier, *The Heart of Hamlet, The Play Shakespeare Wrote* (New York: Thomas Y. Crowell, 1960).
3. David L. Rosenhan, "On Being Sane in Insane Places," *Science* 179 (1973): 250–258.
This Stanford psychologist recruited three female and five male colleagues/volunteers and trained them to briefly simulate auditory hallucinations to get admitted to twelve different psychiatric hospitals in five states. These "hallucinations" were a same-sex voice indistinctly saying only "empty," "hollow," "thud," and nothing else. In hospital, the pseudopatients complained of no further hallucinations and exhibited no other distinctive behavior than public note-taking. The psychiatric staff in these hospitals failed to unmask a single pseudopatient, although some remained hospitalized for months. (Many other actual patients, however, did suspect the pseudopatients for what they were.) In a sequel, a crossover experiment, Rosenhan told staff of one of the study's hospitals that they were going to randomly be sent pseudopatients. Over 2 weeks, the staff "detected" more than forty out of nearly 200 pseudo-fake patients admitted when in fact none were sent.
4. G.R. Elliott, *Scourge and Minister: A Study of Hamlet as Tragedy of Revengefulness and Justice* (Durham: Duke University Press, 1951).
5. Harold Searles, "The Effort to Drive the Other Person Crazy—An Element in the Aetiology and Psychotherapy of Schizophrenia," in *Collected Papers on Schizophrenia and Related Subjects* (New York: International Universities Press, 1965), 254–283, 274–275.
6. Sigmund Freud, "Psychopathic Characters on the Stage," in *The Standard Edition of the Complete Psychological Works of Sigmund Freud*, vol. 7, James Strachey, Ed. and trans. (London: The Hogarth Press, 1905/1966), 305–310.
7. Ibid, 308, 309, 310.
8. Harold Bloom, *The Anxiety of Influence: A Theory of Poetry*, ed. 2 (New York: Oxford University Press, 1973/1997), xxii.

6

ROSSENCRAFT & GILDERSTONE

Destiny's Happy Dupes

People can't keep them straight. Claudius confuses them and has to be corrected by Gertrude. The "Bad" Quarto calls them *Rossencraft* and *Gilderstone*. In authorized versions they are variously Rosencraus, Rosincrance, Rosencran, and Rosincrane; Guyldensterne, Guildsterne, Guyldersterne, and Guildensterne. Their fate is to die in the play—and sometimes before: Laurence Olivier cuts them out altogether—a pity. Ornamental hangers on, they mirror the mannerisms and falseness of the court. In a savage mood, Hamlet mocks their pretentiousness, goading Guildenstern to play a recorder—and of course he can't. Taunting his erstwhile chum, the Prince says, "It is as easy as lying."

The problem is, they aren't good at it. Lying can save your life, but to do it well you need self deception too, which they lack. At the outset they declare they're happy they're not too happy (meaning lucky). They sense the danger of too much luck, and as the play proceeds their unease deepens. They're like a Greek chorus, saying things nobody else can: Hamlet's ambition is problematic, as they say, the more so for being denied. Perversely, the world *has* grown honest upon their arrival because of what they elicit from Hamlet. Within minutes he tells them the truth about his melancholy. It's a mistake to play them as fools. They aren't bad men; they just can't rid themselves of naive honesty. In a play with a hero that's a frustrated actor, they were his audience; Hamlet used to like them, now they're miscast. If they were brutally cynical it might save them. Unperfect actors, they flub their lines.[1]

We meet the Wittenberg pals with the King and Queen just after Hamlet's bizarre intrusion into Ophelia's bedroom.

Queen Good gentlemen . . . sure I am two men are not living
To whom he more adheres. If it will please you
. . . expend your time with us awhile.

Rosencrantz	Both your majesties Might, by the sovereign power you have of us, Put your dread pleasures more into command Than to entreaty.
Guildenstern	But we both . . . lay our services freely at your feet.
King	Thanks Rosencrantz, and gentle Guildenstern.
Queen	Thanks *Guildenstern*, and *gentle* Rosencrantz, And I beseech you instantly to visit My too much changed son.

II.ii.19 TLN 1038–1057

This is all in the elevated register of courtly discourse, but nobody's fooling anybody, these boys are for sale. With low bows they leave to seek the Prince. Hamlet greets his schoolfellows with excitement and real warmth and within seconds they are into their usual bawdy badinage.

Hamlet	My excellent good friends! Good lads, how do you both?
Rosencrantz	As the indifferent children of the earth.
Guildenstern	Happy in that we are not over-happy. On Fortune's cap We are not the very button.
Hamlet	Then you live about her waist, or in the middle of her favors.
Guildenstern	Faith—her privates we.
Hamlet	In the secret parts of Fortune. Oh most true, she is a strumpet. What have you, my good friends, deserved at the hands of Fortune that she sends you to prison hither?
Guildenstern	Prison, my lord?
Hamlet	Denmark's a prison. . . . in which there are many confines, wards, and dungeons—Denmark being one of the worst.
Rosencrantz	We think not so, my lord.
Hamlet	Why then 'tis none to you; for there is nothing either good or bad, but thinking makes it so. To me it is a prison.
Rosencrantz	Why—then your ambition makes it one. 'Tis too narrow for your mind.
Hamlet	O God, I could be bounded in a nutshell and count myself a king of infinite space—were it not that I have bad dreams.
Guildenstern	Which dreams indeed are ambition.

II.ii.223 TLN 1269–1303

Hamlet has bad dreams. This is the truth, although commentators think he's toying with his chums since he never mentions nightmares again. In the earlier *Ur-Hamlet* performed in the 1590s, which is lost to us and on which Shakespeare bases his play, there was apparently a dramatic device whereby Hamlet could be mad and could misdirect his enemies, but he could never lie to them outright.

This is a convention that Shakespeare followed faithfully in his later versions, so whenever you think Hamlet might be lying, look again.

The schoolfellows are stunned by his candor. He immediately spots the hook in their comments about ambition. After bitter remarks about sycophants in Claudius's court, he forces an admission. They are shills of the King and Queen. Brushing aside their manipulation, Hamlet shocks them with a direct response to their prying. "I have of late . . . lost all my mirth," he says. Affliction sits so heavily on him that the world is "a sterile promontory," the heavens "a foul and pestilent congregation of vapors." Melancholy, in other words. The schoolfellows are speechless. As the Prince gets tetchier by the second, they placate him. Rosencrantz tells him they passed a company of actors on the road to Elsinore, the same players he used to love in the city. Hamlet's melancholy vanishes in an instant. The arrival of the Players is heard off stage. Hamlet exiting takes a moment to assure his friends that, no matter what the King and Queen think, he is "but mad north-northwest. When the wind is southerly, I know a hawk from a handsaw."

Rosencrantz and Guildenstern stand for deceptiveness and inadequate self deception, but they also stand for fate. "Fate" implies immutability. It pits *determinism* against *fatalism*—determinism, following a causal chain with choice points—and fatalism as predestined, beyond human control. Determinism describes a causal sequence along which are points where free will may deflect the course of events. ("The fate of the child is in her hands.") The individual has a sense of agency that may not be entirely an illusion. But fatalism obtains when there are no choice points at all. ("He submits himself to his fate.")[2]

And that is the question: Is the universe completely unpredictable, like the roll of the dice—or is it deterministic like an intricate clock? And, does it matter? As for the beautiful jeweled movement of the universe, once it's wound and the pendulum nudged, isn't any sense of personal agency just self-deception? His relationship with the schoolfellows mirrors Hamlet's swerve from a heavy sense of responsibility early in the play to a kind of fatalism toward the end. After his sea voyage, Hamlet returns to Denmark with what almost amounts to serenity. And everywhere there's irony. His pals are in Hamlet's power as he is crushed by forces beyond himself. They're at the crux of mushy character and rotten luck, *Nature's livery* and *Fortune's star*. They embody the contradictions inherent in *could have done otherwise*, the seductive illusory "validity" of the counterfactual. If *determinism versus free will* has now proved too deep for even philosophers to sound, the schoolmates must be forgiven as they lose their nerve. They're snared in the tangle of tragic destiny described by Aristotle; they embody tragic knowledge, a growing hopeless recognition of the will of the gods.

Classical tragedy is always in the background with Freud. Like Hamlet, he thinks about Nature, Fortune, Providence, and Fate—biological determinants, random events, divine will, and sheer coincidence. Freud's universe, like Hamlet's, teeters between the complete randomness of the dice game and the hard determinism of the fixed paths of the planets; he read the Greeks and believed in the dramatic collision of fate and chance. The ensuing catharsis, he thought, brings purgation through pity and terror, emotional healing, moral cleansing, and hygienic physical release. For maximal effect, the tragic myth needs to faithfully imitate real life. Aristotle says it's best when "events come on us by surprise; and. . . . tragic wonder will then be greater than if they happened of themselves . . . for even coincidences are most striking when they have an air of design."[3]

Freud has a single paper on what he calls the "compulsion of destiny" or the "fate neurosis." The concept never generated much interest and it faded from view. Freud says it occurs in the occasional normal person, the asymptomatic non-neurotic individual.[4]

> The impression they give is of being pursued by a malignant fate or possessed by some 'daemonic' power; but psycho-analysis has always taken the view that their fate is for the most part arranged by themselves [and this] 'perpetual recurrence of the same thing' causes us no astonishment when it relates to *active* behaviour on the part of the person concerned.

Freud is describing the rare instance when there's no apparent agency of the patient in the repetition, "cases where the subject appears to have a *passive* experience, over which he has no influence, but in which he meets with a repetition of the same fatality." He distinguishes the garden variety symptom-producing neurosis—the repetition compulsion—from the asymptomatic neurosis of destiny: These people repeat a pattern but don't have psychogenic impotence or hysterical conversions. Oedipal conflicts don't seem to be driving the repetition.

> Thus we have come across people all of whose human relationships have the same outcome: such as the benefactor who is abandoned in anger after a time by each of his *protégés* . . . or the man whose friendships all end in betrayal by his friend . . . or again, the lover each of whose love affairs with a woman passes through the same phases and reaches the same conclusion.[5]

The patient seems to possess an "essential character-trait" that awaits destiny and is entangled in the fated outcome but doesn't unconsciously cause it; for Freud "character" has internal consistency. He's following Aristotle: Even in the snares of coincidence, "a person of a given character should speak or act in a given way. . . . according to the law of probability or necessity."[6]

But Aristotle pays little attention to distinctiveness in character. His critics say that tragic drama represents the *destiny of the individual* because action "is a product of the characters and of the circumstances in which they are placed." In real life, it's rare that "outward circumstances are entirely dominant over the forces of the spirit. If it is true that 'things outward do draw the inward quality after them,' it is no less true in tragedy that things inward draw the outward after them." Aristotle said plot elicits inward qualities of character, but he's criticized for ignoring the way character traits reach out and capture life's plot elements to drive the action:

> This inevitable sequence of cause and effect is the link that character forges as it expresses itself in action. A man's deeds become external to him; his character dogs and pursues him as a thing apart. The fate that overtakes the hero is no alien thing, but his own self recoiling upon him for good or evil. . . .[7]

One's own self recoiling on itself. This is the tension between character and plot. Coincidentally this tension is also the divide between the first two centuries of *Hamlet* criticism, which focused on plot, and the second two centuries that focus on the character of the Prince. It wasn't until Hazlitt's time that something complex within Hamlet was supposed to cause him to hesitate.[8]

In psychoanalysis, there's a tension between character and symptom. Freud never completely resolved it, being content to describe character as distinctive behavioral presentations behind which deeper instincts conflict. The problem with character clinically was that it hardened transference resistances. Freud discerns a deeper "core" self manifest by peculiarities in the patient "which he had seemed to possess only to a modest degree" yet which are suddenly "brought to light in surprisingly increased intensity, or attitudes [that] reveal themselves in him which had not been betrayed in other relations of life."[9]

So character was left as muddy in psychoanalysis as it was in tragedy—distinctive "peculiarities" of interaction and stylistic "attitudes" particularizing an individual's social intercourse. Neurotic symptoms of the "compulsion to repeat" had a coherent oedipal plot line, but the fate neurosis was murky, like tragic character, and got no definitive explanation. Freud never repudiated it but relegated it to the same metaphysical attic as the death instinct. It was gradually absorbed into another fuzzy concept, the "character neurosis," and forgotten.[10]

Despite general indifference to the "fate neurosis," there was someone who was taken with it. Helene Deutsch, born in Poland in 1884, moved to Vienna and eventually became a member of Freud's inner circle. In her youth Deutsch was a great beauty who had a penchant for a certain type of man. Fiercely independent and unconventional, she tended to pursue—and win—the older, powerful kind of man who was not just a leader, but a radical, a revolutionary. Her first romance (starting at age fourteen) was with the much older Polish Socialist Herman Lieberman. This species of triangular relationship was a pattern in Deutsch's life and the subject of some of her writing in which she sometimes used her experiences disguised as clinical material.[11]

Helene Deutsch's life might at times have seemed to her guided by destiny. Her papers concern women in a love triangle who try to pull a man away from the rightful wife—which was her own story; it mirrored her family constellation of attachment to her father and rivalry with her mother. After becoming a physician in order to become an analyst, she entered psychoanalysis with Freud in Vienna, where she lived out ironies that evoke the idea of a "compulsion of destiny." Concurrent with her own analysis with Freud, she psychoanalyzed the gifted Victor Tausk whom Freud himself refused to analyze. Freud had rejected Tausk because he didn't have the time, but there are questions about Freud's disinclination to take on a younger man of some promise who also was attractive to the women in Freud's coterie. (For instance, Lou Andreas-Salomé, who had affairs with, among others, Rilke, Nietzsche, and Tausk.) So 6 days a week Deutsch had Tausk on her couch for his analysis, then she went to lie on Freud's couch to talk about Tausk.[12]

The early psychoanalytic movement had a lot of blurring of social and doctor-patient boundaries, and there does seem to have been some major denial by Freud, Tausk, and Deutsch. But what actually happened in their complex relationship is conjecture. Tausk's overall contribution to psychoanalysis is hard to assess a century later, although he did write one brilliant paper still read today. Freud's detractors paint Tausk as a victim of Freud's malefactions. There is reason to suppose Tausk had post-traumatic stress disorder upon return from World War I. But Tausk was evidently a man who both demanded Freud's attention and resented his help. Refused by Freud for analysis, he turned down Freud's first two suggestions for an analyst for himself, suggesting Helene Deutsch instead—which Freud reluctantly agreed to. Since she herself never spoke of it, there is mystery about Tausk's analysis, which Deutsch abandoned under pressure after 3 months. Freud said it served as a resistance in her own ongoing analysis: All she could talk about was Tausk. Such countertransference makes sense in light of her history, since Victor Tausk—5 years older than Helene—was one of the most elegant, creative, and credentialed men of Freud's circle. And, of course, Tausk was unhappily married, something she looked for in a man.

Tausk killed himself 3 months after Freud told Deutsch to terminate Tausk's analysis—which she did the day after Freud's mandate. Then over the next 3 months, Tausk seduced a patient of his, got her pregnant, and was a week away from marrying her, apparently choosing to kill himself instead. His suicide he accomplished by hanging himself with a curtain cord, at the same time shooting himself in the head—after writing a tender suicide note to Freud.[13]

A gunshot to the temple. The index case for Helene Deutsch's papers on the fate neurosis is a woman in her twenties, "beautiful, cultured, and rich." She came to the first interview with a fresh superficial gunshot wound to her temple after a suicide attempt. She wasn't depressed and she had no idea why she had tried to shoot herself. She had a conviction that it was her destiny to die under her present circumstances (she was about to marry the man she had so long pursued). Although she had no symptoms, as she told Deutsch her story she gradually started to feel "there was something mysterious and apparently morbid in her life, something which convinced her that she was after all in need of analytic treatment." It ran through her life "like an inscrutable decree of fate" that she could love and be loved but something always went awry.[14]

The patient had tried to shoot herself on the eve of her marriage to a man she won away from another woman—a triangle personally familiar to Deutsch. But over the course of the patient's long and ultimately successful analysis, what had appeared to be the workings of external fate turned out to be internal after all—

there was nothing mysterious or supernatural about it. What appeared as a lack of conflict and absence of symptoms eventually emerged as an old unconscious attachment that held the patient in an endless cycle of repetitions—her fixation on her father. She always chose men who resembled him, although the men had to be superficially different in order not to arouse conscious guilt about incestuous desires.

Deutsch's formulation embarks from Freud's idea that oedipal conflicts give rise to "ego alien symptoms." Neurotic *character*, on the other hand, may be manifested in repeated self destructive patterns experienced as beyond the individual's intent, "not my fault." These repeated patterns are made up of "ego syntonic" behaviors that seem to "just happen." But over the years Deutsch thought about this case, she eventually concluded that what appears to be fate is actually unconscious intent, that the "fate neurosis" was no more than a garden variety "repetition compulsion." It was just that the patient's agency was at first invisible. Thirty years later "quite by chance," Deutsch had the opportunity for a follow-up interview with her fate neurosis patient, who had done well in both her career as a physicist and her life as wife and mother. Deutsch was curious about what had happened to the transference in the decades since the analysis.

> Toward me she showed a certain condescending benevolence, as to a good, old aunt. When I pointed out how successful her analysis had been, she said, again with a benevolent smile: "You have helped me a great deal, but analysis gave me nothing. I don't believe in analysis at all—it is a hoax—all bunk—purely constructions in your own mind."[15]

The interpretation of these devaluing remarks is typical Deutsch: For her, the female Oedipus complex is a refusal to identify with the *type* of woman the mother was. Deutsch firmly believed (contra Freud) that a daughter's identification with her father was healthy. She felt that the daughter of a masochistic mother always blamed her for not making the daughter a son, obviating the necessity for shameful identification with a weak woman. So this patient's competitiveness with her mother was still present decades later "despite a thorough analysis of the negative transference." She expressed the "devaluation in displacement from my role as woman and mother into the sphere in which she herself feels secure: in the professional life where she achieved so much (as physicist) and I so little ('nothing') (as analyst)."[16]

This is how Deutsch retooled the concept of "penis envy", configuring it to her own clinical experience. For her it was not so much a literal feeling of inferiority over lacking a penis as the attempt by a little girl to gain power and status equal to boys. But she understood the little girl's sharp awareness of symbolic markers of gender inequality. Deutsch speculated that the scar of this awareness persists in the patient's apparent bitterness that analysis hadn't changed the biological fact of her femininity. Deutsch had the wisdom to admit there was a limit to what she and this patient could understand together. The distinction between a repetition compulsion and a fate neurosis is blurry; the difference between a symptom neurosis and a character neurosis is also indistinct. She used to teach novice analysts that symptomatic people enter therapy because they want to change; and that people with deep character problems enter treatment because they *wish* they wanted to change.

Into her eighties Deutsch carefully preserved letters from her first love when she was fifteen, Herman Lieberman—there are some things people don't even *wish to* want to change. Although she was writing about the fate neurosis, she could just as well have been writing about herself. She, and her patient, always chose a man like her father who put her on a pedestal and made the same high expectations of her that she had of herself. But—there was a problem—the unconscious guilt toward her mother that made her always punish herself.

> In the inner awareness of her . . . deeply rooted masochistic attachment to her father, she was panicky at the thought that she might be unable to meet her lover's intellectual and moral demands. [She would rather shoot herself] than to adopt toward her lover the masochistic attitude of her mother to which she was compulsively driven.[17]

Helene Deutsch had a practice of putting forth her own history as case reports. Reading her letters you see her taming impulses as she grows year by year and comes to terms with life's realities. She was her own best patient—and her own best analyst. "The hysterical fate neurosis," Deutsch said, "is a form of suffering imposed on the ego apparently by the outer world with a recurrent regularity. The real motive of this fate lies, as we have seen, in a constant, insoluble inner conflict." So oedipal conflict—not fate—gives rise to the neurosis of destiny.[18]

The schoolfellows are poor actors and worse liars. And they're dreadful sycophants. They realize they're in a tight spot, but it's even worse than they imagine.

Guildenstern We will ourselves provide
To keep those many many bodies safe
That live and feed upon your majesty.
Rosencrantz The lives of many . . . Dies not alone but doth draw
. . . ten thousand lesser things. Never alone
Did the king sigh, but with a general groan.
*III.iii.*7 TLN 2279–2296

Claudius must inwardly wince; they depict him as a bloated lump, with wormy subjects feeding off him. And they've failed to control Hamlet, so now they're starting to sweat.

There's a better way to play Rosencrantz and Guildenstern than most productions attempt—a concept that doesn't sacrifice their comedic or choric functions. It assumes their motivation at Elsinore is based on greed, yes, but that the key element is a conflicted relationship with Hamlet. Suppose at university Rosencrantz and Guildenstern had just the right amount of deference toward a prince, yet irreverence and wit enough to get Hamlet to laugh. They share confidences and bawdy humor. Rosencrantz and Guildenstern "being of so young days brought up with him" would be friends ready at hand to "draw him on to pleasures." For their part, the schoolfellows are thrilled the Prince has taken them up, he laughs at their jokes, he is seen in public with them, they all go to theater. The fourth of the group, Horatio, balances at the edge of their little clique, listening at a bit of a distance. (Hamlet addresses him with the more formal *you* until the middle of the play but he calls Rosencrantz and Guildenstern the familiar *thou* from the beginning.)

Look how they greet Hamlet—*God save you sir! Mine honored lord! My most dear lord!*—doesn't it seem their exaggerated courtesy might be the same playful irony they used to bridge differences in status back at Wittenberg, the private wit they used to loosen the public demands upon a prince? When they arrive at Elsinore, Hamlet falls upon them, starved for companionship. It's easy to believe, on their part, his old playmates had grown to love Hamlet—as indeed who does not? They're pulled several directions, but the motivation that shouldn't get lost onstage is their regard for Hamlet. They've been told on high authority that he's mad. Horatio, for one, our truth litmus, never devalues the schoolfellows, and he silently disapproves Hamlet's destroying them. They deserve better than they get. After his rash impulse to shut them out, the Prince never again takes them into his confidence, so they believe they're acting in Hamlet's interest serving the rightful king. "My lord, you did love me once," says Guildenstern with quiet dignity, and there's no reason to disbelieve him.

Sympathetic schoolfellows make it more difficult for the actor playing the Prince, and it makes more shocking their useless deaths and unshriven souls. He destroys them like an angry child breaking toys. It's ironic they're murdered, because there was a way out: Had these bad actors stepped out of Claudius's play into Hamlet's, they might have remembered the Prince's trick of creating reality. They are capable of it—that's why Hamlet liked them in the first place. The plays within plays in *Hamlet* create riddles, so it takes a riddle to solve them. The key is the liar's paradox: *This statement is a lie.* It's inherently non-sense. If it's true, it's false; if false, it's true. They know how to use it—we see them do it just after they first greet Hamlet *happy in not being too happy*—but they don't think to use it to save their own lives.

The crazy-making paradox is Hamlet's method with Polonius, and he uses it on Rosencrantz and Guildenstern: "I would obey the Queen were she ten times my mother." *Were she my mother* means she's not his mother, a counterfactual. Pitch perfect, it's a grammatically lawful sentence with a logically unlawful meaning. You think he's about to tell them he'd obey her even if she weren't his mother. But she is his mother, so he will obey her, yet he wishes times ten she weren't—so he won't—or will he? The hyperbole of *ten times my mother* also ironically falsifies the proposition. Hamlet knows *how to do things with words* (in J.L. Austin's nifty phrase), and the Wittenberg chums could have turned the Prince. Perhaps their easy familiarity back at school has made them take him a bit for granted. It may be this more than anything that dooms them. They should have loved Hamlet less and feared him more. It's a nice touch that the schoolfellows announce the Players' arrival at Elsinore; but they needed to decide which stage they're on, Wittenberg or Elsinore. They try to be all things to everyone and end up as nothing.

There is a moment when inside Hamlet a door that was open shuts forever.

Hamlet What's the news?
Rosencrantz None, my lord, but that the world's grown honest.
Hamlet Then is doomsday near—but your news is not true.
Let me question more in particular. . . . In the beaten
way of friendship, what make you at Elsinore?
Rosencrantz To visit you, my lord, no other occasion.
Hamlet Beggar that I am, I am even poor in thanks, but I thank you.
And sure, dear friends, my thanks are too dear a half-penny.
Were you not sent for? Is it your own inclining? Is it a free
visitation? Come, come. Deal justly with me. Nay, speak!
Guildenstern What should we say, my lord?
Hamlet Why, anything but to the purpose. You were sent for, and
there is a kind of confession in your looks which your
modesties have not craft enough to color. I know the good
King and Queen have sent for you.
Rosencrantz To what end, my lord?
Hamlet That you must teach me—but let me conjure you by the
rights of our fellowship, by the consonancy of our youth,*
by the obligation of our ever-preserved love —
Be even and direct with me. . . . if you love me, hold not off.
Guildenstern My lord, we were sent for.

II.ii.36 TLN 1281–1339
* by bond of our younger days

They were sent for. The play needed them, and the playwright gives them better lines than Horatio or Polonius. Without them the Prince would lack a platform for some of his best invective. And an audience for his essay on man, a cry from the depths. It's hard to know what Hamlet loves—or used to love—but Rosencrantz and Guildenstern catalyze what amounts to love poetry. In the script, the speech is prose but recast into verse it shows its lyric bones:

Hamlet What a piece of work is man —
How noble in reason, how infinite in faculties,
In form and moving how express and admirable,
In action how like an angel,
In apprehension how like a god:
The beauty of the world, the paragon of animals —
And yet to me, what is this quintessence of dust?

II.ii.292 TLN 1349–1356

Notice the indefinite article before *man*—there isn't one in our version. Earlier to test a reading, we used the First Law, *If there is one perfect way to say something, Shakespeare will have found it.* Here, it licenses us to drop the article. The Quarto of 1603 has it without the *a*, three times within six lines, just *man*—as when Hamlet tells Rossencraft and Gilderstone, "No, nor man that is so glorious a creature contents not me." Only Shakespeare can inspire ink wars over the indefinite article. Freud called such quibbles "the narcissism of minor differences," and Hamlet says men will die "even for an eggshell." For Shakespeare at least, people will fight over one syllable, so here we'll drop the *a*.

Poetry at its most perfect is words in a tight spot—but the right words in the right spot. We have to be grateful to Rosencrantz and Guildenstern not just for their cautionary example but because they elicit Hamlet's most heart stopping poetry.

Notes

1. Helene Deutsch, "Some Forms of Emotional Disturbance and Their Relationship to Schizophrenia," *Psychoanalytic Quarterly* 11 (1942): 301–321.

   Sonnet 23 says, "As an unperfect actor on the stage/ Who with his fear is put besides his part . . . So I, for fear of trust forget to say/ The perfect ceremony of love's rite." Deutsch gave the name *as if* to a type of chameleon-like individual. The "as-if personality" is a conformist whose character is shaped by others' expectations rather than a coherent self image. Their lives run along "as if" normally, but they're highly suggestible, superficial in conscience, often depersonalized, and emotionally shallow. Such people act *as if* they're what people want them to be. Sometimes they play their roles so well they never realize they're actors.
2. Espen Bjerke, "Victim of Fate?: A Presentation of the Concept of 'Fate Neurosis'," *Scandinavian Psychoanalytic Review* 18 (1995): 80–90.
3. Aristotle, *The Poetics*, S.H. Butcher, trans., ed. 2 (New York: Macmillan, 1898), 39.
4. Sigmund Freud, "Beyond the Pleasure Principle," in *The Standard Edition of the Complete Psychological Works of Sigmund Freud*, vol. 18, James Strachey, Ed. and trans. (London: The Hogarth Press, 1920/1955), 1–64.
5. Ibid, 21, 22.
6. Aristotle, *Poetics*, 35, 55.
7. Ibid, Butcher's critique, 346–347.
8. Margreta de Grazia, "Hamlet's Thoughts and Antics (draft version)." http://emc.eserver.org/1-2/degrazia.html, accessed February 9, 2012.
9. Sigmund Freud, "Some Character-Types Met with in Psycho-Analytic Work," in *The Standard Edition of the Complete Psychological Works of Sigmund Freud*, vol. 14, James Strachey, Ed. and trans. (London: The Hogarth Press, 1916/1957), 310–333.
10. Ruth F. Lax, ed., "Introduction," *Essential Papers on Character Neurosis and Treatment* (New York: New York University Press, 1989), 1–20.

    Donald M. Kaplan, "Reflections on the Idea of Personal Fate and its Psychopathology: Helene Deutsch's 'Hysterical Fate Neurosis' Revisited," *Psychoanalytic Quarterly* 53 (1984): 240–266.

    Lawrence B. Inderbitzin and Steven T. Levy, "Repetition Compulsion Revisited: Implications for Technique," *Psychoanalytic Quarterly* 67 (1998): 32–53.
11. Helene Deutsch, "Hysterical Fate Neurosis," in *Neuroses and Character Types: Clinical Psychoanalytic Studies* (1930; reprint, New York: International Universities Press, 1965), 14–28.

    Helene Deutsch, "Psychoanalytic Therapy in the Light of Follow-up," in *Neuroses and Character Types: Clinical Psychoanalytic Studies* (1959; reprint, New York: International Universities Press, 1965), 339–352.

Paul Roazen, *Helene Deutsch: A Psychoanalyst's Life* (New York: Anchor Press/Doubleday, 1985).

12. Victor Tausk, "On the Origin of the 'Influencing Machine' in Schizophrenia," Dorian Feigenbaum, trans., *Psychoanalytic Quarterly* 2 (1919; reprint 1933): 519–556.

    Tausk anticipated the concept of ego boundaries and of what came to be called "identity" that influenced object relations theorists. He's credited with the insight that a child's first lie, a lie that's believed, is a milestone in selfobject differentiation because it proves the privacy and integrity of the self. Children with overly intuitive parents good at "mind reading" make it harder for the child to have a sense of privacy and me/ not-me distinctions.

13. Paul Roazen, *Brother Animal: The Story of Freud and Tausk* (New York: Alfred A. Knopf, 1969).

    James W. Hamilton, "A Reconsideration of the Freud-Tausk-Deutsch Relationship," *Psychoanalytic Review* 78 (1991): 267–278.

14. Deutsch, "Fate," 17, 24.
15. Deutsch, "Follow-up," 347.
16. Ibid, 343.
17. Ibid, 349.
18. Deutsch, "Fate," 27.

7

THE FAIR OPHELIA

Truth or Transference?

Distortions in how we perceive important people in our lives, "transference," is the hardest concept in psychoanalysis. But what is it really, does it even actually exist? In a century of psychoanalytic hairsplitting, despite Freud's writ and warrant, the key fact of transference kept getting lost: *Normal, healthy people form transferences all the time.* That's because we need to deceive ourselves. Deception is an adaptation evolved for survival. Widespread over many species are strategies that optimize fitness by deceiving enemies—or mating partners—and counter-strategies for cheater detection, and counter-counter-strategies. Transference is our subjective distortion of the image of others in relation to ourselves. But it must find a balance; there can't be too much denial. Nor too little—we can't stand to look naked reality in the face.

Freud's first important engagement with psychopathology was hysteria, described by Hippocrates and manifested by some of the women (mostly women) of turn-of-the-century Vienna. Its symptoms were a crazy quilt of physical ails—varied, mysterious, and impossible to ignore because they had to be presumed physical to rule out serious medical conditions. Hysteria was a diagnosis of exclusion. Initially Freud thought hysteria was caused by childhood seduction. Later he decided the sexual abuse was imaginary, a false memory. (Hysterics were so plentiful, and he couldn't believe there was that much child molestation.) He concluded that sexual conflict was being *converted* symbolically into the language of the body; unconscious displacement of emotions onto various body parts resulted in "conversion symptoms."[1]

Freud then moved from treatment by hypnosis to free association, the flow of which he repeatedly observed was impeded by *resistance* related to the transference. Unconscious transfer of thoughts, feelings, and defenses from parents onto later stand-ins can distort all human relationships but its resolution in analysis, especially the patient's *transference neurosis* toward the analyst, was supposed to cure the underlying hysterical neurosis.[2]

The literature on transference begins in 1895 when Freud and his friend Joseph Breuer were trying to understand failures in the treatment of the hysterical cough and paralysis of "Anna O." What Freud and Breuer neglected to mention in their published work was that Anna O developed a psychotic transference and a hysterical pseudopregnancy with Breuer as the "father." This precipitated Breuer's panicky termination of therapy, his flight out of town with his jealous wife, and his abandonment of psychoanalysis as a career. Breuer and his wife then went on their second honeymoon and conceived a daughter they named Dora, born the same year as the "Dora" in Freud's case.[3]

In fact the history of transference is rooted in such disasters. Janet Malcolm writes,

> Freud stumbled on the concept of transference while desperately casting about for an antidote to the epidemic of iatrogenic lovesickness that had spread through his practice in the 1890s. When, one by one, all of his women patients stopped doing the work of free association that they had at first enthusiastically taken up and began shyly and then importunely to declare their love for him he shrewdly surmised that it was not "the charms of my person" that were the cause of the disturbance but, rather, that the women were in a state of readiness to fall in love. . . . Freud's clearsightedness about the profound impersonality of romantic passion was not an original insight. . . . Where Freud's genius came into play was in his extension of the metaphor of unseeing, solipsistic passion to the whole of human interaction. It began to dawn on Freud that it is not only love that is blind: *all* our feelings toward and ideas about one another are marked by a magnificent obliviousness to reality.[4]

An obliviousness at times including Freud. Steven Marcus calls *Dora* "one of the great works of literature." He focuses the lens of literary criticism on the negative transference, "as the account progresses, Freud has never been more inspired, more creative, more inventive; as the reader sees Dora gradually slipping further and further away from Freud, the power and complexity of the writing reach dizzying proportions." At the center of Freud's "modernist novel" is the fact that every character (including at times the analyst) has betrayed her. After many reversals Dora, in an act of pure revenge, abruptly leaves Freud stunned behind his couch, gasping like a spurned lover. She breaks off treatment as he's about to make his biggest breakthrough. In a dramatic sense it's deeply satisfying. Dora's is an overdetermined conclusion that strikes out at her father, her mother, Herr K and Frau K—and, most of all, at Freud himself.

> What went wrong with the case . . . was something to do with the transference. . . . On Dora's side. . . . there was the failure on her part to establish an adequate positive transference to Freud. She was not free enough to respond to him erotically—in fantasy—or intellectually—by accepting his interpretations: both or either of these being prerequisites for the mysterious

> "talking cure" to begin to work. And in the second, halfway through the case a negative transference began to emerge, quite clearly in the first dream.[5]

Something to do with transference. But Marcus is wrong when he talks about Dora's inability to connect intellectually. Transference has nothing to do with the intellect, it's sexual at root, entirely involuntary, and fundamentally irrational.

It's odd there's no critical literature on transference in *Hamlet.* Nobody describes a clear instance of "transference," "*the* transference," "a transference neurosis" or anything close. But transference is there—vividly. Picture the scene in Gertrude's bedroom, Hamlet stabs Polonius hiding behind an arras. Isn't this the projection of wishes and fears onto parent surrogates? Isn't this Shakespeare's metaphor for transference—suddenly to transform Polonius (really nothing more than a lump in a rug) into the suppositious Claudius? Yes and yes. You miss "transference" if you're looking for a single example. But in plain sight is instance after instance. It's also the root of some of the play's "problems" endlessly debated by scholars. It is the knottiest of concepts, and even its discoverer came to hate it.[6]

Dora is Freud's first, best description but he missed her negative transference, obvious in retrospect in the famous first dream. And he couldn't bear to publish the case for years, disclaiming it as a "fragment." Two decades later in 1923, when he tacked his last convoluted misremembered footnote to the "Postscript," he made one final rueful stab at justification: His blind spot came from a secret his patient still hadn't told him: *Dora was in love with Frau K.* Even the father of psychoanalysis, was exasperated with transference.[7]

Hamlet's schoolfellows report to the royal couple the good news of their son's reaction to the arriving actors and his plans for a play before the court. Claudius is now persuaded by Polonius to use Ophelia to get information. Polonius arranges for his daughter, reading a prayer book, to be stationed where she'll encounter Hamlet. Polonius and Claudius hide behind a tapestry. He enters deep in a conversation he is having with himself. *To be or not to be*? At his most inward, he's weighing known sufferings against an uncertain afterlife.

He notices Ophelia praying. *Soft you now, the fair Ophelia.* But, after Hamlet at his most appealing, Shakespeare shows us Hamlet at his most vicious. The delay in revenge has been called the "problem of problems," but the most painful problem is the way he treats her. He has a savage aspect to his character, seen in the murder of Rosencrantz and Guildenstern and his chilling vow in Soliloquy 6 not just to kill Claudius but to destroy his soul. And it has its climax with his sustained abuse of his mother. But the fact is, this most difficult problem—the abuse of these two females—is also the most striking example of transference from one to the other.

The play doesn't say whether Ophelia obeyed her father's orders to avoid the lord Hamlet, but nothing could justify his rage. Dover Wilson feels it's entirely pretended, Hamlet is throwing Claudius and Polonius off the track. Some critics have the hunch that, unless it's a feint, Hamlet's behavior toward Ophelia has to do with anger toward Gertrude. But how? When scholars think the scene depicts

Hamlet's true feelings, most let it go as conscious displacement; he's enraged at Gertrude and takes it out on Ophelia. The larger issue is, does Hamlet really love her? Nowhere does he show remorse. And those celebrated soliloquies from the center of his soul? Love goes unmentioned, Ophelia doesn't exist.

Three episodes show transference from his mother to Ophelia—the Nunnery scene, Soliloquy 5, and the Closet scene with Gertrude. The scene in his mother's bedroom comes later, but we reverse scene order to look at the relationship, prototype for the transference. With Gertrude, he doesn't trust himself—he might kill her. He pictures stabbing her.

Hamlet 'Tis now the very witching time of night
When churchyards yawn and hell itself breathes out
Contagion to this world. Now could I drink hot blood.
Soft, now to my mother. . . .
Let me be cruel but not unnatural.
I will speak daggers to her, but use none.
III.ii.388 TLN 2259–2268

Hamlet goes to her bedroom, he stabs Polonius, and then he's speaking daggers. She's pleading to know what wrong act she's done.

Hamlet Such an act
That blurs the grace and blush of modesty,
Calls virtue hypocrite, takes off the rose
From the fair forehead of an innocent love
And sets a blister there. . . . to live
In the rank sweat of an enseamed bed
Stewed in corruption, honeying and making love
Over the nasty sty. Not this, by no means . . .
Let the bloat King tempt you again to bed,
Pinch wanton on your cheek, call you his Mouse,
And let him for a pair of reechy kisses
Or paddling in your neck with his damned fingers
Make you to ravel all this matter out.
III.iv.40 TLN 2423–2562

The *blister* Hamlet refers to is venereal, a sore acquired in an *enseamed* bed—between sweaty greasy sheets like a pigpen. The mix of honey and manure is juxtaposed with Claudius's pillow talk and bad breath—*call you his Mouse*—and stinking steamy kisses, caresses on her neck with bloated, stubby fingers.

Now, keeping in mind this image of Hamlet and Gertrude, we go back to Ophelia.

Ophelia Good my lord,

	How does your honor for this many a day?
Hamlet	I humbly thank you, well—well. Well.
Ophelia	My lord, I have remembrances of yours That I have longed long to redeliver. I pray you now receive them. *[offering his letters]*
Hamlet	No, not I, no, I never gave you aught.
Ophelia	My honored lord, you know right well you did, And with them words of so sweet breath composed As made these things more rich. Their perfume lost, Take these again, for to the noble mind, Rich gifts wax poor when givers prove unkind. There, my lord. *[she offers them again]*
Hamlet	Ha, ha—are you honest? *[he flings them to the floor]*
Ophelia	My lord?
Hamlet	Are you fair?
Ophelia	What means your lordship?
Hamlet	That if you be honest and fair, your honesty should admit no discourse to your beauty . . . for the power of beauty will sooner transform honesty to a bawd than . . . honesty can translate beauty into his likeness—I did love you once.
Ophelia	Indeed, my lord, you made me believe so.
Hamlet	You should not have believed me—I loved you not.
Ophelia	I was the more deceived.
Hamlet	Get thee to a nunnery, why wouldst thou be a breeder of sinners? I am myself indifferent honest, but yet I could accuse me of such things that it were better my mother had not borne me: I am very proud, revengeful, ambitious, with more offenses at my beck than . . . time to act them in. What should such fellows as I do crawling between heaven and earth? We are arrant knaves all. Believe none of us. Go thy ways to a nunnery! *[he hears something]* Where's your father?

III.i.89 TLN 1745–1785

Hamlet's misogyny didn't just start with his mother marrying Claudius. Dover Wilson's interpretation of the Nunnery Scene is that Hamlet overhears the conspiracy between Claudius and Polonius early in the play, so Hamlet's aware he's spied on the whole time with Ophelia; he's putting on a performance for the eavesdroppers. This way Dover Wilson justifies all his behavior as a ruse to trick them into thinking him mad and ineffective. But Hamlet's just happening to stumble onto a conspiracy isn't the kind of graceful plotting Shakespeare does in his mature plays. No indication of overhearing occurs at any point until Hamlet's abrupt *Where's your father?*—one of the play's embedded stage directions. Something happens behind the arras.

In their films Branagh, Richardson, and Brook put Hamlet's discovery of the eavesdroppers precisely here with a sudden noise or a glimpse of Claudius or Polonius. It works.

Hamlet	Where's your father?
Ophelia	At home, my lord.
Hamlet	Let the doors be shut upon him That he may play the fool nowhere but in his own house!
Ophelia	O help him, you sweet heavens!
Hamlet	If thou dost marry, I'll give thee this plague for thy dowry: Be thou as chaste as ice, as pure as snow, thou shall not escape calumny. Get thee to a nunnery—go—farewell. Or —marry a fool, for wise men know . . . what monsters you make of them: To a nunnery go—and quickly too. Farewell.
Ophelia	O heavenly powers, restore him!
Hamlet	I have heard of your paintings well enough. God has given you one face and you make yourselves another. You jig and you amble and you lisp . . . and make your wantonness your ignorance. Go to—it hath made me mad. I say we will have no more marriage! Those that are married already, all but one shall live. The rest shall keep as they are. To a nunnery—go! *Exit Hamlet.*

III.i.109 TLN 1785–1805

Eavesdropping theories aside, we still have the Nunnery problem. Antic disposition plus spies are insufficient to explain Hamlet's rage. Dover Wilson says Hamlet has no choice but to savage Ophelia—pretending madness—once he spots the conspirators. But this brilliant, noble, desperate Prince has other ways to fool the spies without sacrificing the love of his life. Hamlet could whisper to Ophelia a quick plea for her to go along—there are other asides—or Hamlet could dash to the arras and expose the spies and, on discovering them, become even more insane.

But there's another approach to his motivation: Hamlet sees Ophelia and they speak. The tenor is sweet until she returns his remembrances, *There, my lord.* Suddenly he is enraged. Branagh has him knocking the tokens out of her hand. *Ha, ha—are you honest?* His tirade goes on till another sudden switch: *I did love you once*, sadly. Then she replies, *I was the more deceived.* Hamlet grows reflective; women's frailty is caused by such "arrant knaves" as all men are. The meditative tone continues until *Where's your father?* From Ophelia's point of view, this is a non-sequitur. *At home, my lord* she says, startled and protective of her father. Her apparent siding with Polonius triggers Hamlet's second tirade, this time sexualized. He blames women not for dishonesty but lust. *Get thee to a nunnery!* Men are victims of seductive women. Ophelia calls for divine help, but all she gets is abuse. (As he had asked, she has now prayed for him—twice.) After a second flood of rage, he storms out.

In the First Quarto version Hamlet uses *nunnery* eight times, in the Folio, five times and, in the Second Quarto, five times. Dover Wilson cites a line of criticism that interprets "nunnery" as "brothel," standard Elizabethan slang, so Hamlet is accusing Ophelia of being a whore. Some scholars claim "nunnery" only means "convent" and are indignant anybody could think Hamlet means "brothel." They point out with pristine logic the thrust of Hamlet's usage is to protect Ophelia's virtue, that he wants her not to be a "breeder of sinners." But Hamlet means both things at different points, depending on his feelings. Dover Wilson is correct here, and any defense of Hamlet against charges of sexual cruelty fails utterly. When Hamlet uses "bawd" he means *slut*, and "breeder of sinners" isn't so delicate either. It's bizarre to insist Hamlet's always a gentleman, considering his offer at *The Mousetrap* to lie in Ophelia's lap, speaking of "country matters" and the "nothing" that lies between a maid's legs.

Boiling the Nunnery scene down to its bones reveals three mood switches: A few moments of tenderness, then Ophelia returns his letters and Hamlet instantly explodes. Another few moments, his rage ebbing, Hamlet reverses the implication of brothel. Now "nunnery" is back to its literal meaning. A convent will protect her from the knavery of men, including him. Catching sight of the spies, he's enraged again. He vilifies all marriages, he curses Ophelia's marriage, he hints at killing Claudius. Hamlet accuses her of being a face-painting temptress and storms off.

This is transference, pure and simple. This is exactly Hamlet's problem with his mother. She's abandoned him and sided with another man. Remember from his conversation with the skull of Yorick how he pictures Milady in her chamber painting her face an inch thick. He forgets anything positive about Gertrude. He has the same mental splitting of Ophelia, she is madonna and whore.

Psychoanalytic listening is like close textual analysis. Surface reality makes no difference in erotic relationships when emotions take over. Don't let logic do your thinking for you. When Ophelia gives Hamlet's letters back, she doesn't expect it to be taken at face value—but Hamlet does! He expects to be rejected as he unconsciously remembers his mother. When Hamlet says, *I never gave you aught*, he means, I didn't give them for you to give back, keep them. When he says, *I did love you once*, he means he did—and still does. When he says, *I loved you not*, he means I wish I hadn't loved you, this hurts too much.

What Hamlet reacts to is his own internal cues and *interpretation of*—his transference to—Ophelia. For a therapist, transference is like that. At first you don't see it, then, suddenly, you can't miss it. And often you get the clue unconsciously before you know it consciously. But once you're watching for it, what leaps out is this singular fact: The first time Hamlet explodes at Ophelia, it is for one reason. *He becomes enraged when she returns his love letters.* This rejection switches on the negative maternal transference.

Now another man dealing with a woman's rejection, Freud psychoanalyzing "Dora." We cut to the transferential center of the case, Dora's first dream.[8]

> A house was on fire. My father was standing beside my bed and woke me up. I dressed quickly. Mother wanted to stop and save her jewel-case; but

> Father said: "I refuse to let myself and my two children be burnt for the sake of your jewel-case." We hurried downstairs, and as soon as I was outside I woke up.

Picture it. A girl just eighteen is lying on a couch in a second floor doctor's office. She has a small purse in her hands and keeps snapping it open and closing it, running her fingers around its rim, and dipping her fingers in and out of the opening. She's talking about her father and his very handsome friend, Herr K. Behind her sits another attractive middle-aged man repeatedly urging her to say what ever comes into her mind. She notices the smell of cigar smoke on him, a familiar odor.

She says it's a recurrent dream, but it didn't start with a real fire. He makes her repeat the dream and give associations to it. *A house was on fire.* She tells Freud that she first dreamt it in the mountains when she and her father were vacationing with Herr and Frau K 2 years earlier. One day she and Herr K had gone for a walk around an alpine lake. Stopping to rest, they shared a cigarette. He began to make overtures to Dora, saying his own wife was cold to him—but Dora slapped Herr K mid-sentence and hurried off in a rage. She can't explain to Freud why his saying *my wife gives me nothing* so angered her, but she remembers that each time she awoke from the dream, she had smelt smoke. Freud prompts her to continue free associating.

Her mother's wanting to go back for her jewel case reminds her that in real life this strange compulsive woman endangered her brother by locking him in his bedroom; her father objected because it was so dangerous in case of fire. Her way of talking about *something dangerous that could happen in the night* tells Freud he's on the right path. From behind the couch Freud watches Dora stroking her purse in her lap, her fingers going around and around the lips and dipping in and out of its opening. Dora says that the jewel case in the dream is like the expensive one Herr K had given her for Christmas. Freud points out that a German expression for virginal female genitalia is *jewel case*; he says the explicit term aloud. Dora says that hurrying downstairs reminds her of *something about stairs*. When she was thirteen Herr K got her alone in his second floor office and rubbed his erect penis against her, but she escaped to the stairs and hurried out into the street. Freud associates fire in the dream with Dora's bedwetting, her father's waking her in the night to prevent it—and with the sexual wetness he is sure she must have felt with Herr K.

In the unconscious, each element of a dream turns out to be represented multiple times in different guises. Overdetermination, multiple causality, of symptoms and dream elements is a major theme of *Dora*. Suppose *beside my bed* also refers to "behind the couch." Freud's pointing out *jewel case* is slang for the maiden vulva makes the girl anxious. She has denied that she masturbates. She fingers her purse, protecting her lap with it. For Freud, Dora is masturbating her purse, "a fact which I did not fail to use against her." She smells Freud's cigar smoke. Does she not want to hurry down the stairs and escape to the street? *As soon as I was outside I awoke* may also mean "leaving your office is like waking from a bad dream."[9]

Smoldering in the background of *Dora* was the fact that her father had tacitly agreed to swap Dora's "jewel box" to Herr K in exchange for sexual access to Frau K. *A house is on fire.* This family's myths recapitulate ancient themes, the mastery of fire and exchange of a daughter. *Papa is standing beside my bed and wakes me up. I dress quickly.* As she wishes in her dream, Dora's father saves her instead of his wife's jewel box. *Mama wants to stop and save it; but Papa says: "I refuse to let myself and my two children be burnt for the sake of your jewel-case."* Here is the wish to replace her mother among her father's riches. Dora so well understands these taboos and is so anxious about them that *as soon as I am outside I wake up.*

Dora fell ill at age eight, well before her family met Herr and Frau K. This couple dominates Freud's narrative, but her father's affair with Frau K doesn't start until Dora is twelve. Already Dora suffered conversion symptoms. For the next 50 years the psychoanalytic literature focused almost exclusively on Freud's sexy triangular centerpiece, ignoring Dora's relationship with her mother. Freud's story of Dora's symptoms, dreams, treatment, and how they tie together is a rhetorical masterpiece though not necessarily veridical truth.

Freud traces a causal chain back from a symptom, Dora's breathlessness and feeling of pressure on her chest, to sexual trauma, Herr K's sexual assault when she was thirteen. "The experience with Herr K.—his making love to her and the insult to honour which was involved—seems to provide in Dora's case the psychical trauma which" Freud had long thought to be "the indispensable prerequisite for the production of a hysterical disorder." Her chest pressure is, in Freud's view, an upward displacement of the memory of Herr K's erect member during his unwanted embrace. The lump of Herr K's penis was displaced up from her genitals, avoiding sexual excitement but causing sensations of pressure and shortness of breath. Her avoiding sexual arousal by means of upward displacement of libido was symptomatic of hysteria.[10]

Another association Freud makes concerns Dora's chronic limp going up or down stairs. This Freud connects with a pregnancy fantasy. Its onset 9 months after Herr K's attempted seduction at the lake reveals her fantasy of having Herr K's baby, and the limp symbolizes her misstep. It stands for the wish she had stumbled and given in and for the punishment for that wish. But Freud never connects the limp on the stairs with the stairs in both of Dora's dreams, nor with the stairs by which she escaped Herr K's assault, nor with the stairs she ascended and descended 6 days a week to Freud's office.

There is a second triangle in *Dora*, Freud, Dora's father, and the "prepossessing" younger friend Herr K. Much of what Freud knew firsthand about Herr K he tucks into footnotes. Herr K was in fact the source of the referral of Dora's father in the first place. Years earlier he had accompanied Dora's father to Vienna to see Freud. For some reason Freud had in mind from the beginning that Herr K would be a good match for Dora, would relieve her dammed up sexuality, and resolve this "fine poetic conflict" with everyone living happily ever after.

But up at the lake Herr K had begun his seduction with, "I get nothing out of my wife—"and Dora slapped him and stormed off. But why? Freud was sure Dora fancied Herr K, but he was at a loss to explain why she would refuse such an appropriate match. He felt the explanation lay in Dora's dreams. He was correct, but the reason doesn't come out until Dora's second dream—and the truth was not at all what Freud—or the reader of *Dora*—thought.

Dreaming is to protect sleep, Freud thought. When anxiety over sexual wishes starts to emerge and awaken the dreamer, symbol formation censors the dream and buffers the anxiety. The main tools for censorship in the unconscious are *condensation* and *displacement*; and when censorship of forbidden desire is inadequate, a nightmare ensues and the dreamer wakes. Except for traumatic dreams, a dream is "invariably the satisfaction of an infantile sexual wish." It's censored to keep incestuous aims hidden. Not only do all dreams express erotic wishes, Freud says, but many dreams are bisexual; they "unquestionably" reveal homosexual impulses.

The sexual wish underlying a dream is the unconscious *dream thought*. It's edited and censored by the *dream work*. When dream thoughts are translated from "latent" to "manifest content," the dream work uses two defenses to disguise hidden wishes, *condensation* and *displacement*. These are censors and also the translators of unconscious thought into dream imagery. The unconscious thinks in symbols; those symbols making up dream thoughts are then assembled into a series of images by the dream work.

Condensation is the first dream work element Freud noticed. Dreams are truncated compared with the range and complexity seen in even simple dreams when decoded, so a single idea has been made to stand for related ones. And condensation disguises as well as compresses: The dream work censors by using a fundamental ability of all natural languages, *metaphor*. Condensation by metaphor acts as a disguise because multiple overdetermined elements expressing the forbidden wish are compressed into a less explicit image. Metaphors also tend to dodge concrete expressions and take cover in abstract ones. Condensation converts elements symbolizing sexual wishes into a single suggestive image, one emotionally less guilt-inducing but still evocative enough for sexual discharge.

In Dora's dream, the dream work is using condensation to compress slang for feminine parts, *jewel* and *case*, into the German word for *jewel case*—which stands, first, for Dora's *genitals* and, second, the *actual case* to hold jewelry given by Herr K as a love token and, third, her mother's genitals not given to Dora's father. Also condensed into the jewel case image is a three part story about jewelry that she had told Freud—concerning the bracelet her father gave Dora's mother instead of the pearl drops she actually wanted; jewels for Dora, supposedly gifts from her father but picked out by Frau K; and the jewels her father gave Frau K. One dream jewel case contains at least six instances of condensation.[11]

The second major tool of the dream work besides condensation is *displacement*. Unconscious desire is displaced to an apparently trivial symbol to avoid dream censorship. Attached to a different image, the emotion is partly tamed, partly gratified. Displacement depends on the same symbolizing mechanisms that give rise to poetry and jokes. It depends on natural languages' ability to recombine parts of linguistic elements while still preserving their meaning. A metaphor compares wholes with wholes—*this* is like *that*—while displacement pulls apart emotion laden wholes and rearranges the parts, diluting and redistributing their emotion through other chains of association.[12]

Interpreting Dora's dream with Freud's formula, the dream work would be using a *fire in the house* as a symbolic displacement of Dora's passion *away from Herr K* in order to damp her desire. Her mother's wish to *save her jewel case* from the fire would be a displacement—by reversal—of Dora's wish to *give hers to her father.*

But what of transference? Of fundamental importance in dreams in treatment are embedded wishes toward the analyst; these reflect childhood traumas as well as imagined *and real* enactments between patient and analyst during the treatment. The transference also re-enacts old defenses used with the parents. Freud came to see a dream as the apex of a tripod, the legs of which are, first, the transference, second, the recent trigger for the dream and, third, the childhood trauma involved in the underlying neurosis. Free associating to a dream image leads to recent conflict, distant trauma, and transference. Freud recommended any resistance detected in the chain of associations be interpreted right away, working on resistance first, then content—fear first, then wish. Dora's dream—escaping the burning house followed by the smell of smoke on awakening—is a specimen transference dream. Freud himself saw in it her wish to flee therapy. In retrospect he knew he should have preemptively warned her not to run away, he should have interpreted her fear—then wish—for a smoky kiss from him so that she didn't have to *act it out* rather than *enact* it. He didn't act quickly enough, and he didn't detect in the dream her understanding of *his* unconscious. Freud missed Dora's attempt to "cure" his countertransference by means of her dream warning him to save her virtue.[13]

From the point of view of "psychoanalytic neutrality" a century later, Freud doesn't dispassionately place himself "equidistant from id, ego and superego" but sees Dora from the vantage of his punitive superego. More problematic, Freud seems unaware of how much his own id is driving the process. That said, Janet Malcolm, rebutting modern critics of Freud, says those who second guess *Dora* are unwittingly praising him. They "should understand the extent to which their own understanding of and sympathy for the girl are artifacts of Freud's rhetoric." Seldom mentioned is the basic humanity of the relationship. Freud, though traditional and hidebound about sex roles, was one of the most open minded adults Dora could have encountered in buttoned up, hypocritical Vienna.[14]

As a Jew like him, Dora's proximity to Freud's abundant self-regard perhaps buffered the antisemitism surrounding her. By his lights, Freud had acted like a physician and a gentleman. While he placed his needs first, a quest for psychoanalytic knowledge, Freud at least tried to honor Dora's. Her father attempted to trade Dora's sexual favors to Herr K. Frau K pretended to like Dora in order to suborn her. And Herr K was a serial seducer of young girls.[15]

Absent in Freud's *Hamlet* citations is any mention of transference; the play evoked the Oedipus complex for him often, so it's odd Freud didn't see transference in it. The Oedipus complex was an invention of which he was justly proud, but its universality is far from proved. In a paper unique in all the literature, Brian Bird wondered why Freud lost interest in transference. Bird sees transference as a major ego function and "the basis for all human relationships." Since transference is a human universal, it's "always present, active, and significant in the analytic situation. . . . everything that goes on in analysis has a transference meaning."[16]

Bird's paper is little mentioned; not only is it ferociously difficult, but in it Bird diagnoses Freud's secret conflicts. He noticed that Freud's important writing on transference began in 1905 but was mostly over by 1917. His 4-year delay in publishing *Dora* was owing to difficulty understanding the transference. In 1905 Freud's observations on transference are confident and his opinions declarative and firm, but in his later writings he mostly neglects the subject. Several times Freud demonstrates obvious blind spots in connecting clinical data to the transference. In 1937 he pessimistically alluded to his own personal frustrations with the subject. Yet, even near the end of his life, Freud put it at the center of psychoanalysis and never stopped believing that the analysis of transference is the *sine qua non* of psychoanalysis.

Bird compares transference with the even harder concept of transference *neurosis*.

> When I think of transference, I think of feelings, reactions, and of a repetition of past events; but when I think of transference neurosis, I think literally of a . . . new edition of the patient's original neurosis, but with me in it.

It's as if the analyst becomes a piece of the patient's superego criticizing the patient and a piece of the patient's defenses, logic, and ego functions. "I come to represent *the patient himself*." But the kind of bitter struggle that overswept Freud and Dora is not mere obstructive negative transference. Going into danger may be a necessary stage of healing. Bird feels that

> only when the analytic situation becomes, in a sense, an adversary situation, should we expect the kind of transference neurosis to develop that can admit to it a representation of destructive impulses strong enough and faithful enough to permit this aspect of the patient's neurosis to be effectively analyzed.[17]

It's a crisis situation, but just knowing it may give the analyst strength to get through a "dark and ominous time, when both patient and analyst are about ready to call it quits." Arriving at this place may be the only way to the heart of the patient's neurosis.

Freud's description of transference in *Dora* was such that it could be attributed only to the ego. Oddly, Bird's insight has had no impact on psychoanalytic theory. Yet, there it is in plain sight. *Transference comes from the ego.* Not the id, not the superego. Since the ego makes and manages transference, not only is the ego the agency that makes us forget, it also lets us remember. As an ego function, transference is the stage manager of defenses. Paradoxically, it's the ego's main anti-repressive device too, helping us retrieve memories—a two-way conduit.

The obvious is hard to see: Normal people have transference. It's a healthy function of the psyche for making attachments. It distorts from both ends to make the coupling fit, a two-way modulating filter for reshaping information about the self and others to connect them.

Hamlet explodes when Ophelia returns his love letters. But why does she return them? Shakespeare loves to rack his audience by star-crossing his lovers, by having them do things that cause the opposite of what they intend. Ophelia doesn't know why he came to her room terrified—or love-struck—or mad. But she has her hopes. She's devised a test pretending to return his tributes. She hopes he'll refuse them and renew his courtship.

Transference functions as a necessary deception of both self and others, and this distortion peaks in erotic love. Love is blind, mad, and transference. Consider Hamlet's poem Polonius reads aloud to the King and Queen.

Polonius To the Celestial Ophelia —
Doubt thou the stars are fire,
Doubt that the sun doth move,
Doubt truth to be a liar,
But never doubt I love.
O dear Ophelia, I am ill at these numbers.*
I have not art to reckon my groans, but that I love thee best,
O most best. Believe it, adieu, thine evermore, most dear Lady,
Whilst this machine is to him,
Hamlet

II.ii.110 TLN 1137–1152
* verses

Polonius (and some scholars) considers this doggerel, so its amateurishness in the hands of a natural poet like Hamlet is a convention. Analogous to the mixed metaphors in his soliloquies, its faux-naivete invites trust. It goes with the role of the fool for love. The theme is deception: I am not deceiving you, you can believe I love you, as you can take for granted that the stars in the sky are fire and the sun moves across heaven. And if there's something you don't understand, at least never doubt my love. Does he really doubt she loves him? We don't, this simple sweet girl. Hamlet praises her excellent white bosom which will hold his poem. Referring to his person as a machine is irony of the subtlest sort, sexy and wry: His body is *a love machine*. But *O most best* is from the heart.

One insight Freud had is unique in all the critical history of the play, his theory of the transference meaning of the poem. On the manifest level, Hamlet asks her not to doubt his love. But just as when he says *I doubt some foul play*—I suspect foul play—he's warning her not to believe his love. Freud thinks Hamlet feels insecure in his *ability* to love, hence the choice of doubt as an unconscious warning to Ophelia: *Never suspect I love. Beware.* Freud invented the analysis of overdetermination and was a master of mixed motives. Leave it to Freud to spot deep in the erotic thrust of Hamlet's numbers a darker side, the *negative transference* he's always feeling for Ophelia. And he even unconsciously warns her about it.

Freud's portrait of Dora's family is brightly lit by his masterful use of dialogue. Another painterly touch is his own mental process, intimately confided to the reader.

> When I set myself the task of bringing to light what human beings keep hidden within them . . . by observing what they say and what they show, I thought the task was a harder one than it really is. He that has eyes to see and ears to hear may convince himself that no mortal can keep a secret. If his lips are silent, he chatters with his finger-tips; betrayal oozes out of him at every pore.[18]

The writing of *Dora* is so brilliant you almost don't notice Freud oozing self-betrayal. He often praises his own straightforwardness, then dives into obfuscation the next sentence. He's almost self-parodying when he describes a dream as standing on two legs, one in current reality, the other in past trauma. And the dream up in the naughty place where the two legs meet. Freud's discourse on Dora is full of adolescent sexual imagery—the lock and the key, the tangled bushes, the picklock—his countertransference chatters from his fingertips. He's neutral about Dora's father and Herr and Frau K, and their affairs, and with scientific objectivity talks about treating Dora's father's syphilis. But he's scathing toward the mother's cleaning and mentions only once in passing the link between her obsessive housekeeping and how she might have felt contracting her husband's venereal disease. He does note Dora's identification with her—and the shame when she developed a vaginal discharge—but here too, he's affectively flat.

Part of the suspense in *Dora* comes from questions Freud didn't ask. A few months after Dora left Freud, one of Herr and Frau K's children died. Dora uses the loss to make a condolence call, and they greet her as if nothing happened over the past 3 years. Freud says she makes it up with them and also gets her revenge. She tells Frau K she knows about the affair with her father. She brings up Herr K's attempt to seduce her, and she extracts from him the long-awaited admission that Dora's version of the story is the truth, his a lie.

Dora's calling on Herr and Frau K upon the death of their daughter is high gothic; and Freud narrates it flat, uninflected. Is it art or countertransference? You picture two bereaved parents paralyzed by Dora's visit, too stunned to deny their guilt. Freud the narrator is opaque, you can't tell whether he approves Dora's getting closure or disapproves her revenge. Did he interpret her confrontation of parents who had just lost a child as vicious? Or did he excuse her because of her age and suffering at their hands? We never find out. He's impassive as the Fates.

Intentional art or unconscious transference? A last example: One day, a few months after her analysis ended and she had already confronted Herr and Frau K, Dora encountered Herr K face to face on the street in Vienna. When Herr K saw her, he stood transfixed. In his paralysis, he was knocked down by a passing carriage.

Dora turned and walked away. She tells Freud she believes Herr K was unhurt, but Freud seems incurious why she left Herr K's fate unresolved. He is more interested in bringing the story to a close. Dora had actually come to ask Freud to take her back into analysis. But, with courtly elegance, he refuses to see her—and in the process promises "to forgive her" for depriving him of a completed case history.[19]

Freud's patients "were in a state of readiness to fall in love," Malcolm's definition of transference. And to hate as well. Transference is the surface of approach-avoidance evolved in the deepest layers of the organism. Positive transference is the disposition to approach, negative transference evolved from avoidance. Fight or flee? Friend or foe? To be, or not to be? These are basic questions. Hamlet was in readiness to kill Claudius. But it was Polonius behind the arras.

Janet Malcolm has a theory why Freud called his patient "Dora." The word means *gifts*; she is *Pandora*, who of course opened her jar and loosed upon humankind the plagues and pains afflicting us. The only thing remaining was hope, hiding under the lip of the container. But was it good that hope stayed? Or should it have followed the other plagues? Transference is also two edged, that "magnificent obliviousness" we have—gift to human beings, or plague? But in any case it remains, hiding under the lip of the jar.[20]

When without understanding it, Freud noticed the symbolic substitution of one person for another, we might say he *invented* transference. He fashioned something novel when he observed it, coined the term, and formulated the explanation. But when he understood the symbolic interchange, what it really meant, and what to do with it therapeutically—then we could say Freud *discovered* transference, he found the eternal. *Readiness is all* as Hamlet says. You have to be prepared to see transference before you can see it. Freud's genius lies in making us ready. Shakespeare's genius lay in making Freud ready.

Notes

1. Joseph Breuer, "Fraulein Anna O: Studies on Hysteria," in *The Standard Edition of the Complete Psychological Works of Sigmund Freud*, vol. 2, James Strachey, Ed. and trans. (London: The Hogarth Press, 1893/1955), 21–48.
2. Lester Luborsky, James Mellon, Kenneth D. Cohen, Paul van Ravenswaay, Anita. V. Hole, Anna Rose Childress, Stephanie Ming, and Paul A. Crits-Christoph, "A Verification of Freud's Grandest Clinical Hypothesis: Transference," *Clinical Psychology Review* 5 (1985): 231–246.
3. Lucy Freeman, *The Story of Anna O* (New York: Walker, 1972).
4. Janet Malcolm, "The Patient Is Always Right" (review of Merton M. Gill, *Analysis of Transference*) 31 (December 20, 1984): 13–18, www.nybooks.com/articles/5622, accessed April 20, 2015.
5. Steven Marcus, "Freud and Dora: Story, History, Case History," in *Essential Papers on Psychoanalysis and Literature*, Emanuel Berman, Ed. (New York: New York University Press, 1974/1993), 36–80, 75.
6. Brian Bird, "Notes on Transference: Universal Phenomenon and Hardest Part of Analysis," *Journal of the American Psychoanalytic Association* 20 (1972): 267–301.
7. Sigmund Freud, "Fragment of an Analysis of a Case of Hysteria," in *The Standard Edition of the Complete Psychological Works of Sigmund Freud*, vol. 7, James Strachey, Ed. and trans. (London: The Hogarth Press, 1905/1953), 18–122, 120, fn.

8. Ibid, 64.
9. Ibid, 39.
10. Ibid, 26.
11. Sara Steinberg, "The Master Tropes of Dreaming: Rhetoric as a Family Affair," *American Journal of Semiotics* 4 (1986): 29–51.
12. Displacement conveys whole concepts with prototypal parts or single parts with aggregates. In rhetoric, this type of figurative language is *metonymy*. The variety made possible by displacement in dreams increases their narrative scope, just the way metonymy enriches natural languages. Metonymy reframes bald statements of reality into tactful allusions. This "displacement" in language makes possible a layer of indirect emotional utterance necessary for social group living. Figurative analogs of displacement include, among others, use of a part to represent the whole (*swords* for *soldiers*) or the whole for the part (*smiling year* for *spring*), effect for cause (*tears* for *grief*), material for the thing made (*glass* for *mirror*), naming one instance to imply a whole category (*a Moll* for *a girlfriend*), or naming the class to represent a member (*law* for *sheriff*).
13. Daniel M. Begel, "Three Examples of Countertransference in Freud's Dora Case," *American Journal of Psychoanalysis* 42 (1982): 163–169.
    Robert Langs, "Misalliance and Framework in the Case of Dora," in *Technique in Transition*, Robert Langs, Ed. (New York: Jason Aronson, 1978), 233–252.
14. Janet Malcolm, "Dora," in *The Purloined Clinic: Selected Writings* (New York: Vintage, 1972), 3–30.
15. Hannah S. Decker, *Freud, Dora, and Vienna 1900* (New York: Free Press, 1991).
16. Bird, "Transference," 267.
17. Ibid, 281, 295.
18. Freud, "Fragment," 77–78.
19. Patrick J. Mahony, *Freud's Dora: A Psychoanalytic, Historical, and Textual Study* (New Haven: Yale University Press, 1996).
    He possibly already knew Herr K's fate. Freud is conspicuously critical of everybody in *Dora*, including himself, but there's not a negative syllable toward Herr K. Freud emphasizes his handsomeness and youth while being oddly silent about his behavior toward teenaged girls. Through the whole case Freud feels Dora should have been attracted to Herr K. He eventually even concluded Herr K's intentions at the lake were honorable but never tells us why. Mahony thinks Freud was treating either Frau K or Herr K in the months after Dora's analysis. This would coincide with Freud's internal struggle over publishing the case.
20. Janet Malcolm, "Reflections: J'Appelle un Chat un Chat," *The New Yorker Magazine* (April 20, 1987): 84–102.

8

"WILD AND WHIRLING WORDS"

Freud's Phobia, Dora's Dream

In the center of every dream, Freud says, there's one place that can't be fathomed, "a navel, as it were, that is its point of contact with the unknown." But he can't see that his own neurosis stops him from plumbing that unknown. The second dream Dora told him—when we reanalyze it—shows how his phobia for railroad travel blinded him to the obvious train symbols in it. Her first dream had been a nightmare in which her father saved her from a burning house. Her second dream comes when only 2 more analytic hours remain, just before Dora breaks off treatment.[1]

> I come into a house where I live, go to my room, and find Mama's letter lying there. She says that as I had left home without my parents' knowledge, she didn't wish to write to me to say that Papa took ill. "Now he is dead and if you like . . . you can come." I then go to the train station and ask about a hundred times, "Where is the station?" I always get the answer: "Five minutes." I then see a thick wood before me which I go into, and I ask a man whom I meet there. He says to me: "Two hours more." He offers to accompany me. But I refuse and go alone. I see the train station in front of me and cannot reach it. Then I am at home. . . . The maidservant opens up to me and replies, "Your mama and the others are already at the cemetery." I see myself particularly distinctly going up the stairs. I go to my room, but not the least sadly, and calmly begin reading a big book that lies on my writing-table.

The associative trigger for the dream is Frau K's actual letter inviting Dora to join them at the alpine resort where occurred the events Freud (and his followers, ever after) called "the scene by the lake."[2]

The Scene by the Lake. It has the ring of legend, as indeed it is for Freudians. The setting of Dora's tragic crisis, the break with family and friends, the end of her childish trust in her father, the locus of her humiliation, and her cue for revenge. After reading her mother's letter, Dora goes to the wooded shore. Unable to penetrate the thick woods around the lake and get to the train station, she refuses the help of a stranger who offers to accompany her but goes home alone. The family have already left for her father's funeral but—not at all sadly—she ascends the stairs to her room and starts to read a big book on her writing desk.

Again, the stairs. Dora was thirteen when Herr K staged a seduction scene—his deserted second floor office, shutters drawn, doors to lock at closing time—and himself. But Dora was "already entirely and completely hysterical" before she met Herr K, says Freud, and her disgust with his kiss and her flight to the stairs and out of his office proved it. But Freud's theories on hysteria were in flux. By the time Dora came along, Freud had decided that the flood of hysterical women in Vienna was not caused by their sexual molestation as younger children, that these outrages would have to be "immeasurably more frequent" than was realistic. But since Freud is unwilling to discard his seduction theory, he modifies it: The seduction is the *wish* of the child, a fantasy remembered as historical fact. Painful as this retraction is, Freud submits to the truth about the unconscious. One can never know beyond any doubt the truth of something remembered. In listening to the patient, there is no infallible test for reality, only fickle memory (something he forgets as the case unwinds).[3]

Setbacks don't deter Freud. Interpreting Dora's index symptom when she was 8 years old, her shortness of breath, Freud charges ahead. From no other evidence than a couple of patients he treated, he traces these attacks to the "primal scene." He concludes Dora was frightened as a young child on hearing the noises of her parents having intercourse; and she was also sexually excited by the sound of heavy breathing. The primal scene was a major *eureka* in Freud's quest for psychic pathogens. Like masturbation—a favorite *deus ex machina*—it neatly tied together anxiety, sexuality, and Dora's shortness of breath: The noises of parental copulation had traumatically stuck in Dora's mind and awaited the force of masturbation anxiety to dislodge it and cause it to go careening around her body creating mischief. Her yearning for her father during his absences produced a nervous asthma. By imagining she was short of breath, she symbolically brought her father back, imitating his symptoms of tuberculosis. And her father was medically forbidden to exert himself sexually. Dora—according to Freud—was worried she'd die when her self-produced orgasms caused her to be a little out of breath.

Freud's story of the interlocking of Dora's symptoms, dreams, and psychoanalysis is a tour de force of imaginative literature but not necessarily historical truth. Freud traces a causal chain running backward from Dora's recurrent feeling of pressure on her chest to Herr K's sexual assault when she was thirteen. Her experience of chest pressure is an upward displacement of the traumatic memory of his erect penis. And her failure to be clitorally aroused Freud ascribed to a kind of early masturbation by thumb-sucking: Her oral zone

> had been over-indulged in Dora's infancy by the habit of sensual sucking. The pressure of the erect member probably lead to an analogous change in the corresponding female organ, the clitoris; and the excitation of this second erotogenic zone was referred by a process of displacement to the simultaneous pressure against the thorax and became fixed there.[4]

For each physical symptom, Freud had to show a symbolic overdetermination of causes. He had to find the disowned emotion, then show the symptom symbolized sexual conflict; and the repressed affect and symbolized conflict had to lead back to a sexual childhood trauma. But along the way, Freud became enthralled by Dora's sexuality.

As one early challenger of Freud's *Dora* formulation put it, Freud's error was "mistaking Dora's defenses to be Dora's conflicts." The missed crux of the case is Freud's neglect of her mother: Dora felt jealous and left out, yearning for the closeness that her brother had with their mother. But she didn't get it, gave up, and turned to her father, "*not out of love for him, but in anger at her mother.*" Her jealous attachment to her governess and passionate ardor for Frau K was a displaced yearning for her mother. And Dora's ambivalent involvement with Herr K over the years was both a displacement from her father and an identification with him; it fulfilled her erotic desire for Frau K, who gave her father the love Dora craved.[5]

Many symptoms suggested Dora's unconsciously placing herself inside her father's illnesses. "Even in the suicide note she imitated her father and his plea for love and attention from Frau K and her mother." What in retrospect is called "probably the most tragic aspect of the entire case" is that Freud had recognized Dora's negative transference to him, but what eluded him was his intensely negative countertransference toward her.

> When Dora, in a panic, returned for help, Freud claimed that one glance at her face could tell him that she was not in earnest over her request for further treatment [but] not even Sigmund Freud could make such a determination in a split second. Freud did not *want* to see her.

Otherwise he'd have recognized her anguished cry for help despite her previous abrupt departure.[6]

Freud's countertransference is brilliantly, if not always intentionally, revealed. The unconscious uses symbols to conceal secrets—and confess them. Dora is telling a story with secret themes Freud may detect, miss, or distort according to his needs and the demands of the art he's presenting. He peeled back layer after layer of his case and in 1923, years after its publication, he realized that he had failed to see the final layer of unconscious determinants, the bedrock—Dora's "gynaecophilic" love for Frau K. He should have seen the homosexual element, something previous experience had shown over and over, a homosexual component in the neuroses reflecting innate bisexuality deep in the human psyche.

But this footnote seems amnesic for a passage years earlier and sixty pages back. Freud says the same thing, that behind Dora's conscious train of thought, desire displaced from her father to Herr K, "there lay concealed a feeling of jealousy which had that lady as its *object*—a feeling, that is, which could only be based upon an affection on Dora's part for one of her own sex." Only later did Freud recall that when "Dora talked about Frau K., she used to praise her 'adorable white body' in accents more appropriate to a lover than to a defeated rival." He remembered and then forgot parts of the case as he wrote the report; and he came back several times over the years to amend it. He lost track of the infantile deprivation aspects of the case the more he was struck by Dora's adolescent sexuality.

But during the first weeks of the analysis he had described her quite accurately to Fleiss. Along with seeing her infantile regression to "pronounced sucking tendencies," Freud had also succinctly sketched her bisexual dilemma, her "opposition between an inclination towards men and towards women." He sees it, then he represses it, then he sees it again and forgets he repressed it. He has two different countertransference responses to Dora that mirror her two different transference responses to him: To Freud as her father-Herr K and—what he couldn't keep consistently conscious—her other transference to Freud as her mother-Frau K.[7]

From the point of view of therapists a century later, Freud seems unaware how much his own id is driving it. He's like a green psychotherapist in training, and there are a number of errors a first-year trainee would quickly learn to avoid: The general rule is *interpret the fear before the wish*. Patients are more willing to admit a fear of punishment than a wish for forbidden gratification. Freud pounds her with her shameful wishes right away. He's also lacking a century of clinical experience later found in the lore, understandably, techniques that don't appear in texts but are part of the oral tradition. One is how the dream work disguises *nouns* versus *verbs*: Nouns are easier to symbolize than verbs, so verbs more often appear undisguised in the dream narrative. Action, being more abstract, is harder to disguise. Keeping this unwritten rule in mind, the experienced modern therapist would perhaps hear something like this:[8]

> I came home and found a letter from Mommy. Daddy was ill. "Now he is dead, and if you like, you can come." I then go to the train station and ask about a hundred times, "Where is the *noun*?" I always get the answer: "Five minutes." I see the train station in front of me and can't reach it. Then I see a thick *noun* before me which I go into, and there I ask a man. He says to me, "Two *nouns* more." He offers to come with me. But I refuse and go on alone. . . . I see the train station in front of me and cannot reach it. . . .

What are those nouns? Dora's dream now starts to feel more plausible as a story of sexual frustration. She goes toward the train station in search of something she can't find. She can't penetrate the thick wood. There are maddening delays, and she's always told, just a little longer. She can see the train station in front of her. Inside the station is what she's looking for but can't touch. Then at last, a man tells her that ahead lie the two things she is searching for—at a distance. He can't give her what she wants, yet he does offer to come. But she goes on alone.

Thus heard, the dream becomes more coherent—and sexier. The dream work tries to tell the story while concealing its meaning. Freud came to one key interpretation only after Dora had quit analysis. *The thick woods was Frau K's pubic hair.* This was a dream of defloration, and Dora, identifying herself as male, finally possesses the object of her desire. But Freud doesn't take the interpretation far enough. By convention, a stranger encountered in a patient's dream is always the doctor. In Dora's dream, *it's not a man she wants*, she doesn't trust Freud and goes on alone. She is trying to get to the train station; it is a container, a female symbol, and within it are a number of long cylindrical objects that go through tunnels that are themselves containers.

You almost have to be asleep not to see it. Freud suffered from a phobia of traveling by train for a dozen years (1887–1899), a symptom he was eventually able to cure by self analysis, tracing it back to having witnessed his *matrem*, as he evasively put it to Fliess, *nudam* during a train trip from Leipzig to Vienna when he was four. Repression may explain Freud's failure to connect *Bahnhof*, train station, to sexuality and his nude mother (and he must be allowed his defenses) but it's odd that over a century of *Dora* commentary fails to notice.[9]

That's how the unconscious works. It's not the least embarrassed by clichés. Dora is looking for two—two mothers, her own and Frau K—two governesses as there are in *Dora*—two—of something she lost long ago, from her mother's body. Commentators have speculated about why Freud needed to make Dora male deflowering Frau K rather than a girl wanting to make love to Frau K. Did the lack of a penis make Freud too anxious? Freud did, however, understand why Dora made Frau K into a virgin in her associations to the dream; on some level he appreciated Dora's need for a mother, especially a kindly Virgin Mother. Part of Freud genuinely cared for Dora and did want her to find the mother she had been searching for.

The coda of the second dream fulfills her wish to be left alone to ascend to a calm place and read in peace. Freud suggests the book is an encyclopedia of sex, but it is more likely a book written by Sigmund Freud. Dora must have known he was studying her, writing about her. Reading and writing were central themes in her life. How could she not burn with curiosity to see herself through his eyes, even if she had to kill the dream Freud off, to possess him through his immortal writings?

When Dora lay down on Freud's couch that last day of 1900, she told him this was her last session. He was shocked, of course, but on some level, the foreshadowing of her flight from the burning house must have given him a feeling of deja vu. And it was in that final hour that Freud came to understand the real reason Dora slapped Herr K up at the lake. Freud asked Dora when she had decided that this would be her last session, and she told him that she had made the resolve to end the analysis 2 weeks back. A fortnight, Freud noted, exactly the amount of time a servant girl must give before she left employment. Then Freud probed the complaint of both Dora's father and of Herr K, *I get nothing from my wife.* It turns out that, as Freud intuited, Dora's slapping Herr K covers a deeper mystery. He learns in the waning minutes of Dora's analysis that the slap marked a crossroad in the paths of gender and class.[10]

Dora told Freud that Herr K had indeed seduced someone, the governess taking care of the two children of Herr and Frau K. During that summer at the lake, the girl had tearfully warned Dora against him. She had trusted him and then been betrayed. Once Herr K had what he wanted, he discarded the governess. She lingered on in the household to see whether he would change his mind, but he did not. As she was departing, she gave Dora a warning that later came to mind in the scene by the lake: Herr K, in presenting his sexual proposition to the governess, had uttered the fatal phrase. She told Dora that, sure enough, he had played on her sympathy—on the grounds that he *got nothing from his wife.*

Freud now understood. Dora wasn't insulted by being propositioned, she was enraged by his putting her in the place of a servant. Dora thought Herr K was not paying her court honorably but soliciting her with a second-hand come-on to a discarded servant girl. Freud interpreted to Dora that she too was like a servant girl in the analysis, leaving a job upon a fortnight's notice. But what Freud never seemed to fully admit was that he was the servant; in the deepest layer of the transference, it was Freud that was feminized and dismissed without notice.

Melanie Klein took Freud literally when he said the unconscious *thinks in symbols,* and she sensed the deeper implications: To deal with the terror and ecstasy of object relationships, people cope by means of symbols. Symbolization is the unique feature of human bonding, both cause and effect of the way we love and hate each other. And Klein saw that the unfathomable depth of the unconscious and the infinite capacities of language are one and the same.

Hamlet's daydreams and dramatic enactments show genius for symbolization as it bubbles up from a seemingly bottomless unconscious. He fits Mrs. Klein's description of two coping mechanisms, the "manic defense" and "defensive disintegration." She might see "To be or not to be" as the surface of a disintegrative defense, the wish for his too too solid self to melt. For him, *not to be* is a conscious, private choice. But in public using the antic disposition defense, he can combine coping mechanisms and ride them at a gallop—wit, sublimation, rationalization—all conscious, all held together by intense focus and concentrated intellect.[11]

Hamlet is sometimes seen reading, but mostly he is mentally writing. And part of what he's writing is himself. The genius in his fully realized manic defense is how it re-creates him.

Polonius	What do you read, my lord?
Hamlet	Words—words. Words.
Polonius	What is the matter, my lord?
Hamlet	Slanders, sir. For the satirical rogue says here that old men have gray beards; that their faces are wrinkled; their eyes purging thick amber and plum tree gum; and

that they have a plentiful lack of wit . . . all which, sir . . . I hold it not honesty to have it thus set down. For yourself, sir, shall grow old as I am if like a crab, you could go backward.

Polonius (Though this be madness, yet there is method in it.) Will you walk out of the air, my lord?

Hamlet Into my grave.

Polonius Indeed, that is out of the air. (How pregnant sometimes his replies are, a happiness that often madness hits on. . . .)

II.ii.191 TLN 1229–1251

Polonius is correct, and one of the methods in Hamlet's madness is using it to keep himself sane. Samuel Johnson criticizes the antic disposition, saying he accomplishes nothing pretending to be mad that he couldn't do just as well acting sane. Johnson may be right about plot, but to the character of the Prince, feigned madness adds an extra dimension to the play, an oneiric layer. A feeling of hallucination winds in and out of *Hamlet*, especially in its tableaus. After a fight with his mother, Hamlet stabs an intruder through a drape in her bedroom. But when the body tumbles out there's a pause and Hamlet sees—*Claudius*? Or so he thinks at first. This is the manifest content of a nightmare, and in the latent content, Freud says in fantasy Hamlet has killed old King Hamlet. Dreams are inventions to wish with, and Freud's oedipal prince wishes—and fears—he's killed his own father.

Denmark's a prison, Hamlet says, and even more constricting are his nightmares. But they're also liberating. He dreams copiously. He's daydreaming in his soliloquies, where he berates himself as John-a-dreams. He's always using the pictorial language of dreams. His mastery of symbol-making culminates in *The Mousetrap* with its Dumb Show, a nightmare for the King. The figures of rhetoric that Hamlet uses to persuade are exactly the tools of the ego's dream work—*condensation* and *displacement*. The analogous rhetorical devices are *metaphor* and *metonymy*. This relationship between how dreams work and how figures of speech persuade suggests a fundamental relationship between unconscious symbol-making and the natural languages, the source of Lacan's claim that the unconscious is structured as a language.

Freud used *symbol* in its vernacular sense, one thing standing for another. A symbolic relationship exists between two different things—behaviors, images, ideas—joined conceptually by something different from either. Dreams use symbols in a distinctive way for a particular dreamer, but they also utilize stock symbols which come from the culture. The essence of *symbol* is connection. For the ancient Greeks, *symvolo* was a means of identification (between two members of a sect, for instance) that consisted of the two halves of a broken object that could be fitted back together. The crack between is nothing, but it tells everything about the relationship.

For Freud, dream thoughts and dream content are the same subject matter in two different languages. Dream work does "secondary revision" (or narrative smoothing) to transform dream thoughts into visual elements for the purposes of representation. The manifest content or narrative is expressed in consecutive pictures. Symbolization of wishes in dream thoughts with serial images is what poets and artists have always done to represent abstract ideas and feelings. With such image juxtapositions, both art and dreams are able to construct effective paradoxes "where contradictory lines of thought are synthesized into a fuller truth."[12]

While *symbol* is central to dream interpretation, Freud doesn't consider symbols to be the product of the dream work. Symbols are a property of unconscious thinking; they're *already there* in the way the unconscious thinks. Klein believed that symbols are the *basis of all talents*. Especially relational ones. A symbol is the way the child's important people get represented in the mind, preserved, and utilized as objects. The infant identifies the mother with another object that's different but is emotionally the same. By instinctual association of one object with another, a *representation* becomes the stepping stone to objects out in the relational world.

A symbol stands for a thing, it isn't the thing itself, so in a sense, a metaphor never means exactly what it says. It's an analogy, not an identity. Figurative language gives us many ways of saying, *This is more like that.* Or saying, *This is less like that.* Epistemologically, figurative language is a necessary handle on reality. Whenever we see anything, our minds comprehend it by comparing; it must evoke something already in the brain to have meaning. Our world is built up of resemblances; reality is approached through analogy. Metaphor is necessary for knowing, and our mental world is made up of a system of comparisons.

For Klein, symbolization is also how we tame the forces of life and death. The infant's rage at the frustrating "bad breast" and guilt and depressive "concern for the good breast" promote symbol formation: An internal representation, a keepsake, allows the infant to transfer destructive emotions and fantasies from the primary external object to an internal image. This "splitting" preserves the beloved object in the infant's emotional memory. The infant's conflict over love and hate for the mother causes guilt, Klein says, which forces a reinvestment of love and hate out into the larger world by means of symbolic transfers of meaning. These various transformations also enable the differentiation of self from other and make love possible. Symbolization enables not just reflected self love that is narcissism but love in the truest sense, the ability to tolerate the ambivalence inevitable in loving an external object.

Ambivalence: Freud said mental health is the ability to tolerate ambiguity. At the far reaches of human experience lies a world of truths whose opposites are also true. Unconscious symbolic thinking creates paradox, and the unconscious also paradoxically resolves it. The relation between literal expression and figurative language is the same as that between unconscious irrational thinking and logical conscious thinking. All natural languages have the capacity to convey opposites—the thing and the not-thing—binary opposition. But there are instances when the literal reality of a thing and its opposite exist together, and their existence cannot be stated in logical fashion. So there's a linguistic loophole to convey paradox—figurative language. Tropes rationalize paradox. And *irony* is the name we give to the interface.

Classical psychoanalysts felt symbolization served as proxy for the id only, and symbol formation was supposedly inferior because it was driven by the pleasure principle to give vent to feelings that ought better be expressed intellectually. But after Freud's death, a trend started of seeing the primary process thinking of the unconscious as giving expression to the *self*, as a basic need unique to humankind. Primary process thinking came to be seen as like an instinct, intrinsic to the ego, specific to humanness. Symbolization is *how* we dream. Self expression is *why*.[13]

Artists like Hamlet have always understood art's ability to express paradox. Dreams and art mirror the pathogenic phenomena that make people crazy. But paradox has an integrative function for healing that madness. What art shares with dreams is the use of aesthetic sensibility to analyze and synthesize simultaneously, to be and not to be at the same time. Humankind makes a net profit on internal visual and verbal depiction or it wouldn't have evolved, but its price is the knowledge of mortality and our inevitable disillusion.[14]

Mankind means nothing, Hamlet says. "To me, what is this quintessence of dust?" But when Rosencrantz and Guildenstern tell him they passed a company of actors, his melancholy vanishes. A changed and charming Prince greets the actors individually. Hamlet asks the First Player to recite a speech on Pyrrhus's slaughter of King Priam—revenge in full sight of Priam's queen, Hecuba, whose screams would milk tears from heaven. The reading astonishes because the actor can make his face turn pale and his eyes weep real tears.

Hamlet asks them to perform for the court. The agony of Hecuba struck him, and he took note of her loyalty to her husband. This gives him an idea. The play will be *The Murder of Gonzago*. Hamlet, in an aside, orders an addition to the script, "some dozen or sixteen lines" he himself will write. He dismisses everyone and Polonius leads them away. "Now I am alone."

Hamlet O, what a rogue and peasant slave am I.
Is it not monstrous that this player here,
Could force his soul so to his own conceit
That . . . all his visage wanned.* Tears in his eyes . . .
A broken voice—and all for nothing? What would he do
Had he the motive and the cue for passion
That I have? He would drown the stage with tears
And cleave the general ear with horrid speech,
Make mad the guilty . . . and amaze indeed
The very faculties of eyes and ears. . . .

II.ii.550 TLN 1590–1606

* could so fit his emotions to his role that his face went pale

Soliloquy 3 moves from awe at the player's passion to Hamlet's own inertia. This actor is just acting but is more authentically engaged than Hamlet.

Hamlet Am I a coward . . . or ere this
I should have fatted all the region kites
With this slave's offal? Bloody, bawdy villain!
Remorseless, treacherous, lecherous, kindless villain,
O vengeance! *[pause]*
Why—what an ass am I. Sure—this is most brave,
That I—the son of a dear father murdered,
Prompted to my revenge by heaven and hell —
Must like a whore unpack my heart with words
And fall a-cursing like a very drab. . . . Fie upon it. Foh!
About, my brains! Hmm —

II.ii.571 TLN 1611–1629

Is the Ghost tempting him? His melancholy he knows makes him more susceptible to evil spirits. Hamlet must be dead certain of his uncle's guilt. This arrival of the actors presents him with a solution: He won't just test his mother by confronting her with the image of another queen—a queen who is faithful—but he will also snare Claudius.[15]

Hamlet Hmm. . . . I'll have these players
Play something like the murder of my father
Before mine uncle. I'll observe his looks. . . .
If he but blench, I know my course . . .
I'll have grounds . . . The play's the thing
Wherein I'll catch the conscience of the King.

II.ii.589 TLN 1629–1645

If he but blench—Hamlet will determine Claudius's guilt by studying his involuntary physical reactions as they betray him.[16]

All through *Dora* Freud's memory fails him. There are obvious gaps, chronological inconsistencies, and lapses in logic. Still, the case fascinates. Freud is seduced by his own stimulating theories of sexuality and making egregious errors in pursuing them. But as inconsistent, and at times preposterous, *Dora* is, discussions like this could never have existed without Freud giving himself away. There is almost no connection, perception, inference, guess, or dictum that history has left unexamined.[17]

One can go through *Dora* paragraph by paragraph, almost sentence by sentence, and catch Freud stumbling at every juncture, taking the wrong direction at every fork, contradicting text with footnote, and obfuscating one year to the next in revisions. No clinician can be anything but appalled at Freud's turning Dora away when she came again for help—and then as he put it "forgiving" her for cheating him out of a completed case. A related injustice is done Dora by Freud's heirs. The most painful is Felix Deutsch's "Footnote" to Freud's "Fragment." Deutsch mirrors Freud's novelistic twists to create his own little masterpiece, complete with unreliable narrator. It is not surprisingly a complete vindication of Freud.[18]

In 1922 Deutsch was asked by Otto Bauer, the leader of the Austrian Socialist Party, to see his 40-year-old sister, Ida Bauer Adler, bedridden with vertigo and hearing problems. She also complained of migraine, the indifference of her husband, and neglect by her grown son. This son was often out late, and she would wait up nights, listening, till he came home. Recounting this history, Deutsch depicts her as whiny, distrustful, and angry toward men. During the first consultation, Deutsch recognizes the patient as the famous "Dora." Indeed, Frau Adler is delighted to be recognized, and she perks up and starts to act "flirtatious." In the 20 years since Freud, she had made progress in her life, she married, and she reared a son. Deutsch's familiarity with Freud engenders a strong positive transference. *She asks him about his opinion of Freud's interpretation of her two dreams.* Deutsch dodges the question and parries with an interpretation right on the spot: He connects her hearing problems with her listening nightly for her son to come home.

Psychosomatic medicine was practically invented by Felix Deutsch, and he is justly remembered for pioneering this psychiatric subspecialty. Not only is this a brilliant interpretation of Frau Adler's unconscious communication by means of the symptom—linking her *hearing* problem and her *listening* for her son—it mirrors Freud's tying her childhood shortness of breath to *listening* to her parents' sexual intercourse.

At their second meeting, the interpretation has apparently cured her hearing problems and, although still complaining, Frau Adler displays a marked positive transference to Freud. She is proud of being the famous Dora and attempts—unsuccessfully—to engage Deutsch in a discussion of her case. Happy and cooperative, she asks him to come back. Deutsch notes her recycling several old symptoms, but he doesn't mention their likely transferential aim of building an alliance with him. His deafness to the adaptive component of her behavior uncannily mirrors Freud's. Neither Freud nor Deutsch saw the maternal transference that was the real substrate for Dora's "revenge." Deutsch recapitulates Freud's abandonment of Dora two decades earlier and refuses to come again, despite several requests by her brother.

In the second half of his report, Deutsch moves from the first person to the third person, quoting an "informant" who's presented as unimpeachable. The informant told Deutsch that Frau Adler had been one of the "most repulsive hysterics" that he had ever met, and that her death was a relief to all concerned. Deutsch wraps it up with what he calls the facts about Dora: She had a bad outcome, she suffered miserably as a result of terminating her analysis prematurely, and she died lonely and alone.

But there is another way to read Deutsch reading *Dora*: Immediately on encountering him, Dora eagerly asks about the interpretation of her two dreams by Freud. Even at this late date, she is wanting to know their meaning, what Freud held back from her, and what the psychoanalytic world had come to think of her. With Deutsch, as in the second dream, she shows a passionate curiosity about herself viewed through the lens of psychoanalysis. Twenty years later, she still wants to climb the stairs and read Freud's book.

In a sense psychoanalysis is dream analysis, since dreams reflect every aspect of the patient's self image and interface with the world. Not only do dreams provide grist for the mill of transference interpretation, they also reflect progress, or lack of it. Successive dreams over the course of treatment show changes in structure and content. The dream work wants not only to disguise forbidden wishes, it wants to proclaim a narrative that strengthens the self image. The therapist hearing successive dreams at transitions at the beginning, middle, and end of analysis can monitor the progress of treatment. Sequential dreams show changes in self approval, emotional pleasure, and increasing independence from the analyst. Dora's first dream was a nightmare that woke her. Dora's second dream is a "good dream" that plans her future.

> In the Dora case . . . her wish to make love to Herr K . . . articulated with her incestuous wishes for her father. In a postscript, Freud discussed the transferential implications of each dream. In retrospect, he realized that in the second dream Dora was telling him that they had only two more sessions before she would terminate the analysis. Freud concluded the postscript by commenting on the change in Dora's dynamics which the two dreams reflected: [Freud writes] "Just as the first dream represented her turning away from the man she loved to her father—that is to say, her flight from life into disease—so the second dream announced that she was about to tear herself free from her father and had been reclaimed once more by the realities of life."[19]

Despite the fairy tale ending, Freud was ambivalent about the prognosis. It was bad because she broke off the analysis, so she was destined to suffer the rest of her life. It was good since Freud the analyst had forced her to admit she was in love with Herr K as a displacement from her father. The unconscious was made conscious and thus lost its power to disable her. Now Dora had a decent chance of living happily ever after.

Notes

1. Sigmund Freud, "The Interpretation of Dreams," in *The Standard Edition of the Complete Psychological Works of Sigmund Freud*, vols. 5 and 6, James Strachey, Ed. and trans. (London: The Hogarth Press, 1900/1953, 1960), fn 143.
2. Patrick J. Mahony, *Freud's Dora: A Psychoanalytic, Historical, and Textual Study* (New Haven: Yale University Press, 1996), 86–87.

   He translates the dream more literally, using the original present tense; he objects that Strachey makes Dora older by substituting *Mother* and *Father* for the original *Mama* and *Papa*.
3. Sigmund Freud, "Letter 69, to Wilhelm Fliess, 21 September 1897," in *The Standard Edition of the Complete Psychological Works of Sigmund Freud*, vol. 1, James Strachey, Ed. and trans. (London: The Hogarth Press, 1966), 259–260.

4. Sigmund Freud, "Fragment of an Analysis of a Case of Hysteria," in *The Standard Edition of the Complete Psychological Works of Sigmund Freud*, vol. 7, James Strachey, Ed. and trans. (London: The Hogarth Press, 1905/1953), 18–122, 30.
5. Karl K. Lewin, "Dora Revisited," *Psychoanalytic Review* 60 (1973): 519–532.
James W. Kern, "Transference Neurosis as a Waking Dream: Notes on a Clinical Enigma," *Journal of the American Psychoanalytic Association* 35 (1987): 337–366.
Freud fits clinical descriptions of a transference neurosis, his oft-noted "symptomatic acts" as they appear through the 11 weeks of analysis. He forgets key dates having to do with Dora's mother, dismisses the importance of her grandmother's letter and, in an enactment, tests Dora by placing a match holder in her line of sight to prime the pump for her "fire/wetness" associations.
6. K. Lewin, "Dora," 529.
7. Freud, "Fragment," 59–61, fn 120.
8. David Gelman, "Dreams on the Couch," interview with Edward J. Brennan, *Newsweek*, August 14, 1989, 45–47.
Not entirely unwritten. I first encountered this technique in a seminar of Edward Brennan at the American Psychiatric Association Annual Meeting in New York, May 6, 1996.
9. Bertram D. Lewin, "The Train Ride: A Study of One of Freud's Figures of Speech," *Psychoanalytic Quarterly* 39 (1970): 71–89.
10. Mahony, *Dora*. He thinks Freud actually treated Frau K or Herr K around the time of Dora's analysis; and there are two curious sentences, *Dora* 119, where Freud tries to account for Dora's abrupt termination as an "acting out" of revenge on Herr K, a transference reaction to some "unknown quantity" in Freud himself which reminded Dora of Herr K: "What this unknown quantity was I naturally cannot tell. I suspect that it had to do with money, or with jealousy of another patient who had kept up relations with my family after her recovery." Who might Dora have been jealous of and what was this individual's connection with Freud's family? Dora's family? Herr and Frau K's family? If it wasn't Herr K, most likely it was the young and beautiful Frau K. And there is a sequel to Dora and Frau K's story. They resumed their friendship, and in the 1930s they teamed up as card partners and competed against other teams when a contract bridge craze swept Vienna. When later "Dora," Ida Bauer, as the sister of a Socialist leader, was escaping to France, Peppina Zellenka, "Frau K," took her in and hid her from the Nazis.
11. Hanna Segal, *Introduction to the Work of Melanie Klein* (New York: Basic Books, 1964), 12, 17–18, 69–70.
12. Alan Roland, "The Context and Unique Function of Dreams in Psychoanalytic Therapy," *International Journal of Psycho-Analysis* 52 (1971): 431–439.
13. Alan Roland, "Imagery and Symbolic Expression in Dreams and Art," *International Journal of Psycho-Analysis* 53 (1972): 531–539.
He quotes Suzanne Langer's observation that "symbolic expression can be conceptualized as a basic capacity and function of the ego, crucial to human development. [This] 'basic need, which certainly is obvious only in man, is the need for symbolization'," 533.
14. Hannah Segal, "On Symbolism," *International Journal of Psycho-Analysis* 59 (1978): 315–319.
Marion Milner, "Aspects of Symbolism in Comprehension of the Not-Self," *International Journal of Psycho-Analysis* 33 (1952): 181–195.
15. Sara Steinberg, "The Master Tropes of Dreaming: Rhetoric as a Family Affair," *American Journal of Semiotics* 4 (1986): 29–51.
Soliloquy 3 is full of Freud's tools of the dream work and their analogous figures of speech. (1) Condensation/metaphor: *rogue and peasant slave*—comparing wholes with wholes, Hamlet condenses himself metaphorically into two people of lowest status, peasant and slave. (2) Displacement/metonymy: *cleave the general ear*—uses the anatomical part for the whole populace listening (and incidentally underscores the theme of eavesdropping that runs through *Hamlet*). (3) Overdetermination/symbolization: *like a whore unpack my heart*—feminizing himself as *whore*, he castrates himself and uses only *words* for weapons; his *heart* is a container of foolish love (which refers also to swords

and cups—in literature, myth, and dreams—symbols of male and female). (4) Secondary revision/irony: *this is most brave*—the bravery is ironic self mockery (both irony and secondary revision allowing the subtext to show through).

16. R. Thomas Boone and Ross Buck, "Emotional Expressivity and Trustworthiness: The Role of Nonverbal Behavior in the Evolution of Cooperation," *Journal of Nonverbal Behavior* 27 (2003): 163–182.

    Darwin cites *Hamlet* on voluntary and involuntary displays of emotion in deception and cheater detection; he quotes Soliloquy 3 at length.
17. Except Freud's repressing the significance of *Bahnhof* which I can find no mention of.
18. Anne E. Thompson, "The Ending to Dora's Story: Deutsch's Footnote as Narrative," *Psychoanalysis and Contemporary Thought* 13 (1990): 509–534.
    Felix Deutsch, "A Footnote to Freud's 'Fragment of an Analysis of a Case of Hysteria,'" *Psychoanalytic Quarterly* 26 (1957): 159–167.
19. Myron L. Glucksman, "The Use of Successive Dreams to Facilitate and Document Change During Treatment," *Journal of the American Academy of Psychoanalysis* 16 (1988): 47–70.

9

TO BE OR NOT TO BE?

Conscience and the False Self

After he roils the court of Denmark with his antics; after the schoolfellows and players arrive; after Polonius and Claudius install Ophelia in the shadows and themselves behind an arras to eavesdrop, Hamlet walks to the edge of the thrust stage and stands looking out at the horizon. He's in a conversation with himself—as it happens, the axial meditation of western literature.

Time is suspended. This is not a Hamlet we've seen before. There's no cue for this, no trigger, no antecedent. All passion's spent that he showed in previous soliloquies; now he's drawn to think on existence—*to be*—for humankind. Is it nobler *in the mind* to endure life's misery, or end suffering with a single stroke? He answers his own question—it's better to die.

Hamlet 'Tis a consummation
Devoutly to be wished: To die, to sleep —
To sleep perchance to dream. Aye, there's the rub,
For in that sleep of death, what dreams may come
When we have shuffled off this mortal coil
Must give us pause. There's the respect
That makes calamity of so long life.
For who would bear the whips and scorns of time,
The oppressor's wrong . . .
The pangs of despised love, the law's delay,
The insolence of office . . .
When he himself might his quietus make
With a bare bodkin?

III.i.62 TLN 1717–1730

If only death were a dreamless sleep. But dreams may come in that undiscovered country from which no traveler returns. (Hamlet and his audiences are never bothered by the contradiction of a ghost from that country, though critics labor to explain it.) This is a hypothetical suicide, no one expects him to pull out a bodkin and kill himself. But is he talking himself into rash action?

Oddly, despite its juxtaposition of self analysis with sleep and dreams, Freud's not interested. He has one brief mention of it, otherwise, he lets the soliloquies speak for themselves.

> *Hamlet* Who would . . . grunt and sweat under a weary life,
> But that the dread of something after death
> (The undiscovered country from whose bourn
> No traveler returns) puzzles the will
> And makes us rather bear those ills we have
> Than fly to others that we know not of?
> Thus conscience does make cowards of us all,[1]
> And thus the native hue of resolution
> Is sicklied o'er with the pale cast of thought,
> And enterprises of great pitch and moment
> With this regard their currents turn awry
> And lose the name of action.
>
> *III.i.75* TLN 1730–1742

Overfamiliar as the soliloquy is, Northrop Frye says it's the kernel of the play, organized around a stream of infinitives. An infinitive is a "mysterious part of speech that's neither a verb nor a noun, neither action nor thing," so it reflects the nothingness Hamlet fears is at the center of being. He has the sickness of melancholy, as Shakespeare's audience would know, an excess of cold dry humors, associated with philosophy, poetry, and madness. In someone with his "complexion," Elizabethans knew excess of black bile led to *melencholia.* His temperament is dark and earthy, not light and airy (despite Horatio's apostrophe to flights of singing angels—angels, Frye observes, that can hardly have seen the play up to that point).[2]

Frye thinks Hamlet would delay even if he had no excuse. So he persuades himself to doubt the Ghost and take a detour, chasing after his mother's complicity. The Ghost warns him to focus on revenge and not digress ("Leave her to heaven"). Later, the Ghost appears in Gertrude's closet to direct him back to the task. That the play itself never leaves Elsinore emphasizes the claustrophobia of the court. The Prince is quite alone at Elsinore, except for Horatio. Frye believes Hamlet was trying to make Ophelia his confidante in the visit to her closet. But on seeing her childlike face he decided not to bring her into his dangerous tangle.[3]

Vacillation, procrastination, and every sign of doubt are in the lines of the Fourth Soliloquy. Hamlet's debate must be shared by directors and actors who feel obliged to give a novel reading. Modern film *Hamlets* show the attempt of each to escape the influence of previous ones. More recent performances, Tennant directed by Doran, for instance, are desperate, pleading to be judged in the moment. But there is no cultural amnesia for earlier versions, and no pity in the viewer who has inevitably seen it done better.

The seven soliloquies do nothing to advance the plot. And this soliloquy would fit naturally into the play here where it is—or earlier, or late. Try reading the first two scenes but substituting *To be or not to be* for *Too too solid flesh.* It fits surprisingly well. Or put it in place of *How all occasions do inform against me.* It works. Because of its lack of antecedent and absence of cues from the plot, Soliloquy 4 can be, and has been, moved around in production without damage to its impact. This may relate to its odd absence of the first-person viewpoint. It's strange that a passage of self-examination at the depth of Augustine or Montaigne has neither *I* nor *me* nor *myself.* It manages to be personal without direct self reference. And it cements Hamlet's relationship with the audience. Whether in film (with or without voice-over) or in the theater (with or without eye contact) the soliloquy brings the audience closer and closer until the listener is inside Hamlet's head.

Another oddity is the effect of the soliloquy on critics. Samuel Johnson flatly said the speech "is connected rather in the speaker's mind than on his tongue," but even he got drawn into debating whether Hamlet is sketching general principles or working out personal problems. Both are true, of course. Critics over the centuries have fretted about its untidy profusion of figures of speech. Victorians went to some lengths to rationalize "incongruous" metaphors "from which good sense and good taste have long recoiled" by providing emendations. One suggests "Or to take arms against *the seat* of troubles, And by *a poniard* end them?" where *seat* is *heart* and *poniard* is a *bodkin.*[4]

The soliloquies exemplify the quest for self knowledge in the Renaissance. There was a revival of interest in classical ethics and a fashionable push for noble conduct. Recipes for moral improvement were the self help literature of the day, and under the baleful glare of the Puritans even poetry needed justification. Elizabethan drama was interested in moral calibration through self study. In Shakespeare, direct references to self knowledge "occur with some frequency in his dramas and poems—fifteen times altogether, and considerably more often if variations are included, such as finding oneself, being oneself, and forgetting oneself." The particular context "makes clear that self-knowledge had for Shakespeare and his audience a different emphasis." An emphasis on using reason to master passions and humility to tame pride. The elite were reading treatises on manners in the original French and Italian and keeping little memoranda where they recorded elevated slogans. ("My tables! My tables—I shall set it down.") The Tudor gentleman looked to a superior being as his model, and in turn was supposed to be a model for others. What was advised in self help books was to look to an admired object for moral examples as a mirror for self correction.[5]

Suddenly, and for no obvious reason, Hamlet dismisses the schoolfellows and seizes upon his friend, who's obviously been sent for.

Hamlet What ho, Horatio!
Horatio Here, sweet lord, at your service.

Hamlet Horatio, thou art even as just a man
As ever my conversation coped withal —
Horatio O my dear lord —
Hamlet Nay, do not think I flatter,
For what advancement may I hope from thee
That no revenue hast but thy good spirits . . .?
Since my dear Soul was mistress of her choice
And could of men distinguish her election,*
She hath sealed thee for herself. For thou hast been
As one in suffering all that suffers nothing —
A man that Fortune's buffets and rewards
Has taken with equal thanks. And blest are those
Whose blood and judgment are so well co-mingled
That they are not a pipe for Fortune's finger
To sound what stop she please. Give me that man
That is not passion's slave and I will wear him
In my heart's core—aye, in my heart of heart —
As I do thee.

III.ii.52 TLN 1902–1925

* ever since my soul could discriminate among men

He's as honest a man as Hamlet ever met. And it's here that Horatio is addressed by the intimate "thou" for the first time. Blushing, the Prince stops himself, "Something too much of this," and changes the subject.

The Elizabethan audience is getting more sophisticated. A woman is on the throne, there's cultural identification with the female. Even Hamlet's soul is gendered by convention, mistress of choice. Sharp gender roles and moral absolutes were the norm, but there was growing tolerance for ambiguity. In drama, situations dripping irony were engrafted onto pre-existing heroic conventions; ironic and classical modes began to blend—as did, to some extent, comedy and tragedy. For the first time, "Shakespeare holds the mirror up to nature in not separating completely the tragic and comic worlds, which, we know, cannot be completely separated in life." In 1600 when Shakespeare addressed himself to reconciling such antinomies, or rather the impossibility of doing so, the soliloquies fell on receptive ears.[6]

The play opens with "Who's there?" so we know this is going to be about identity. Soon Hamlet's telling his mother that he doesn't know what *seems* means, that, unlike the court, what he shows is an exact depiction of the inner man. He's denying a gap between his outward manifestations and his true self—impossible, of course, nobody's exactly the same on the inside as outside. It's this difference of "that within" from his "outward shows" which constitutes the concept of *the gap* that starts to emerge in modern literary discussions of selfhood.

Hamlet has been at the center of controversies of self for two centuries. Scholar John Lee examines whether Shakespeare's greatest achievement is the creation of "interiority." Is the mark of his genius the depiction of human character, of self? Up to the early nineteenth century, the "answer to 'Who's there?' was 'character,' which, in its meaning, underwent a gradual process of interiorization." Key to such meanings was the belief that he was a real person, independent of Shakespeare. "Prince Hamlet was the liminal point at which art merged with life. He was the point of the most intense interrelationship between the fictive and the actual. And so the claim was made that Prince Hamlet was the first modern man."[7]

Lee disputes that claim. What after much ado he comes up with is a "self-constituted" self for Hamlet rather than one that's "self-fashioned." But *constituted* versus *fashioned* is a distinction only academic postmodernism could love. And related to the *self* is the nettlesome issue of "the gap" in Hamlet's character. There is a large and contradictory literature that argues over empty spaces and discontinuities in his personality. One school of thought is that the interiority of the Prince is the *product* of these accidental gaps. But the big problem for Lee is how the modern vocabulary differs from descriptions of self in the text of *Hamlet*. He concludes that the limited lexicon of Elizabethan English precludes in *Hamlet* and Hamlet the nuanced depiction of interiority that only modern psychology can achieve.

But notions of identity and interiority always existed, though expressed in different words, ideas we take as defining *self*, "character," "personality," "human nature," "individual," "self awareness," or the other terms psychology and philosophy use to mean the human subject. *Self* necessarily implies consciousness, which in turn implies consciousness *of something*; and the *OED* directly links *self* and *consciousness* in a definition where *self* is the persistent, durable experience of successive, different conscious states.

Selfhood and consciousness have never been pinned down by philosophy and psychology, so it was inevitable that advances in scientific medicine and neuroscience would be added to the mix. But its definition remains at least circular if not impossible: A self thinks, it feels, it remembers itself and others, it deceives itself and others, it forgets itself entirely, it is preoccupied with itself; it depicts itself variously with symbols and internal conversations. Self has conscience as well as consciousness—and within itself passions and, some say, a part that's immortal. The human brain is the interface of biology and culture where language constructs the self-conscious human. *The mind is what the brain does*: Neuroscience now posits that this self-regarding agency is built out of symbolic language by means of the interaction of body and environment.[8]

Besides having thoughts, feelings, and behaviors, *self* is experienced as having layers. We sense when we are in our "deeper self." Self has breadth and depth and distinctiveness. And its impact on other selves is of immense concern to itself. Because Elizabethans didn't refer to "self" exactly the way we do, some claim they lacked a concept for all the various meanings and functions catalogued here. It's argued that the lack of a perfect synonym for *self* meant nobody could conceive of himself or herself as we do—only toward the end of the seventeenth century does selfhood in our sense begin to come into being. This claim is made in disregard of the songs of Sappho, the plays of Sophocles, and the confessions of Augustine.

A definition that sees selfhood as conceptually out of reach of people that hadn't started to use our precise words has to ignore Chaucer, Spenser, and Montaigne.

But more astonishing is the argument that Hamlet cannot be a modern self because he doesn't use the jargon of self consciousness coined in the early nineteenth century. Lee doubts Hamlet's ability to characterize "that within" without the modern psychological lexicon of selfhood. Hamlet's descriptions of himself are missing "a self-constituting interiority possessed of agency," so he rejects Hamlet's ability to speak as a modern man, disallowing among other terms "soul" as a synonym for *self* because

> it lacks any sense of psychological or other individuation. 'Soul', used some forty times in *Hamlet* [connotes] the basic element of energy, what gives motion or life . . . or it can be the quality that allows the person to feel, or to think; or it may represent the part of the person that is immortal. . . . It could be involved in dialogues with the body, yet its purpose was not to differentiate people from each other, but rather to show one the path that led humankind to God.[9]

A purpose that doesn't *individuate or differentiate people*? The play contradicts this, line on line. "Soul" is used in multiple and nuanced ways that add up to self exactly as we mean it. The dozens of times "soul" appears (here, by TLNs) even show different characters using *soul* according to the speaker's self definition: Hamlet's nuanced usage spans many meanings, especially connotations of *self* characteristic of the modern:

> 458 Till then, sit still my soul—*my anxious emotions*
> 641 Thoughts beyond the reaches of our souls—*thoughts beyond our imaginings*
> 728 O my prophetic soul—*oh my intuitive self*
> 1137 To the celestial and my soul's idol—*the angel my passions worship*
> 1593 Force his soul so to his whole conceit—*bend his emotions to his acting role*
> 1930 Even with the very comment of thy soul—*along with your keenest judgment*
> 2108 We that have free souls, it touches us not—*we that have skeptical intellect*

whereas Polonius is more concrete, instrumental, descriptive, prescriptive—and medieval,

> 528 Grapple them to thy soul with hoops of steel—*hold them tight in friendship*
> 1068 I hold my duty as I hold my soul—*as I value moral principles.*

And Laertes, schooled in Paris, has a sophisticated physiological notion of it when he counsels Ophelia (TLN 476) that self knowledge matures with the body, that the "inward service of mind and soul/ Grows wide withal."

At prayer in TLN 2344 Claudius gets how his guilt snares him, "O limed soul . . . struggling to be free," as does Gertrude in 2629 and 2762, "Thou turnst mine eyes into my very soul" to reveal "To my sick soul as sin's true nature is," *what sin is.*

The Ghost, like Hamlet, powerfully nuances "soul," giving it multiple meanings at once:

> 701 Would harrow up thy soul, freeze thy young blood—*would terrify your whole innocent being, mind and body*
>
> 770 Taint not thy mind, nor let thy soul contrive—*don't debase your thinking or let deep suspicions move you to trickery*
>
> 2493 Step between her and her fighting soul—*intercede in her emotional and spiritual crisis.*

And finally, skeptical Horatio, true to his function as dramatic prop, never uses "soul."

In *Hamlet* "soul" is a person; the seat of emotions; romantic passion; the immortal spirit; one's deepest being; the conscience; a ghost; self knowledge; fraternal love; the tender affections; the beloved; the essence of something; one's principles; the source of imagination; the mind; one's intellect; and the capacity for discernment. These should satisfy Lee's criteria for an "interiority possessed of agency" leading to personal responsibility. Even where the inward language of selfhood is archaic, the voice of a modern personal self is clearly audible.

There's a profusion of ideas about consciousness in *Hamlet* and more ways of parsing them than there are commentators. Nuttall finds in the play the font of modern thought. Bate sees it as the bedrock of western humanism. Bloom calls Hamlet the ultimate "hero of consciousness." One approach to this mysterious consciousness is to observe it as it emerges from Hamlet's *true self* through his language, his poetry.[10]

Nigel Alexander constructs his study of consciousness in *Hamlet* around three concepts, *poison*, *play*, and *duel*. He says these dominant symbols gather plot and character so tightly that a production neglecting one fails in all three. Besides plot, these extended metaphors reflect Hamlet's consciousness. Alexander understands why many conclude the dilemma is insoluble; but he doubts that Shakespeare is content to solve the dramatic problem "by representing Hamlet's divided mind and to leave his audience in the same confusion as his character."

He believes *Hamlet* is a search for the moral core of humanity and finds for *Hamlet* a quasi-therapeutic function. He doubts the riddles of the play ought to be easily solvable; he thinks Shakespeare wanted the audience to grapple with them and—in passing—get in touch with their own unconscious.

> This is precisely Hamlet's own response to the problems of the play. Since Hamlet is unable to bring the inner debate of the soliloquies to a final and satisfactory conclusion, psychology has sought for a final answer to the problem in Hamlet's unconscious.

The character emanates from his problems. The drama grows out of the audience's puzzlement. Alexander's idea about delay, the "problem of problems," is simple.

> Hamlet's delay is a dramatic device which allows the dramatist to question the nature of the act of revenge. This has escaped the notice of many . . . because they are persuaded that they know the right answer to one of the play's most important and exacting questions. In their view Hamlet ought to kill the King.

But the audience needs time to grow psychologically and morally. For Alexander, the problem is its own solution, the question contains its own answer, and this answering a question with a question is key to the play's dramaturgy: Hamlet's conflicts are *equivalent to a separate character.* The internal debate becomes personified. "The deliberate creation of Hamlet's 'unconscious' is a technical triumph. . . . Hamlet's argument with himself, conducted in soliloquy, is deliberately inconclusive because the dramatist needed to create an unconscious as well as a conscious side of Hamlet's mind." This play, he says, is not meant to provide final answers, it's to make the audience ask questions.[11]

Modern neuroscience has found that the partitioning of cognitive functions in the human brain into explicit and implicit compartments (conscious and unconscious operations) is related to symbol formation and language—which fits nicely with how unconscious thinking has the dialectical structure of natural languages. This division is thought to give rise to the unique human gift (and curse) of self consciousness. This partition we might call a *gap.* Now we find Alexander independently developing a theory of Hamlet's consciousness that's almost identical: Hamlet's "divided mind" creates a gap or "center of consciousness" out of which arises his ability for self-reflection. The "instrument" of this consciousness is Hamlet's authorship of the inner-play *The Mousetrap*, his artistic creation.[12]

Cognitive neuroscience and postmodern literary interpretation converge neatly in the notion of "the gap." Ellen Spolsky says the "divided mind" that evolved to facilitate consciousness also leads to poetry, that

> the vacancies between fragments of understanding not only permit but actually encourage transformation and innovation. . . . a culture's most powerfully imaginative texts are understandable as the heroic efforts of particularly responsive minds, goaded by the inevitable asymmetry and incompleteness of mental representation to vault the gaps in brain structure thus surpassing the limitation of the biological inheritance. The mind itself can hurt you into poetry. The inevitable slippage we have come to acknowledge between words and the world has at least an analogue, and presumably also a source in the workings of the human brain.[13]

The mind can hurt you into poetry. Literary theory has long acknowledged these slippages, limitations, and asymmetries. But she's interested in the occasions when the gaps aren't filled conventionally, but creatively, as in literary texts. She says that "innovation in literary systems can be understood as evidence of the mind's responses to incompatible representations." She thinks a metaphor (or any trope) acts in crucial ways as if it were visual, having the same impact as something seen. The impact is irresistible because the image is evoked reflexively. Different brain functions and information processing by their nature create a gap between the visual and the linguistic. The gap between the imagistic and the propositional suspend between them the simultaneous meanings of both.[14]

The field of linguistics sees the "self" as created within this gap. Creativity depends on the self experiencing itself from within and observing itself from without at the same time. The center of Hamlet's self consciousness is the aching gap within him, reflected in *The Mousetrap*. Spolsky's "slippage between word and world" goes to the painful heart of his mystery.

Winnicott said psychoanalysis could penetrate the deeper mysteries of the self if the analyst was able to tolerate a regression to extreme dependency by the primitive patient. (And if you're picturing a patient in the fetal position on the couch, you're not far off.) He sites the origin of the self in the first months of life before a distinction exists between the inner world and the outer world. Normally the infant experiences primitive "id-demands" as its core. But disturbances in the mother-child relationship prematurely fragment parts of the self. He describes grown people in analysis who have a very successful False Self but feel all their lives that they haven't started to exist because they can't experience authentic passionate feelings at the deepest level.

The "successful False Self" has the function of a caretaker, a proxy mother. In the course of a good-enough analysis, it can hand its function over to the analyst. The False Self is what other people think is the real person. Up close in intimate relationships the False Self starts to fail and the individual gets symptomatic. In analysis there may come a crisis when the person can see across to the promised land of authentic selfhood but can't get there, and there's despair and potential suicide to avoid loss of the True Self. "When suicide is the only defence left against betrayal of the True Self, then it becomes the lot of the False Self to organize the suicide."

We're convinced of Hamlet's whips and scorns of time, we know he's endured slings and arrows. And yet over the course of the play, he will emerge as a true self (specifically at the resolution of the Closet scene with his mother). In favorable circumstances, either in psychoanalysis or good enough environmental conditions, the False Self has been built on identifications with the True Self of a person in the environment, a nanny or grandparent, for instance, (or a court jester) that augments the mother who is not good enough.

In health, the False Self presents as polite social behavior and the maintenance of healthy privacy. A special danger during transformation into True Self occurs when the False Self is organized around a high intellect. The mind becomes its locus, causing

> a dissociation between intellectual activity and psychosomatic existence. . . . The world may observe academic success of a high degree and find it hard to believe in the very real distress of the individual concerned, who feels phony the more he or she is successful. When such individuals destroy themselves . . . this invariably produces a sense of shock.

This brings Winnicott to the relationship among True Self, False Self, and the actor. The "ordinary devoted mother" reacts to the "spontaneous gesture" of the infant—loving or hating, destructive or erotic—with unconditional love and allows the True Self to be creative and feel real. This requires a rudimentary ability to use symbols, to play. When there is a False Self hiding the True Self, there is difficulty in using symbols and transitional objects. In analysis this leads to a time of danger, when a period of extreme dependency may ensue. In this crisis Winnicott enters into the psychosis with the patient. He tells of a man who had "a considerable amount of analysis before coming to me. My work really started with him when I made it clear to him that I recognized his non-existence." All his previous analysis was useless "because it had been done on the basis that he existed, whereas he had only existed falsely."

But Hamlet is not deeply ill, he's regressed from trauma to a developmental low ebb. There exists a range of self guises from psychotic to well, and Hamlet would be at the healthier end. Winnicott talks about a compliant False Self that's a defense but is taken for the whole, so that sometimes it forms the basis for a kind of sublimation, as when a child grows up to be an actor.

> In regard to actors, there are those who can be themselves and can also act, whereas there are others who can only act, and who are completely at a loss when not in a role, and when not being applauded. Health here is closely bound up with the capacity of the individual to live in an area that is intermediate between the dream and the reality.[15]

Still, Hamlet's narcissistic defenses have a toxic effect on some. D.H. Lawrence hates Hamlet. He sees the Prince as the embodiment of all that's wrong with the modern world, a failure to act on instinct that inadvertently sweeps up blameless bystanders and destroys them.

> I had always felt an aversion from Hamlet: a creeping, unclean thing he seems. . . . His nasty poking and sniffing at his mother, his setting traps for the King, his conceited perversion with Ophelia make him always intolerable. The character is repulsive in its conception, based on self-dislike and a spirit of disintegration.

A creeping, unclean thing. Hamlet's flaws are modern flaws for Lawrence, a repellent mixture of frigidity paradoxically fused with sexual obsession. Hamlet is suspicious, "isolated, self-nauseated, labouring in a sense of physical corruption." But he disowns his own corruption, "letting his mother know he had discovered her incest, her uncleanness, gloated in torturing the incestuous King. Of all the unclean ones, Hamlet was the uncleanest." This disowned but inescapable

> sense of corruption in the flesh makes Hamlet frenzied, for he will never admit that it is his own flesh. . . . The whole drama is the tragedy of the convulsed reaction of the mind from the flesh, of the spirit from the self.

This echoes Freud's initial diagnosis of Hamlet as frigid hysteric. Most clinicians can think of patients, anorexics or self-mutilators for instance who, just as Lawrence says, hate their own bodies, deny their own flesh, and paradoxically are incarcerated in it. But then after his long, acid critique, Lawrence takes an abrupt turn: *To be, or not to be*? Even Lawrence is under the spell. Hamlet, with his self reflection and pursuit of consciousness, has the one thing modern humankind would do well to emulate. Lawrence says modern man

> has still to let go, to know what not-being is, before he can *be*. Till he has gone through the Christian negation of himself, and has known the Christian consummation, he is a mere amorphous heap. For the soliloquies of Hamlet are as deep as the soul of man can go, in one direction, and as sincere as the Holy Spirit itself in their essence.[16]

As deep as the soul of man can go. Hamlet returns to this again in Soliloquy 7. A person can't be free to say *yes* without freedom to say *no*. Someone can't really do evil without ability to choose otherwise; choice is the litmus of responsibility, agency, and therefore knowledge of sin.

Neuroscience's idea of consciousness as a product of the gap in a bicameral brain seems right. But perhaps the consolidation of human consciousness comes of wrestling with choices. *I am me myself choosing right and not wrong*. Hamlet is in a circular process in which conscience creates consciousness and consciousness creates conscience. This is the heart of his mystery. The concepts of free will, right and wrong—these depend on a considered unconstrained moment alone with whatever gods he has—a silent pause followed by an intuitive leap. A soliloquy.

Hamlet How all occasions do inform against me*
And spur my dull revenge. What is a man
If his chief good and market of his time
Be but to sleep and feed? A beast—no more.
Sure he that made us with such large discourse,
Looking before and after, gave us not
That capability and godlike reason to fust in us unused.

IV.iv.33 TLN 2743+26–33

* all events accuse me

Large discourse, looking before and after. A quarter of the play later, a thousand lines after *To be or not to be*, another meditation on the divine will, a search for his creator's plan. Hamlet knows inside him "noble reason" and "infinite faculties" are rusting. Asking why he hesitated earlier, he thought he was all tangled in thought. Is it still true, or is it the opposite?

> *Hamlet* Now, whether it be bestial oblivion or some craven scruple
> Of thinking too precisely on the event —
> A thought which quartered hath but one part wisdom
> And ever three parts coward—I do not know
> Why yet I live to say, "This thing's to do,"
> Since I have cause and will, and strength and means
> To do it.
>
> *IV.iv.40* TLN 2743+33–40

None of the seven soliloquies is more true to the character of the Prince, not even the fourth. But the Folio of 1623 discarded it. From the end of the Tudor era, culture changed, and English drama evolved over two decades of Stuart rule, from early performances to the Folio's publication. And considering the length of the play, it would be a logical cut. Still, Soliloquy 7 finds its way back into productions. It comes as a burst of energy just when the play needs it. It's in Gielgud's film, and Branagh's. Nowhere in Shakespeare are there lines more stirring.

Simmering in Freud's mind with *Hamlet* was a great thick stew of concepts—the uncanny, conscience, consciousness, ego, superego, guilt, crime and punishment. His practice was a peephole through which he observed loosened inhibitions and forbidden acts of the patient.

> Analytic work then brought the surprising discovery that such deeds were done principally because they were forbidden, and because their execution was accompanied by a mental relief for their doer. He was suffering from an oppressive feeling of guilt, of which he did not know the origin, and after he had committed a misdeed, his sense of guilt was at least attached to something. Paradoxical as it may sound . . . the sense of guilt was present before the misdeed, that it did not arise from it, but conversely—the misdeed arose from the sense of guilt. These people might justly be described as criminals from a sense of guilt.[17]

Criminals from a sense of guilt. Crime and punishment are reversed. A strong, vague feeling of guilt, which has always been present, then seeks a cause. As if in a trance, a powerful impulse lashes out. The individual awakens to a nightmare. There is blood on the hands, the sheriff at the door, the eyes of the world witnessing a crime that was never intended.

Freud here is at his darkest. As Plato observed, good people dream what bad people do. The relief in waking from a dream in which one has done something horrible makes it easy to see: This guilt comes from the reproaches of the superego. It develops from the ego as a self-observing capacity during the later stages of ego development. A "special agency" is gradually formed which is able to stand apart from the rest of the ego "which has the function of observing and criticizing the self and of exercising a censorship within the mind, and which we become aware of as our 'conscience.'" The fact that an agency of this kind exists "able to treat the rest of the ego like an object [has the result] that man is capable of self-observation."

Freud locates the superego in relation to the *uncanny* through the familiar sense of dread that comes in life and in dreams when repressed desires are about to erupt. In the unconscious there is "a 'compulsion to repeat' proceeding from the instinctual impulses . . . a compulsion powerful enough to overrule the pleasure principle, lending to certain aspects of the mind their daemonic character. . . ."[18]

Hamlet calls his melancholy by name as a disease. He "knows *whom* he has lost but not *what* he has lost in him." Mourning is conscious, but melancholia has unconscious identification with the departed object. Freud notes that the melancholic's self-reproach is immune to reason, there's "a delusion of (mainly moral) inferiority." But along with it, a keener sense of reality.

> We only wonder why a man has to be ill before he can be accessible to a truth of this kind. For there can be no doubt that if anyone holds and expresses to others an opinion of himself such this (an opinion which Hamlet held both of himself and of everyone else), he is ill. [Freud's footnote: 'Use every man after his desert, and who shall scape whipping?']

Freud concludes that what permits this is the splitting off from the ego of a part of itself, a part that sets itself against the ego and judges it critically,

> the agency commonly called 'conscience'; we shall count it, along with the censorship of consciousness and reality-testing, among the major institutions of the ego, and we shall come upon evidence to show that it can become diseased on its own account.

In melancholia, there was not the normal withdrawal of the libido from the lost object over time and a displacement of it onto a new one. Rather, the libido was turned on itself and

> served to establish an *identification* of the ego with the abandoned object. Thus the shadow of the object fell upon the ego, and the latter could be henceforth be judged by a special agency, as thought it were an object, the forsaken object. In this way an object-loss was transformed into an ego-loss. The self-tormenting in melancholia, which is without doubt enjoyable, signifies . . . a satisfaction of trends of sadism and hate which relate to an object, and which have been turned round upon the subject's own self.[19]

Freud has the Prince in mind in "Mourning and Melancholia" and footnotes the play to show how object loss—which might normally only cause mourning—can be turned against the self to cause melancholia. Hamlet's introspection is deepened by grief. But what introspection might reveal is criticized by a superego pathologically swollen by identification with his father's righteousness. His superego is also inflamed in the fight to keep hidden his guilt over having unconsciously wished him dead. Even if his normal father-son rivalry doesn't entirely cause his procrastination, it may help explain Hamlet's melancholia. *The shadow of the lost object fell upon the ego*, and then melancholia led to conscience, and conscience led to consciousness.

The soliloquies utterly refute Ernest Jones's claim that Hamlet's "apparently causeless inhibition," his "paralysis arises . . . not from physical or moral cowardice, but from that intellectual cowardice, that reluctance to dare the exploration of his inmost soul." Hamlet? *Intellectual cowardice*? There are always places in us we cannot look. The inability to completely pluck out the heart of Hamlet's mystery proves he's a truly modern character, and his inability to penetrate his own enigmas makes his character fully human.[20]

Notes

1. Shakespeare uses *conscience* throughout his works—and conspicuously in *Hamlet*—in both its connotations of "inwit," or awareness within self and "pravity," the moral sense. (The *OED* quotes the Fourth Soliloquy to illustrate its use as moral sense.) The word *conscience* had already been used for three centuries to mean either *inwit* or *pravity*—and Hamlet as usual intends both.
2. Francesca Bugliani, " 'In the Mind to Suffer': Hamlet's Soliloquy, 'To Be or Not To Be,' " *Hamlet Studies* 17 (1995): 10–42.
3. Northrop Frye, "Hamlet," in *Northrop Frye on Shakespeare* (New Haven: Yale University Press, 1986), 82–100.
4. Bernice W. Kliman, *Enfolded Hamlet*, 1996. www.leoyan.com/global-language.com/enfolded/output4.php?file=hworks1700/hw-1713cn.xml, accessed May 1, 2013.
5. Rolf Soellner, *Shakespeare's Patterns of Self-Knowledge* (Columbus: Ohio State University Press, 1972), xiii–xiv.
6. Ibid, xvii.
7. John Lee, *Shakespeare's Hamlet and the Controversies of Self* (Oxford: Clarendon Press, 2000), 150–151.
8. Mary Thomas Crane, *Shakespeare's Brain: Reading with Cognitive Theory* (Princeton: Princeton University Press, 2001).
9. Lee, *Controversies*, 155–156.
10. A.D. Nuttall, *Shakespeare the Thinker* (New Haven: Yale University Press, 2007). Jonathan Bate, *Soul of the Age: A Biography of the Mind of William Shakespeare* (New York: Random House, 2009).
11. Nigel Alexander, *Poison, Play, and Duel: A Study in Hamlet* (Lincoln: University of Nebraska Press, 1971), 9–12.
12. Mark Solms, "What Is Consciousness?" *Journal of the American Psychoanalytic Association* 45 (1997): 681–703.
13. Ellen Spolsky, *Gaps in Nature: Literary Interpretation and the Modular Mind* (Albany: State University of New York Press, 1993), 2–3.
14. Ibid, 7.

15. Donald W. Winnicott, "Ego Distortion in Terms of True and False Self," in *The Maturational Processes and the Facilitating Environment* (New York: International Universities Press, 1965), 140–152.
16. D.H. Lawrence, *Twilight in Italy* (London: Duckworth, 1916), 122–124, 134.
17. Sigmund Freud, "Criminals from a Sense of Guilt," in *The Standard Edition of the Complete Psychological Works of Sigmund Freud*, vol. 14, James Strachey, Ed. and trans. (London: The Hogarth Press, 1916/1957), 332–333.
18. Sigmund Freud, "The 'Uncanny,'" in *The Standard Edition of the Complete Psychological Works of Sigmund Freud*, vol. 17, James Strachey, Ed. and trans. (London: The Hogarth Press, 1919/1955), 219–252, 238.
19. Sigmund Freud, "Mourning and Melancholia," in *The Standard Edition of the Complete Psychological Works of Sigmund Freud*, vol. 14, James Strachey, Ed. and trans. (London: The Hogarth Press, 1917/1957), 243–258.
20. Ernest Jones, *Hamlet and Oedipus* (New York: Doubleday Anchor Books, 1949), 103.

10

HAMLET WRITES *THE MOUSETRAP*

Method Acting and Metatheater

Nearly one-fifth of *Hamlet* involves metatheater—plays within plays, performances about performing. These dramatic insertions begin well before the Prince produces *The Mousetrap*. Such devices add a layer of realism at the same time they break the conventions of drama and multiply plot ambiguities. Most ambiguous of all is the meta-metatheater of the Dumb Show, the play within a play within a play that's completely redundant and unnecessary—or is it?

Dozens of images evoke actors, scripts, roles, entrances, exits, lighting, makeup, and costumes (including clown shoes with rosettes Hamlet would wear if he were to run off with an acting troupe). Performance is omnipresent. There's music—snatches of two or three popular songs by Hamlet, several by Ophelia, sacred and profane. Trumpet fanfares are played, and oboes; recorders are played and conspicuously not played. Jigs are at first scorned, then forbidden, and finally danced by a gleeful Hamlet.

Much of the lifelikeness of *Hamlet* comes from ambiguities created metatheatrically. And besides references to drama *Hamlet* is full of references to poetry, writing, and journaling. There's a crucial epistolary element, as some dozen letters are material to the plot (three of Claudius—one forged—a letter from Old Norway, one from Polonius to Laertes, and letters from Hamlet to Horatio, to Claudius, to Gertrude, and several to Ophelia). Metatheater inserts irony into the play. When we first meet the Prince he's denying to his mother that he *seems*. This he quickly reverses by enacting madness through the whole middle of the play. The Third Soliloquy deals with drama's effect on "guilty creatures sitting at a play" (ourselves, if you hadn't guessed). And metatheater leverages suspense: As bait to trap his mother, Hamlet writes some dozen or sixteen lines to insert into *Gonzaago*. Besides her guilt, underlying *The Mousetrap* is the question whether the Ghost is the spirit of his murdered father.

The Prince is at his happiest around theater. And real: After the players come to Elsinore and are made welcome, Hamlet says, "they are the abstract and brief chronicles of the time. After your death, you were better have a bad epitaph than their ill report while you lived." It's a touching moment as it feels like Shakespeare's tribute to his profession and his own company, an abstract and chronicle now four centuries old.

Metatheatrical devices mirror the textures of real life. Shakespeare has actors on his stage refer to the fact that theater exists, actors act, plays are played. This one opens with us watching people watching—for a ghost. It closes with us watching people watching—Hamlet's body lying in state—and Horatio is ordered to assemble an audience to hear Hamlet's story. A fundamental convention in drama is that actors ignore the audience and the audience pretends not to exist. In *Hamlet* there are places the playwright breaks these illusions and then glues them together stronger than ever. When Hamlet swears Marcellus and Horatio to secrecy "upon my sword," the subterranean Ghost cries, "Swear!" And the Globe audience heard *Swear* booming out from under the stage. The five feet of headroom under the stage entered by a trap door was called the *cellarage*: "Come on, you hear this fellow in the cellarage," cues lines from under the platform: *Swear*. Hamlet doesn't say "this fellow under the earth." When he says *cellarage*, he is calling the space under the stage by its theatrical name.

Theater commenting on theater runs right through to Hamlet's final words, "You that look pale and tremble at this chance/ That are but mutes or audience to this act . . . Oh, I could tell you—but let it be. Horatio, I am dead." As audience we become extras ("mutes" in Elizabethan theater). When actors on the stage refer to themselves as "actors" metaphorically and their "lives" as like theater, they bend dramatic convention. Paradoxically, metatheater increases the illusion. When an actor on a stage says, "I feel like I'm an actor on a stage," it makes the audience less, not more, conscious of being an audience because in "real life" we so often use figures of speech about theater. When Hamlet bids Horatio to report his motives to the world, it tethers *Hamlet* as the chronicle of Shakespeare's own time. The Prince is thought to be the character that was the playwright's personal favorite, but Hamlet is not Shakespeare. As much as he might want to be, Hamlet is no professional, he's an amateur. He teaches the players techniques different from the first player's method. Hamlet directs them to perform consciously willed behaviors, to *imitate* emotion (feelings driven by thoughts).[1]

Hamlet asks the first player to recite lines he knew and loved, a scene about the killing of King Priam in full sight of Priam's wife, Hecuba. The performance is a tour de force. Hamlet, deeply touched, asks him to perform *The Murder of Gonzago* before the whole court the following evening. The agony of Queen Hecuba has struck Hamlet, and he especially notes *her* loyalty to *her* husband. This gives Hamlet an idea. He says aside to the first player that he wants to add some dozen lines he himself will write. The player says, yes, they can work with the changes for the court performance.

Hamlet is in awe of the first player because he knows imitation alone can't achieve perfectly natural effects. In Soliloquy 3 Hamlet is trying learn acting (and, of course, better know himself, why he delays). The first player's streaming tears and blanched face are more than mere imitation. Hamlet senses extra mastery as he observes the actor taking from life a "cue for emotion" (experience remembered and re-imagined). Mimicry makes for a contrived character; but the first player *becomes* the character by mastering guided empathy, asking, What are my real-life cues for this emotion? When have I felt these feelings before? Hamlet can't teach the player's method because he hasn't grasped the distinction. So when he's directing the players he settles for imitation and its limitations, teaching acting through conscious intent.[2]

> Speak the speech I pray you as I pronounced it to you—trippingly on the tongue. But if you mouth it as many of our players do, I had as lief the town crier spoke my lines. Nor do not saw the air too much with your hand—thus—but use all gently, for in the very torrent, tempest and, as I may say, the whirlwind of your passion, you must acquire and beget a temperance that may give it smoothness.
>
> *III.ii.1* TLN 1849–1856

There's value in Hamlet's direction, but he can't quite take it up to the next rung, the ability to actually turn pale, to cry actual tears. With an imitative technique, character is constructed from the outside; because of the limitations of surface simulation, not empathic performance—actors hit the wrong note. As a result Hamlet over directs and because, as director, he's forcing upon the players his own line readings rather than allowing theirs, he must warn them against overacting.

> O it offends me to the soul to hear a robustious periwig-pated fellow tear a passion to tatters . . . to split the ears of the groundlings who are capable of nothing but inexplicable dumb shows and noise. . . . Be not too tame neither, but let your own discretion be your tutor. Suit the action to the word, the word to the action that you o'er-step not the modesty of Nature. . . . O there be players that. . . so strutted and bellowed that I have thought some of Nature's journeymen* had made them, and not made them well, they imitated humanity so abominably.
>
> *III.ii.10* TLN 1864–1883
>
> * apprentices

Imitation is a basic instinct. As *Hamlet* unfolds, the Prince must become more and more a method actor. The process stabilizes him blowing off steam. But at times Hamlet enacts madness so convincingly that he fools himself. In the final scene, what else could he mean in his apology to Laertes, when he says he wasn't really himself, that Hamlet was taken away from Hamlet?

Freud doesn't care about the soliloquies. Hamlet's self analysis doesn't come up even when Freud applies psychoanalysis to drama, even modern "psychopathological drama." Such plays—and Freud claims *Hamlet* is the first—are about conflict between a conscious impulse and a repressed one. This is *The Mousetrap* too. The trap's spring is conflict between a conscious impulse and one lurking unseen. Hamlet feels women are poisonous weeds gathered at midnight. He's obsessed by the conscious picture of his mother on a bed of bridal flowers with Claudius. This becomes the inspiration for the lines he dreams up to insert in *Gonzago*.

Trumpets and oboes sound. The King, Queen, Polonius, Ophelia, Rosencrantz and Guildenstern enter and take their seats, the court arrayed behind them.

King	How fares our cousin Hamlet?
Hamlet	Excellent, in faith. Of the chameleon's dish I eat—the air . . .
King	I have nothing with this answer. . . . These words are not mine.
Hamlet	No, nor mine now, my lord—Be the players ready?

III.ii.92 TLN 1948–1961

When Hamlet says he's tired of eating only promises, the King ignores the reference to thwarted ambition. Polonius, at Claudius's ear, is urging him to watch for evidence that the Prince is mad for love. With this pleasant banter, Gertrude is starting to relax. Hamlet's like his old self.

Gertrude	Come hither, my good Hamlet. Sit by me.
Hamlet	No, good mother, here's mettle more attractive.
Polonius	O ho! Do you mark that?
Hamlet	Lady, shall I lie in your lap?
Ophelia	No, my lord.
Hamlet	Do you think I meant country matters?
Ophelia	I think nothing, my lord.
Hamlet	That's a fair thought: To lie between maid's legs.
Ophelia	What is, my lord?
Hamlet	Nothing.*
Ophelia	You are merry, my lord.
Hamlet	O God. . . .what should a man do but be merry? For look you—how cheerfully my mother looks—and my father died within's two hours.
Ophelia	Nay, 'tis twice two months, my lord.
Hamlet	So long? Nay then, let the devil wear black. . . . O heavens, die two months ago and not forgotten yet? Then there's hope a great man's memory may outlive his life half a year.

III.ii.108 TLN 1963–1987

* pronounced no-thing, a bawdy Elizabethan pun

This is excruciating. Hamlet's refused to sit by Gertrude, where he can't watch Claudius's face, but lies at Ophelia's feet looking up her skirt. Ophelia tries to deflect his lewdness, but his answers are satiric and hostile. This bawdry confirms Polonius's theory about love-madness. *The Murder of Gonzago* begins, oboes announcing the Dumb Show pantomime.

> Enter a king and a queen very lovingly, the queen embracing him, and he her. She kneels and makes show of protestation unto him. He takes her up and declines his head upon her neck. . . . She seeing him asleep leaves him. Anon comes in another man, takes off his crown, kisses it, pours poison in the sleeping king's ears, and leaves him. The queen returns, finds the king dead, and makes passionate action. The poisoner, with some three or four, comes in again, seeming to condole with her. The dead body is carried away. The poisoner woos the queen with gifts. She seems loath and unwilling awhile, but in the end accepts his love.
>
> *III.ii.135* TLN 1991–2002

There's no reaction from the Elsinore audience. Exit the Dumb Show players. The player king and queen enter, and the king recalls the years they've been married. The player queen worries about his recent sickness, but he tells her to remarry after he dies. The queen says, "None wed the second but who killed the first." *A woman who remarries must have killed her first husband.* The player king says her good intentions will change with time.

> *Player King* I do believe you think what now you speak,
> But what we do determine, oft we break.
> Purpose is but the slave to memory,
> Which now like fruit unripe sticks on the tree
> But fall unshaken when they mellow be.
> Our wills and fates do so contrary run
> That our devices still are overthrown,
> Our thoughts are ours, their ends none of our own.
> So think thou wilt no second husband wed,
> But die thy thoughts when thy first lord is dead.
>
> *III.ii.186* TLN 2054–2083

This passage is torture for a modern audience; three-fourths of the speech is cut here but you certainly don't miss it. The emotions of the king and queen are unplayable (unless the actors disobey direction and ham it up). The poetry isn't sublime, though experts say it's indisputably Shakespeare, perhaps taking after Ovid; it would have seemed archaic even to the Elizabethans. The first half dozen lines establish only that they've been married 30 years. This is the setup for the player king's saying that, despite what the queen claims, she will change her mind. The player queen's response is so exaggerated that when Hamlet asks his mother what she thinks, Gertrude quotes an old (slightly naughty) proverb, " 'The lady doth protest too much,' methinks." And Hamlet counters, "But she'll keep her word."

No she won't. The Dumb Show says *she goes away with another.* Why does Hamlet undercut his dramatized accusation of unfaithfulness? Editors are useless here. We have to shrug it off as a Freudian slip, a wish opposite the conscious message.

After all, Hamlet is in a nightmare. Deep in his unconscious every wish is unwished, every *no* also becomes a *yes*. And at the climactic entrance of the poisoner, Hamlet will make another slip, calling Lucianus nephew to the king, not brother.

During the play Gertrude doesn't react, but the game is starting to dawn on Claudius.

King Have you heard the argument? Is there no offense in it?
Hamlet No . . . they do but jest, poison in jest, no offense in the world.
King What do you call the play?
Hamlet "The Mousetrap." This play is the image of a murder done
in Vienna. Gonzago is the duke's name. 'Tis a knavish piece of
work, but we that have free souls, it touches us not.
[enter Lucianus
This is one Lucianus, nephew to the king. Begin
hamming it up]
murderer! Pox. Leave thy damnable faces and begin!
Lucianus Thoughts black, hands apt, drugs fit, and time agreeing,
Confederate season else no creature seeing,
Thou mixture rank, of midnight weeds collected . . .
Thy natural magic and dire property
On wholesome life usurps immediately. *[pours poison in his ears]*
Hamlet He poisons him in the garden for his estate. His name's
Gonzago. The story is extant and written in very choice
Italian. You shall see anon how the murderer gets the
love of Gonzago's wife.

III.ii.231 TLN 2100–2136

Onstage Lucianus pours poison in Gonzago's ears as Hamlet narrates. He's about to describe the wooing of the widow when Claudius jumps up shaking. "What?" Hamlet jeers, "Frighted with false fire?" The King calls for some light, and the court follows as he lurches out amid calls of "Lights! Lights! Lights!"

After the long king and queen speeches, there are six short bursts of dialogue and a dozen people scramble off stage. Hamlet and Horatio are alone. There's silence. Hamlet erupts in glee at Claudius's reaction to the onstage crime, but Horatio is calm. He understands this doesn't constitute a public confession. The audience at Elsinore will think the King couldn't tolerate Hamlet's insults. But now at least, Hamlet is certain it's an honest Ghost.

Nigel Alexander says mounting *The Mousetrap* is one of the "dominant symbols" of the play. Successful productions must persuasively mimic a court performance within the larger play's dramatic action. "The audience . . . must be made to grasp the distinction, and the relationship, between the play and inner-play, between the 'poison in jest' played by the actors and the acts of poison performed by the characters." He thinks the metaplays perform functions similar to the soliloquies. They depict in pictures the subtexts of the soliloquies.[3]

> If, in *Hamlet*, the great instrument of awareness is the centre of consciousness created in Hamlet's divided mind, the great instrument of conscience is the inner-play. *The Murder of Gonzago* expresses in exact dramatic form the considerations of conscience which cannot be completely dramatized in the soliloquies.

The center of consciousness is Hamlet's divided mind. Consciousness has to be depicted in visual symbols, the way a dream depicts the self's wishes in conflict. This is what Alexander means by the inner-play being the instrument of Hamlet's consciousness, that it's like the dreamwork, spinning Hamlet's hidden desires—Freud's "dream thoughts"—into images. Figures of speech convey meaning using other figures of speech. These are recognized using hidden symbolic processes whose surface manifestations are figurative. Freud saw it—obvious but paradoxical—*the unconscious mind thinks in symbols*. These symbols get translated into a story that explains the world through analogies.

This is external awareness. But how about self awareness, does the same machinery that perceives the world also perceive the self? When Hamlet perceives Polonius, he compares the old counselor in the present moment with all experience of what he knows of Polonius's *desires, beliefs, and intentions*. He perceives him through a "theory of mind," an informed guess about future behavior based on past patterns. Hamlet is "reading" Polonius's mind. This split-second assessment of complex motives is reflexive and guided by Hamlet's own desires, beliefs, and intentions. This reflexive social appraisal of self and other represents 100,000 years of human evolution. How ever complex culture has become and how ever powerful its impact on evolution of the species and individual development—still, it starts with the basic neural wiring of the early human. We can't *not* read each other's minds.

But how is Hamlet's perception of Hamlet different from his assessment of someone else? Not much, the same assessment of desires and beliefs is going on; the same comparison of memories of experiences and threads of concepts; the same observation of feelings about self and others. The only difference is that "Hamlet looking at Hamlet" looks inward. This self construction depends on a "theory of mind" too, but a theory of one's own mind as it mirrors one's own desires, beliefs, and intentions. Now, Hamlet perceives Polonius. He can also perceive himself perceiving Polonius—in imagination he can place himself at a third point separate from them. And in the same way Hamlet can perceive Hamlet. By imagining himself in triangulation with his perceiving self and his self *as perceived*, he can *observe his own self awareness*. And through the re-creation of this triangle outside himself symbolically—let's say with puppets—Hamlet can even see his own process of self perception and anticipate where it could lead. (This model of consciousness should start to remind you a little of *The Mousetrap* and the Dumb Show.) The phenomenology of human consciousness, abetted by language, is unique, like nothing else in Nature. It implies awareness *of* something; as William James said, consciousness is at root a *knowing* of something, so individual consciousness is not a *thing* but a process, one of knowing and computing with symbols.

Cultures too have "self" and "consciousness." What distinguishes modern consciousness from the Elizabethan experience of selfhood in poetry and drama? James Shapiro says that an important difference is the concept of literature as an exploration of the author's self through personal disclosure and literary explication. Rightly cautious about the autobiographical fallacy (*They were just like us*), Shapiro says Elizabethan literature did examine the place of the self in religion, history, and government. But what modern culture added is the meta-phenomenon of the examination *of the examination* of the self by means of literature, with the reader looking on and the writer self consciously aware of being read.[4]

But we see Hamlet doing exactly this—watching himself analyzing himself by means of the literature he has available—and then analyzing the analysis. *About, my brain.* The gathering of cultural knowledge is the subtext of the Third Soliloquy. He's heard guilty persons watching a play have been so struck with remorse that they've confessed. Based on that, he writes the dozen extra lines inserted into *Gonzago*. He makes frequent reference to stories, songs, and verse and compares his situation of the moment with them. He likens Ophelia to Jephtha's daughter and Gertrude to Hecuba and from these literary examples fashions cognitive tools. Hamlet shows us how he's shaped by what he writes in his tables or commonplace book, a habit of self examination he alludes to in the Nunnery scene: He knows he's proud, revengeful, ambitious, with a long history of terrible offenses—and his inventory is not something he's doing on the spot, we sense he's done it before.

Some detect a qualitative difference in "selfhood" between Shakespeare's time and ours. The notion is that because so much was different in their culture, there is a discontinuity in their appreciation of *self*. But if there were any real difference, Hamlet wouldn't feel so familiar. That's how we know *Hamlet* is truly modern.

The device of "the play" magnifies and multiplies what Nigel Alexander feels is the most important tool of theatrical depiction, dramatic irony. By means of the inner-play and the Dumb Show in it, what the "spectators" onstage learn is ratified or contradicted by other information known to the audience watching *Hamlet*. Plays within plays not only report an incident taking place in stage time but reinforce the threat Hamlet's making to the King and Queen. They magnify suspense by visually evoking the past and foreshadowing the future.

The play within a play was already old when Shakespeare wrote the revised *Hamlet*. In addition to metadrama's capacity to evoke past memory in an audience, it condenses and intensifies the information. Alexander uses the term "mediated perception" for how a person becomes aware of things outside direct view. This is perception *mediated* by a point of view beside the perceiver, a second set of eyes looking at the same thing (as Hamlet has Horatio watch the King). This second point of view can be done by telling or showing something, but it's especially powerful when they're done together, as Hamlet does with *The Mousetrap*. Metadrama does a good deal of work for of the audience of *Hamlet* by remembering and organizing what they saw earlier. Freud's theory of dreamwork says that condensation disguises information by superimposing two or more concepts, images, or symbols, allowing what they have in common to stand out. What's hidden this way also shows the deeper relationship among elements. But it also reveals as it conceals.

The audience to *Hamlet*—and *The Mousetrap*—don't have to use evocative memory, active data retrieval. They only need recognition memory, a less effortful process—and a more primitive and impactful one. The similarity between Pyrrhus, Lucianus, and Hamlet versus Priam, King Hamlet, Claudius, and the player king all give Hamlet cover through displacement. He can feign not understanding if accused of treasonous speech. ("No, nor mine now.") What Priam, Claudius, and the player king all have in common is kingship and a queen. What Hamlet, Pyrrhus, and Lucianus have in common is jealous hatred, usurpation, and revenge. The audience sees the two categories, kings and avengers, and condenses them down into two id-driven concepts, thinly disguised just as in a dream: Sexual desire and blood lust.

It is also an enacted metaphor that the court of Denmark gathers to watch another court, the one in the inner-play. This is the second of four times it'll assemble. The first was the Council scene. Assembling as a whole group is quite different from coming together in pairs or trios. It says to the audience of *Hamlet*, take notice: Something is happening now that refers to the past assembly and future ones. Alexander's insight is that the four gatherings represent four major plots lines in life and drama—courtship and marriage (the council scene), art as a touchstone for truth (*The Mousetrap*), lost love (Ophelia's funeral), and violent death (the duel).

Critics and scholars have long struggled to understand a redundancy in this very long play. All three texts of *Hamlet* present *The Mousetrap* and, oddly, all call for the Dumb Show too. Either the inner play or the Dumb Show accomplishes Hamlet's aim of mirroring back his mother's frailty; either serves to capture the conscience of Claudius; either tests the Ghost's story. Of the two dramatized poisonings, either one or the other could be omitted without damaging plot logic (something often done in productions). But the careful deliberate reduplication of the ear-poison motif in all three authoritative versions testifies to the firmness of Shakespeare's intentions.

It's now generally accepted that the "bad" First Quarto is an actor-dictated reconstruction pirated from a legitimate performance of *Hamlet*. Although some reconstructions of its speeches are poor (*To be, or not to be. Aye, there's the point. / To die, to sleep, is that all?*) others are almost word perfect. This 1603 printing probably represents the stolen text of a road show performance of *Hamlet* chopped down to a playing time of 2 hours with cuts, transpositions, and interpolations written by Shakespeare himself.

Why this curious preservation of *two* onstage depictions of the king's death in all *three* versions? Why the similarity of two actual playing scripts to a pirated memorial reconstruction? There are small changes but in all three texts Lucianus is "nephew to the King." The stylized painfully convoluted seventy-line dialogue between player king and queen in Q2 and the Folio is shortened by two-thirds in the road show version. The changes are all solidly attributable to Shakespeare, so "There seems, therefore, to be no escape from the conclusion that [the 1603 'bad'] Q1 preserves an authorised replacement whose only perceptible function was to shorten the episode—which it does to the extent of forty lines." Still, the playwright was at pains to preserve the Dumb Show.[5]

Ten years before the opening of *Hamlet*, the dumb show had already gone out of fashion. By 1590 dumb shows were not used by leading dramatists, and this Dumb Show is quite aberrant even as such plays went. They were usually short, easily interpreted emblems of the play to follow, like subtitles. Even in its heyday, a dumb show did not mime the complete action of the ensuing play, as this one does; typically it was just one or two summarizing tableaus. Nigel Alexander's theory is that Shakespeare intended *Hamlet* to derive part of its dramatic impact from a particular and calculated use of silence, from an *enforced pause*. The play within the play's counterpoint of action and speech, "silent deeds and their varied interpretations, is a vital principle of organization in the play. The dumb show is used as a recurring oracular forecast of a developing pattern of disaster."[6]

He itemizes the "dumb shows." The first appearance of the Ghost is a dumb show. Ophelia describes to her father how Hamlet appeared in her closet in a distraught dumb show. The final dumb show is where the spoken word is defeated by death. "In the graveyard Hamlet casts down the jawless skull of Yorick, the King's Jester and master of the spoken word, and advises him that his last joke must take the form of the grinning dumb show of death." His theory is that the theme of deeply nuanced silence is a unique dramatic device Shakespeare invented. And he tethered it to the Dumb Show to weave the play together—Alexander thinks—like the separate characters in Seneca that periodically walk onstage to function as omens.

These are Alexander's claims about consciousness and metatheater: First, that Hamlet's divided mind is the center of his consciousness, that his self awareness arises out of the separation of his conscious from his unconscious mental operations. And, second, that the instrument of that consciousness is *The Mousetrap* and the Dumb Show within it. The various dumb shows function as the soliloquies do, as the necessary machinery of his conscience. But they think in pictures what the soliloquies debate in words—shame versus blame, activity versus passivity, revenge versus conscience, bestial oblivion versus conscious awareness.

Language and dreams both start as cognitive operations arising from one common neurobiological source. Underpinning language production are hidden symbolic processes called "speech planning." At some point language and image production branch off each other, ending up as speech *in words*, on the one hand, and as conscious thought *in images* on the other. Neuroscience believes these two mental activities utilize the same brain wiring because so many studies show that language and dreams are both semantically opaque, that they're similar in how they hide their ultimate meaning: Congenitally blind individuals experience dreams without visual images; on questioning they say they "just know" what their dreams are about (identical to verbally mediated waking knowledge or "inner speech"). Sleep studies indicate that a dreamer is unconscious of the *intention* of the dream while having a sense of its *content*. Dreamers wakened in sleep laboratories "just know" whether a dream is finished or not, so there's a clear narrative coherence between semantics and intention in dreams.

We write plays in our own minds, tableaus, and dialogue. Readers of a novel will picture episodes in it, and then on first viewing a film based on it will have clear opinions about how much the film does or doesn't match the images they expect based on the book. Dreaming is a product of the same symbol forming function that enables our inner playwright to think about and even create people and events in their absence with words and pictures.[7]

Through dreams, Freud came to understand irrational "primary process thinking" in the unconscious (as opposed to the rational "secondary process" of the conscious mind). He was struck by *overdetermination*, the existence of more than one correct dream interpretation. Like all psychological "structures," dreams have several meanings that are mutually contradictory. He had observed that a hysterical symptom could have one meaning viewed from one angle and another from a different vantage. Dreams, symptoms, slips of the tongue, and wit all emerge with their form and content determined by multiple causes working in disparate ways—but working simultaneously. And a-chronologically. The timelessness of the unconscious was a necessary inference from overdetermination. Poets had always depicted unconscious time as not tethered to the present and not linear from past to future. Eventually Freud had to conclude that *the unconscious thinks nonchronologically in symbols*. Symbol formation is *how* the unconscious thinks—not words, not images—but the *relationship* between word and image. He then connected condensation and displacement with that other great symbol based tool, figurative language, specifically *metaphor* and *metonymy*. Both are about the pictures underlying the words, why else would they be called *figures* of speech?

Alex Roland says both art and dreams start off as instinctual wishes (Freud's *dream thoughts*), and they are allowed to emerge from the unconscious because global holistic imagery is able to bypass ego mechanisms of defense better than linear propositional speech. The metaphors of art and dreams are able to give expression to conflicting structures, drives, affects, and layers of personality. Freud called the mechanism for narrating expressions of the unconscious the *dreamwork*. The dream is the most accessible communication in psychoanalysis—with "the incipient makings of a paradox," one which can interpret unconscious communications that contradict each other. In a dream we can analyze the latent content as it falls into the two fundamental opposing elements of structural linguistics—the thing and the not-thing, the act and the not-act—since all natural human languages are constructed of binary elements in opposition. A dream *begins* to put these two opposites together. By the collaboration of analyst and patient, Roland claims, a co-created interpretation can *then* complete the paradox or metaphor into a final form analogous to a work of art, a final editing process Freud called *secondary revision*.[8]

So it wasn't just Lacan who saw that the unconscious is structured as a language; Freud got there first, and structural linguistics had already given him credit for it: The close relationship between how dreams work and how figures of speech persuade shows their biological root. The device of *metaphor* is to the dreamwork's *condensation* as the language device of *metonymy* is to the dreamwork's *displacement.* Even before culture makes its mark, the brain is built to dream, hard wired to speak the symbolic language of the unconscious.[9]

And nearly a century ago one of the greatest scholars of Shakespeare came to the identical conclusion by an entirely different route, the analysis of ambiguity in poetry.

William Empson understood that the unconscious of psychoanalysis and the unconscious of poetry are one and the same. He took as his point of departure the logical contradiction between the literal and the figurative sense of words: The literal meaning of a word always conflicts with its figurative meaning, even if only slightly. It's a lexical fiction that any word can have an exact synonym. In this "extended sense any prose statement could be called ambiguous." His broad use of *ambiguity* is "any verbal nuance, however slight, which gives room for alternative reactions to the same piece of language." Ambiguity is the soul of poetry because "what often happens when a piece of writing is felt to offer hidden riches is that one phrase after another lights up and appears as the heart of it; one part after another catches fire."[10]

And the soul of human relationships is irony, "the subdued appreciation of ambiguity," which is a "generous skepticism" that can believe at once that people *are* and *are not* guilty.

> This sort of contradiction is at once understood in literature, because the process of understanding one's friends must always be riddled with such indecisions and the machinery of such hypocrisy; people, often, cannot have done both of two things, but they must have been in some way prepared to have done either; whichever they did, they will have still lingering in their minds the way they would have . . . acted differently.

You can only understand them by bearing both possibilities in mind, by cultivating *a generous skepticism.* Empson makes a claim for the birth of language out of the womb of ambiguity. Metaphor, he says, "is the normal mode of development of a language." And metaphor (and all tropes and aspects of the dreamwork) arises from unconscious processes.[11]

On antithesis and negation, Empson echoes structural linguistic theories of binary opposition in language, but his ideas come straight from Freud. The idea of an *opposite*, he says, is a comparatively late human invention and is found nowhere in the material world. Words in poetry, like words in primitive languages,

> often state a pair of opposites without any overt ambiguity. . . . Opposites, again, are an important element in the Freudian analysis of dreams; and it is

> evident that the Freudian terminology, particularly the word 'condensation,' could be employed with profit for the understanding of poetry. Now a Freudian opposite at least marks dissatisfaction; the notion of what you want involves the idea that you have not got it. . . . In more serious cases . . . such as are likely to be reflected in language, in poetry, or in dreams, it marks a centre of conflict; the notion of what you want involves the notion that you must not take it [and shows] that you want something different in another part of your mind.

Freud, before he accepted paradox in the unconscious, had to appreciate it in poetry. And *Hamlet,* with its layers of irony—and its ambiguity born of metatheater —was catalytic to his thinking. While it's true, he said, that obsessive symptoms arise when strong love and hate are in conflict, the negative factor of libido still isn't fully understood. "We know too little of the nature of love to be able to arrive at any definite conclusion" especially about the sadistic component.[12]

> Poets tell us that in the more tempestuous stages of love the two opposed feelings may subsist side by side for a while as though in rivalry with each other. . . . We should have expected that the passionate love would long ago have conquered the hatred or been devoured by it. And in fact such a protracted survival of the two opposites is only possible . . . in the unconscious. The love has not succeeded in extinguishing the hatred but only in driving it down into the unconscious; and in the unconscious the hatred is able to persist and even to grow [as if] at a very early age, somewhere in the prehistoric period of his infancy, the two opposites have been split apart and one of them, usually the hatred, have been repressed.

We still don't exactly know why displacement into obsessional doubt is generated rather than hysterical symptoms. Perhaps if intense love and hate coexist, there is paralysis of the will, Freud says, perhaps the obsessive neurotic uses displacement preferentially over condensation. Hamlet serves as an example in his doubt of Ophelia: "A man who doubts his own love may, or rather *must,* doubt every lesser thing." Still, Freud admits, *We know too little of the nature of love to be sure.*

And in not knowing, we become more human. Just as a good deal of the realism of *Hamlet* comes from ambiguities and ironies created by Shakespeare's use of metatheater, much of the realism of the character of Hamlet comes from his unconscious and his struggle to make it conscious: As *The Mousetrap* is to catch the conscience of the King, the Dumb Show is to catch the consciousness of the Prince.

Notes

1. Dan H. Buie, "Empathy: Its Nature and Limitations," *Journal of the American Psychoanalytic Association* 21 (1981): 281–307.
2. "Self-experiential empathy" triggers the evolved emotional responses Darwin described. It engages the autonomic nervous system by means of fantasy; method acting tricks the

"involuntary" nervous system into doing the actor's will. Polonius notes the first player's crying real tears; Hamlet admires the actor's making his complexion go pale in a dream of passion. Horatio turns pale seeing the Ghost. Hamlet is curious about its face—red or very pale? Gertrude's galled eyes attest to her grief. Claudius should blanch if *The Mousetrap* is a true lie detector. Hamlet says the face of melancholia is sickly pale. He shames Gertrude because she hasn't the modesty to blush. On seeing the Ghost Hamlet fears he'll succumb to tears rather than the flushed face of vengeance. Hamlet when he's dying sees the courtiers tremble and look pale.

3. Nigel Alexander, *Poison, Play, and Duel: A Study in Hamlet* (Lincoln: University of Nebraska Press, 1971), 2, 90.
4. James Shapiro, *Contested Will: Who Wrote Shakespeare?* (New York: Simon & Schuster, 2010).
5. J.M. Nosworthy, *Shakespeare's Occasional Plays: Their Origin and Transmission* (New York: Barnes & Noble, 1965), 108, 204.
6. Alexander, *Poison*, 118.
7. David Foulkes, *Children's Dreaming and the Development of Consciousness* (Cambridge: Harvard University Press, 1999).

   Neuroscience sees the function of dreams as practicing survival routines and performing cognitive housekeeping, such as reorganization of memory storage. Dreams are rehearsals continuous with (and not qualitatively different from) consciousness. Consciousness is a process of knowing, and knowing about knowing, "higher-order thought." A mental state's being conscious is its being accompanied by a higher-order thought about that very mental state. Dreaming is no different from our waking ability to voluntarily see images in the mind; *dreaming and visualization are both products of the same infinitely productive brain process* as evidenced by the fact that both dreams and language are astonishingly unpredictable when parsed in sequence. Language is infinitely productive, so in judging later productions from earlier ones, it's not possible to forecast what words in a sentence or associative string will follow from previous ones or what images in a dream will succeed previous ones. And the types of slips in language and in visualizations are similarly unpredictable.
8. Alan Roland, *Dreams and Drama* (Middletown: Wesleyan University Press, 2003).
9. Daniel Chandler, *Semiotics: The Basics*, ed. 2 (New York: Routledge, 2007).

   Roman Jakobson worked out a binary theory of language that states that all natural languages entail an opposition between two "devices" at work in any symbolic process. He identifies these as *metaphor* and *metonymy* and mentions Freud's discovering these same polarities in dream symbols created by *condensation* and *displacement*. He based this on the major types of expressive aphasia (1) *anomic* or fluent aphasia and (2) *non-fluent* aphasia. Individuals with fluent or anomic aphasia speak smoothly but their speech is missing names of things. Instead of *pen*, patients use circumlocution, "The . . . what you write with." They have difficulty meaningfully *sequencing* words in a sentence, but their speech sounds at least superficially normal because grammar is preserved. These preserved capacities correspond to the figure of speech *metonymy* and the dreamwork function of *displacement*. By contrast, individuals with non-fluent aphasia can find nouns but can't fluently put them into a string of easily understood speech. They seem to be using baby talk and make only short sentences, but ones that make logical sense. They can name things, and often their meaningful sentences are only a single word. *Go. Drink. No.* These non-fluent aphasias leave preserved the *selection* of words from a mental lexicon along with *substitution* of one word for another, finding synonyms. For Jakobson this function of *selection/ substitution* of words was in its essence the trope of *metaphor*, and this corresponded to Freud's *condensation*.
10. William Empson. *Seven Types of Ambiguity* (1930, revised 1947, reprint; New York: New Directions, 1966), xi.
11. Ibid, 101, 192–194.

   On *hendiadys*:

   > Consider a linguistic form common in Shakespeare . . . the (noun) and (noun) of (noun); in which two, often apparently quite different words are flung together,

followed by a word which seems to be intended to qualify both of them. . . . in effect a single word which combines two opposite notions. The words are intended for the stage; they certainly convey something to an audience; and there is no time for them to convey anything more definite than this before the soliloquy has swept on to another effect of the same kind. . . . the form itself is so strong that its elements hold together. It is strongest, evidently, when the two first nouns are almost synonyms.

Within the book and volume of my brain. . . .
The pales and forts of reason.
The slings and arrows of outrageous fortune.
The whips and scorns of time. . . .

[and] either word gives the sense alone. This shows a pride in the possession of language. . . . But the form is rare before Shakespeare, and even in Shakespeare before *Hamlet*; it is not likely to be sought for by an author unless he wants to hold a thought in the reader's mind while he plays round its implications.

12. Sigmund Freud, "The Instinctual Life of Obsessional Neurotics," in *The Standard Edition of the Complete Psychological Works of Sigmund Freud*, vol. 10, James Strachey, Ed. and trans. (London: The Hogarth Press, 1909/1955), 238–241.

11

THE DOUBLE SOLILOQUY

Freud's "Compulsion To Repeat"

The Prince's procrastination has long been part of western folklore and literary memory. His hesitation to act was a cultural deep structure waiting to pave the way for Freud's Oedipus complex—a neurosis in which the son's rivalry with his father is not seen but is indirectly detected in symptoms of inhibition, like impotence or fear of success. (Oedipus was not, in fact, inhibited but that's a quibble and Freud found a way around it.) The most interesting thing about it isn't the father-son rivalry but how Freud used it to explain the origins of the guilty conscience.

After *The Mousetrap* we saw Claudius fleeing with his court, calling for light; now he creeps into the darkened chapel, leaving his sword at the door.

King O, my offense is rank, it smells to heaven —
A brother's murder. Pray can I not. . . .
My stronger guilt defeats my strong intent
And, like a man to double business bound,
I stand in pause where I shall first begin —
And both neglect.

III.iii.36 TLN 2312–2319

Like a man to double business bound. It's the bind both King and Prince are in. This is the first time the audience knows the Ghost was telling the truth about Claudius. Now they expect Hamlet will obey its ghostly commandment for revenge with all possible speed.

King What if this cursed hand
Were thicker than itself with brother's blood?

My fault is past, but . . . since I am still possessed
Of those effects for which I did the murder —
My crown, mine own ambition, and my Queen —
May one be pardoned, and retain the offense?
In the corrupted currents of this world
. . . oft 'tis seen that the wicked prize itself
Buys out the law. But 'tis not so Above:
There is no shuffling. What—try what repentance can?
Yet what can it, when one cannot repent?
Bow stubborn knees, and heart with strings of steel
Be soft as sinews of the newborn babe.
All may be well.

III.iii.43 TLN 2319–2348

Enter the Prince on his way to his mother's bedroom. He sees the kneeling King, seizes the sword, and steals up behind him. Hamlet's first thought is to plunge a blade into his back. It's opportune, quick, coincidental, easy—perhaps too easy.

Hamlet Now might I do it pat. But—now he is a-praying.
And now I'll do it. And—so he goes to heaven.
And so am I revenged? That would be scanned:*
A villain kills my father and for that
I, his sole son, do this same villain send—to heaven?
Why, this is hire and salary, not revenge.

III.iii.73 TLN 2350–2355
* that needs rethinking

Claudius would die in a state of grace. Hamlet needs to kill him in the same state of sin as King Hamlet was when Claudius poisoned him, stuffed with sins like a goose for the oven.

Hamlet He took my father grossly, full of bread,
With all his crimes broad blown, as flush as May.
And how his audit stands who knows—save heaven.
But in our circumstance and course of thought
'Tis heavy with him. Am I then revenged
To take him in the purging of his soul
When he is fit and seasoned for his passage?
No.

III.iii.80 TLN 2356–2362

Hamlet will spare the King for the moment and kill him when he's unprepared and unshriven, like old King Hamlet. He will not just destroy his body, but his soul too.[1]

This decision to send Claudius to hell is one of the more contentious issues in *Hamlet*. Is "immortal vengeance" inhumanly evil? Even a murderer facing execution is allowed confession. Or is killing the soul just a dramatic convention of Elizabethan revenge tragedy? Does Hamlet mean it, or is this another excuse? In any case, Hamlet puts the sword aside and backs away.

Hamlet Up sword, and know thou a more horrid hent:*
When he is drunk asleep or in his rage
Or in the incestuous pleasure of his bed,
At gaming, swearing, or about some act
That has no relish of salvation in it
. . . that his soul may be as damned and black
As hell whereto it goes. My mother stays;
This physic but prolongs thy sickly days. *[exit Hamlet]*
King My words fly up, my thoughts remain below.
Words—without thoughts—never to heaven go.

III.iii.88 TLN 2363–2373

* opportunity

Damning Claudius to die like his father, in the blossoms of his sins, Hamlet spares him for now. But he needn't have. It's Claudius that's inhibited: Ironically, the sinful King still can't pray.

The much quoted 1897 letter to Fliess on the oedipal subtext of *Hamlet* comes after the death of Freud's father and after he'd gone through a prolonged period of hesitation and paralysis. His own self analysis was revealing how much his unconscious rivalry with his father affected him—and he's beginning to think this "complex" isn't peculiar to him but quite widespread.

> I am not thinking of Shakespeare's conscious intention, but I believe rather . . . that the unconscious in him understood the unconscious in his hero. How can Hamlet the hysteric justify his words 'Thus conscience does make cowards of us all,' how can he explain his hesitation in avenging his father by the murder of his uncle—he, the same man who sends his courtiers to their death without a scruple and who is positively precipitate in killing Laertes? How better could he justify himself than by the torment he suffers from the obscure memory that he himself had meditated the same deed against his father from passion for his mother, and—'use every man after his desert, and who should 'scape whipping?' His conscience is his unconscious sense of guilt. . . . And does he not in the end, in the same remarkable way as my hysterical patients, bring down punishment on himself by suffering the same fate as his father of being poisoned by the same rival?[2]

The letter is a holy relic, sacred to what came to be called "applied psychoanalysis," literary criticism based on psychoanalytic theories of motivation.

After World War I the humanities embraced Freud. From long experiences with hidden layers in poetry and drama, scholars of English literature accepted notions of conflict in the dynamic unconscious, of ambivalence and overdetermination, of symbolization as a way of speaking what was at deeper levels. By midcentury the academy had incorporated Freud—unconscious rivalry with the father, incestuous desire toward the mother (and sometimes the father), and the "primal scene." They even grasped transference as an explanation of irrationalas displaced behavior, and they had an inkling of the adaptive function of symptoms.

Where scholar Harold Goddard excelled was his feel for poetry. His unique contribution to *Hamlet* studies lay in resolving the paradox of the Ghost's command, which went against the moral code of the Elizabethans: To be saved, one was supposed to renounce revenge. Goddard traces the Prince's evolution from crude avenger at the beginning of the play to Christian humanist at its end, a conversion rooted in Hamlet's natural ambivalence toward violence.

> Now whatever we are "meant" to assume, there is no doubt that nearly every spectator and reader the first time he encounters the play does assume that Hamlet ought to kill the King—and nearly all continue in that opinion . . . we have all stored up within ourselves so many unrequited wrongs and injuries, forgotten and unforgotten, and beneath these such an inheritance of racial revenge, that we like nothing better than to rid ourselves of . . . the accumulation by projecting it. There is no mystery about it. Anyone can follow the effect along his own backbone.[3]

Goddard cites the Ghost on the evils of "Murder most foul, as in the best it is." Is this a slip on the Ghost's part, or is it a projection that reveals the state of Hamlet's mind? *Foul as in the best it is.* Murder is foul, revenge is murder, revenge is wrong how ever human it is; human nature is what civilization wants Hamlet to rise above. Goddard finds within the Prince another instinct equally powerful. All great poetry, he says, has an equal balance. "The greatest poetry has always depicted the world as a little citadel of nobility threatened by an immense barbarism. . . ." But "foul, as in the best it is" had been there in plain sight, and Goddard noticed its deepest implications: The Ghost's demanding murder, even at best, is a sin.

But Goddard is not quite so good at applied psychoanalysis. He fails to understand intent can be unconscious and yet still not be an excuse. For Freud, transgressive impulses are often unconscious, but they can be called to account by the superego; in fact, it's the glimpse of the not-quite-buried that causes neurotic symptoms. For Freud, ignorance of the law is not an excuse, whereas Goddard worries that calling an act unconscious will extenuate it. He criticizes Freud and Jones as reductionist; but ironically, it's he that's forcing simplistic choices between antinomies, nature and nurture, good and evil. That murder and incest are present deep in Hamlet and all of us Goddard doesn't deny, nor that Hamlet is ultimately overthrown by his instincts.

> But . . . when we search [Jones's] essay for an account of that struggle it turns out to be nothing but the struggle of a trapped animal and the Freudian interpretation reduces to nothing but the picture of a man foredoomed to destruction. If this be so, Hamlet may indeed be a supreme treatise on pathology. But it is no longer drama, let alone poetry.[4]

Not so. The Greeks had the same trapped animal basis for their drama. Goddard sees a conflict between the rarified nobility of art and the dark animalism of humankind. But humanity can have both a universal psychology and, on that foundation, a distinctiveness that gives each human being characteristic moral burdens.

Northrop Frye allows that Freud's formulation makes sense but, like Goddard, says there are more subtle aspects to Hamlet than repressed desire and blocked action. Hamlet's "delay" is less important than moral development, which psychoanalysis doesn't address to the satisfaction of scholars. (Or perhaps they're unable to follow Freud on the superego as a product of the resolution of the Oedipus complex.) Frye's aperçu is that at the beginning of the play, Claudius deserves to die—but it isn't till the end that Hamlet has earned the right to kill him. The rub for Frye and Goddard is that they think psychology should explain Hamlet's unique consciousness, just as literary criticism tried to explain the Prince's unique impact upon the world's literature.[5]

But Stanley Cavell is perfectly at home with the Freud-Jones formulation and doesn't see it as oversimplifying the universal character of the Prince. Both a Shakespeare scholar and philosopher, he almost out-Freuds Freud when he suggests Laertes is inseminating Hamlet with the poisoned foil, as Hamlet will soon inseminate Claudius with it. The Prince's actions, he says, are not just Hamlet's dreams, but *our* dreams. He starts with the idea that the core of tragedy is disowned knowledge, what motivates Shakespeare's heroes is an inability to face the "all but undeniable" painful reality. Disowned knowledge and deferred action he compares with Freud's return of the repressed. He uses concepts in psychoanalysis that even some analysts aren't comfortable with—the "primal scene" of repressed parental intercourse, insemination through the ear, and innate unlearned knowledge in the infant.[6]

But Cavell's oddest idea is "deferred representation." This is like a forgotten premonition (*O my prophetic soul*). It's the playwright's way of "presenting in the closing image of a play something denied our sight" in the earlier action. He thinks later tableaus in Shakespeare are the fulfillment of earlier deferred revelations. He instances Claudius's reaction—or non-reaction—to the ear-poisoning in the Dumb Show; he ties the double poisoning in *The Mousetrap* to Hamlet's double murder of Claudius, stabbing him and forcing him to drink up the poisoned chalice. Cavell says this demonstrates to the audience at last why Claudius didn't react when the actor poured poison in the sleeping actor-king's ear: It was because Claudius had done the murder by poisoning old King Hamlet's *drink*, not his ear. Cavell thinks like the unconscious thinks, with two possibilities true at the same moment. Like Freud, he is less drawn to plausibility and more to dark and unwholesome imaginings—so Cavell is much admired but little believed for his strange and shocking double poisoning theory.

William Empson sees the Prince's delay as part of the playwright's dramatic technique, especially the construction of Hamlet's unconscious. He doesn't dispute an oedipal basis for inhibited action but says it's only one determinant among many; Shakespeare intentionally piled up all the excuses for delay he could imagine. It was a bold artistic decision to throw a novel concept of the old revenge play at an already *Hamlet*-jaded audience (the earlier *Ur-Hamlet* had become a byword, causing the running gag "revenge, Hamlet, revenge" to be played for laughs in other plays). Empson imagines the playwright stroking his chin saying to himself,

> "I shall make Hamlet walk up to the audience and tell them, again and again, 'I don't know why I'm delaying any more than you do; the motivation of this play is just as blank to me as it is to you; but I can't help it.' What is more, I shall make it impossible to blame him. And *then* they daren't laugh." [Then—Empson concludes—it] turned out, of course, that this method, instead of reducing the old play to farce, made it thrillingly life-like and profound.[7]

So it became a psychological mystery. What Shakespeare did was to construct a drama that was two plays in one, a parody of revenge drama (with its wink to the sophisticated) "and a real, terrifying, murder-answering-murder."

A.D. Nuttall says that Freud's understanding of *Hamlet* fails to catch how his histrionic behavior creates Hamlet's own sense of self. He's always acting. "Now could I drink hot blood!" is vintage Kyd revenge tragedy. Nuttall says the Prince's "play" before an audience of one, Ophelia, is yet another experiment in being someone else. "Hamlet must be using the black-revenge style to practise upon himself. . . . modes of outside-in motivation. . . . Hamlet's is an essayed self-therapy." And Nuttall says Shakespeare was prescient in anticipating Freud-Jones.

> This bizarre theory, the fruit of a later age, turns out to have extraordinary purchase on the text. In particular, the play of stylistic registers supports it. A good Freudian would predict that such an Oedipally-impeded hero would use the language of the super-ego (conscientious, high-minded) when speaking of his father, because the super-ego presides over the business of repression, tells us what we ought to say as distinct from what we wish. But in moments of passion he will use earthy sexual language, as when he begins to see Claudius . . . as the new lover of Gertrude. And that is exactly what we get.

This "extraordinary purchase on the text" is seen when Hamlet characterizes Claudius as a "mildewed ear," whereas it was old King Hamlet that was overspread with rot, starting from the ear. "Hamlet's mind can slip sideways," he superimposes his mother's two husbands to produce one father. But then after his nimble confirmation of oedipal themes, Nuttall inexplicably recoils from the plausible notion of incestuous desire for the mother, which he calls a "lunatic idea." Shakespeare in creating Hamlet was not creating the universal, he says, but rather "a one-off, a manifestly peculiar case."[8]

Nuttall must be thinking of Olivier's Hamlet, because Shakespeare's Hamlet is both universal and distinctive. Suspense comes not only from whether revenge will succeed, it comes from identification with the hero, even his psychopathology. But is the Prince's delay evidence of a universal Oedipus complex? That is the question.

The Oedipus complex involves anxiety over incestuous impulses, repression, and the repetition of behavior symbolizing the conflict. It's also a motivator for formation of the conscience in the individual and a system of laws in the tribe. A consequence of the Oedipus complex is the *repetition compulsion*. In "Remembering, Repeating and Working-Through," Freud's intuition leapt beyond logic to the paradox of memory and repressed desire: We *repeat* the past in order *not* to remember it. Painful recollections of past events are warded off. They're not consciously remembered but, rather, they're encoded in implicit memory, embedded as a symbolic representation of trauma. Then they're enacted in the present rather than felt.[9]

It's all in the duels with older men. Polonius has come between Hamlet and Ophelia, Claudius between him and his mother. He can't consciously remember a rivalry with his father but he repeats it whenever he encounters the oedipal triangle. He's not consciously aware of King Hamlet as swordsman. But he never really forgets either: Old Hamlet's body is with the worms.

King	Now Hamlet, where's Polonius?
Hamlet	At supper.
King	At supper—where?
Hamlet	Not where he eats but where he is eaten. A certain convocation of politic worms are eating at him. Your worm is your only emperor for diet. We fat all creatures else to fat us, and we fat ourselves for maggots. Your fat king and your lean beggar is . . . two dishes but to one table. . . . A man may fish with the worm that hath eat of a king, and eat of the fish that hath fed of that worm.
King	Where is Polonius?
Hamlet	. . . if indeed you find him not within this month, you shall nose him . . . up the stairs into the lobby. . . . Farewell dear Mother.
King	Thy loving father, Hamlet!
Hamlet	My mother: Father and mother is man and wife, man and wife is one flesh and so—my mother. Come! For England!

IV.iii.16 TLN 2682–2717

Once alone, Claudius writes to remind England of their defeat by Denmark: The English king must obey. This he seals in a letter to accompany Hamlet in custody of the schoolfellows.

King And England, if my love thou holdest at aught
After the Danish sword . . . thou mayst not coldly set
Our sovereign process which imports at full —
By letters conjuring to that effect —
The present death of Hamlet. Do it England!
IV.iii.58 TLN 2723–2730

He reacts as fathers react to oedipal rage in sons. Freud noted how often sons dream of the death of the father—and how often fathers, including himself, dream of the death of the oedipal son.

Freud mined philosophy and religion in search of the universal. Resolution of the Oedipus complex was supposed to result in the superego, which grows out of the ego and can step aside and treat the ego like an object—resulting in the human capacity for self observation. Thus it acts as guardian over the id and prevents "the return of the repressed." But there are instinctual wishes too powerful to be entirely repressed which emerge as a compulsion to repeat, impulses powerful enough to override the pleasure principle (which fears the superego's punishment) and to bring disaster crashing down upon the self.

Freud thought and wrote about Jewishness more and more over the course of his life, but often overlooked is his early exposure to Catholicism. On Sundays Freud's nurse would take him with her to mass, this child of preschool years, brilliant, curious, observant. He would sit in the pew beside her, his most intimate adult connection, and take it all in—with the woman he most credited with his knowledge of sex. He would later write of the libido she stirred up in him.

Perhaps this explains Freud's familiarity with Catholicism in *Hamlet*, Shakespeare's most Christian play. It's natural to him as a part of daily life, the Catholic conscience of Hamlet. *Angels and ministers of grace defend us.* Hamlet falls back on Christian awe, enfolded in line on line of the play. *I must be their scourge and minister.* After killing Polonius, he takes on the role of executioner and judge. Hamlet and all characters in the play are swept up in the tides of faith: A ghost comes from Purgatory. Ophelia is seen at her orisons. Claudius prays. A priest conducts Ophelia's funeral. Scripture is interpreted by a gravedigger. The inquest is rigged to bury a suicide in sanctified ground. Ophelia is to become a ministering angel. And, in the end, flights of angels sing the Prince to his rest. But Christian rituals are violated too, and often. The old king is inadequately mourned. The sacrament of marriage is brought on with unseemly haste. Ophelia reading of a prayer book is bait on a hook of sacrilege. Claudius can't pray. Christian graves are desecrated in fantasy—Old Hamlet exhumed as the marble jaws of his tomb cast him up—and in fact: Polonius can't be buried properly, only hugger-mugger—like Ophelia. And a final insult, Hamlet and Laertes fight in her grave, trampling on her coffin.

These emphasize the play's dominating subtextual debate over an afterlife. Hamlet fears there is no God, and "the play insists on the brute fact in relation to the dead that they are gone for ever." So Ophelia sings of Polonius "And will he not come again?/ No, no, he is dead . . . He never will come again." The Ghost "returns old Hamlet to life . . . whose essential message is 'Remember me' ('Do not forget!') The living owe the dead remembrance because there may be nothing else." This resonates with the pagan side of Hamlet's beliefs, the classical heroic tradition "of death as total oblivion. . . . This anxiety about death makes more poignant the effect of Hamlet's pursuit of revenge . . . in which he becomes the direct or indirect cause of far more deaths than Claudius brought about."[10]

Always close to the surface is Hamlet's obsession with the unprepared death. Doubt of God as a central theme makes perfect sense in this light, so "immortal vengeance" and the fate of the unshriven schoolfellows are even more pivotal. Crawling between heaven and earth Hamlet is afraid of the utter finality of death. But he is even more terrified at the thought of his immortal soul being punished forever. *Hamlet* brings together these threads of conscience, and Freud quotes deeply from the play in discussing oedipal guilt and the superego.

Freud's investment in the Oedipus complex evolved over the course of his life, from theories of id (incest desires) through the ego (symptoms and defenses) to the superego and ego ideal (the birth of conscience in the individual and the tribe). Marjorie Garber approaches his theory of the Oedipus complex through Freud's own neurotic mechanisms and narcissistic defenses: He had to abandon the "seduction theory" of hysteria because he couldn't believe such a high prevalence of father-daughter incest in Vienna, how ever much he might have wanted to support his pet theory. But (Garber hypothesizes) this set him thinking about the Freud family secrets, his father's penchant for younger girls, his mother's suspected affair with Freud's older half brother, and perhaps some well kept secrets and intense relationships Freud shared with his wife's sister and his own daughter. He salved the loss of the seduction theory by investing in another theory, and he solaced himself on the loss by finding universal confirmation for the Oedipus complex in art and letters.[11]

> It can scarcely be owing to chance that three of the masterpieces of the literature of all time—the *Oedipus Rex* of Sophocles, Shakespeare's *Hamlet* and Dostoevsky's *The Brothers Karamazov*—should all deal with the same subject, parricide. In all three, moreover, the motive for the deed, sexual rivalry for a woman, is laid bare.[12]

In *Hamlet* Freud found support for his ideas about repression, remembering, and the compulsion to repeat. *We repeat the past in order* not *to remember it.* Garber catalogs two dozen-plus references to *remembering* in the play, quite impressive pulled together in one place. She puts instances of the return of repressed memory in the same conceptual category as *doubling* and *mirroring*—which nicely fit with Freud's compulsion to repeat. Doubling, much discussed in literary criticism, is another form of remembering. Mirroring, doubling, and return of memory all reinforce each other macroscopically as themes that run through the play. In addition, its language microscopically supports themes of reflection and reappearance.

Garber finds doubling in the deepest layers of the poetry. Constructions called "hendiadys" are scattered all through the play, tropes of the form *noun* and *noun* or *verb* and *verb*, where the two words are near synonyms, often from different language trees, usually romance and middle English. (*Tremble and look pale. Sensible and true avouch of mine eyes. Pales and forts of reason.*) Their nearness in meaning, yet difference, gives a kind of binocular effect to the line of poetry in which they appear. And there are dozens of these subliminal reminders of doubling and mirroring in *Hamlet*, at least sixty. Then she makes a brilliant leap: By means of these, Garber says, the oedipal *triangle* rests on the *dyad* of *hendiadys*. A triangle has three pairs of points, so its definition depends on three dyads, three acts of memory, and any of these scores of dyads subliminally evokes themes of desire, repression, and remembering.

A generation earlier, Nigel Alexander had written *Poison, Play, and Duel*, still the best ever analysis of the Freud-Jones theory by anyone, psychoanalyst or scholar. Not unsympathetic to Freud, he assumes the symptom is overdetermined. The Prince hesitates, Alexander doesn't contest it. Hamlet says so himself and acknowledges he doesn't fully know why. Alexander says that the intentional creation of this very distinctive unconscious is a triumph of characterization.

> Hamlet fails to act, and is unable to explain this failure, because he is suffering from an Oedipus complex. Since he has not resolved his unconscious infantile desires to kill his father and marry his mother he is constitutionally incapable of taking any action against the man who has in fact carried out these fantasy wishes. . . . [But also in fact] Hamlet's delay is a dramatic device which allows the dramatist to question the nature of the act of revenge.[13]

Alexander is responding to what Jones calls Hamlet's "apparently causeless inhibition," saying his "paralysis arises . . . not from physical or moral cowardice, but from intellectual cowardice."[14]

An attempt to refute Jones's theories led Alexander to search out the oedipal triangle in other Elizabethan plays. He found several counterexamples of incestuous triangles with *similar delays*, but for *different reasons*, in other revenge tragedies written around the same time. Then Alexander confronts Jones on his own home ground, ego psychology. *Here*, Alexander says to Jones, *you can't get so bogged down in pathology that you miss adaptation. You mustn't overlook neurosis as a striving toward health*:

> Jones's analysis is inadequate because he has failed to examine one of the major psychological observations of the play. He thinks that Laertes exists in the drama as an example of how Hamlet should have behaved. . . . The audience is . . . bound to desire Hamlet to execute vengeance on the King

> in the same aggressive spirit that Laertes exacts his revenge. The realization that what they desire is a person like Laertes ought to cause the audience more reflection. The reaction of Laertes is a 'normal' and 'human' reaction. It leads to those very normal and human activities of treachery and murder by poison. Jones has made exactly this automatic ethical assumption that the play of *Hamlet* is designed to examine and question. Unthinking aggression is not always necessarily a sign of mental health.[15]

The contest between psychoanalysis and the literary establishment to explain Hamlet's delay resembles a chess tournament. In the deciding match Alexander anticipates Jones's argument that Hamlet's hesitation is entirely oedipal—*check*—and then Alexander pushes forward a piece of evidence from the play itself—*check!*—hidden in plain sight:

> Hamlet does display exactly these symptoms of unthinking aggression when he kills Polonius, believing that he has killed the King. This would suggest that he is not as inhibited in his reactions as the Oedipus complex requires, and Jones goes on to elaborate lengths to explain away the plain language of the play. It is, however, clear that Hamlet's conduct . . . is connected with fundamental instincts of jealousy and sexual affection. The psychology of *Hamlet* is more subtle than the simple observation that infantile relations with one's mother involve sexual feelings which may give rise to adult complications.

His sudden stabbing of "Claudius" shows he's not as globally inhibited in his aggression as the typical unresolved Oedipus complex would dictate. The argument is simple. *Checkmate.*

Over time Freud tested and retested his theory of the Oedipus complex. One of its problems was that, although Oedipus doesn't know who his father is, he's not inhibited and kills Laius without hesitation. Nor does he repress anything, as the oedipal son must; he is all too conscious of what has happened. But Freud wanted to wrap up his theory seamlessly, so he had to protect it from annoying details in the Sophocles story. So he reasoned that repression was a later human invention necessitated by the murder of the primal father and the subsequent institution of the totem feast by the primal horde. This was the march of civilization in which the primitive was repressed and replaced by tamer stuff, at the price of collective discontent. General malaise was caused by free-floating guilt, civilizing guilt dampening impulses, humankind's price for progress. Primitive impulses succumbed to repression in the individual and in the collective, leaving behind its traces in cultural institutions.

Over the history of drama, conscious conflicts between protagonist and antagonist gave way to conflicts between two conscious impulses in the hero, leading to psychological drama. And when conscious and unconscious impulses came in conflict in the same individual, it became a "psychopathological drama" like Hamlet. In an earlier age, he thought, there was nothing unconscious, no repression. Freud's theory evolved:

> In Sophocles' play, "the child's wishful fantasy that underlies it is brought into the open and realized as it would be in a dream. In Hamlet it remains repressed; and . . . as in the case of a neurosis—we only learn of its existence from its inhibiting consequences." Oedipus Rex belongs to an older stage of civilization. Hamlet, in contrast, is the product of a modern mind.[16]

This let Freud have it both ways. The Oedipus complex was universal wherever there was civilization, but there was a difference between ancient and modern cultures. "Shakespeare's Hamlet has its roots in the same soil as Oedipus Rex" but the "changed treatment of the same material reveals the whole difference in the mental life of these two widely separated epochs of civilization: the secular advance of repression in the emotional life of mankind." The secular advance of repression occurred in cultures. But in individuals, id meets superego, incestuous impulses are repressed. Inhibition of associated desires also occurs. The repressed incestuous desire then returns, but under different circumstances and in disguised form.

Freud's writing on the Oedipus complex throbs with energy. And when he kills off the complex for the boy in the process of becoming a man, the imagery is violent. In boys it "is not simply repressed, it is literally smashed to pieces by the shock of threatened castration." Its sexual and aggressive energies are ripped away from their attachments to people, desexualized, rechanneled into productive efforts at work and play, and "its objects are incorporated into the ego, where they form the nucleus of the super-ego and give that new structure its characteristic qualities." The Oedipus complex exits and "even in the unconscious, the super-ego has become its heir." The normal male has taken unto himself what is good and right of civilization. He may have faced castration, but in a swap of passion for law he comes out ahead. He's undergone a symbolic castration bowing to the father, but in exchange he receives the blessings of society.[17]

The precise mechanism for this tradeoff is, Freud concedes, not entirely clear. There are elements of identification with the aggressor; also there must be a renunciation of the father's prerogatives with the boy's mother and displacement of libido toward a substitute. But the details remain fuzzy. Freud fails to explain the final superego solidifying step in the resolution of the Oedipus complex. But the mechanism for transformation of a girl's rivalry with the mother into the female superego is described without qualifiers.

> In girls the motive for the demolition of the Oedipus complex is lacking. Castration has already had its effect, which was to force the child into the situation of the Oedipus complex. Thus the Oedipus complex escapes the fate which it meets with in boys: it may be slowly abandoned or dealt with by repression, or its effects may persist far into women's normal mental life. I cannot evade the notion (though I hesitate to give it expression) that for

> women the level of what is ethically normal is different from what it is in men. . . . that they show less sense of justice than men, that they are less ready to submit to the great exigencies of life, that they are more often influenced in their judgments by feelings of affection or hostility.

Women show less sense of justice than men. Freud's idea that women are ethically weaker defines the limitations in his vision. When he says women are less moral than men, he echoes Hamlet's rant at Ophelia, "You make your wantonness your ignorance." Hamlet's charge against her defective superego is that she excuses promiscuity by claiming she doesn't know any better, while Hamlet confesses to more "offenses at my beck than I have thoughts to put them in, imagination to give them shape, or time to act them in."

For the rest of his life Freud held that his theory of the Oedipus complex should be remembered "among the precious new acquisitions of mankind." The irony is what he seemed to forget: Oedipus comes out blind at the end.

Notes

1. Stephen Greenblatt, *Hamlet in Purgatory* (Princeton: Princeton University Press, 2001). Eleanor Prosser, *Hamlet and Revenge*, ed. 2 (Stanford: Stanford University Press, 1971).
   After the Ghost's description of sins being burnt and purged away, Hamlet is obsessed about dying without absolution. His sparing Claudius at prayer in order to later kill him unshriven appalled Samuel Johnson. Prosser reviews vengeance in dramas from 1585–1642 and finds no support for the notion that Hamlet's vow is mere convention. She says it's quite singular: In dozens of plays of the period she finds no parallel to Hamlet's actions and concludes "immortal vengeance" would seem to an Elizabethan audience an act of pure evil.
2. Sigmund Freud, "Letter 71, to Wilhelm Fliess, 15 October 1897," in *The Standard Edition of the Complete Psychological Works of Sigmund Freud*, vol. 1, James Strachey, Ed. and trans. (London: The Hogarth Press, 1966), 265–266.
   K.R. Eissler, *Discourse on Hamlet and HAMLET: A Psychoanalytic Inquiry* (New York: International Universities Press, 1971).
3. Harold C. Goddard, "Hamlet," in *The Meaning of Shakespeare*, vol. 1 (Chicago: University of Chicago Press, 1951), 331–386, 334.
4. Ibid, 345.
5. Northrop Frye, "Hamlet," in *Northrop Frye on Shakespeare* (New Haven: Yale University Press, 1986), 82–100.
6. Stanley Cavell, "Hamlet's Burden of Proof," in *Disowning Knowledge: Seven Plays of Shakespeare* (Cambridge: Cambridge University, 1987), 179–191.
7. William Empson, "Hamlet," in *Essays on Shakespeare*, David B. Pirie, Ed. (Cambridge: Cambridge University Press, 1986), 79–136, 84.
8. A.D. Nuttall, *Shakespeare the Thinker* (New Haven: Yale University Press, 2007), 197–200.
9. Sigmund Freud, "Remembering, Repeating and Working-Through," in *The Standard Edition of the Complete Psychological Works of Sigmund Freud*, vol. 12, James Strachey, Ed. and trans. (London: The Hogarth Press, 1914/1958), 147–156.
10. R.A. Foakes, *Hamlet Versus Lear: Cultural Politics and Shakespeare's Art* (Cambridge: Cambridge University Press, 1993), 174–180.
11. Marjorie Garber, *Shakespeare's Ghost Writers: Literature as Uncanny Causality* (New York: Routledge, 1987), 157–171.

12. Sigmund Freud, "Dostoevsky and Parricide," in *The Standard Edition of the Complete Psychological Works of Sigmund Freud*, vol. 21, James Strachey, Ed. and trans. (London: The Hogarth Press, 1928/1961), 188–189.
13. Nigel Alexander, *Poison, Play, and Duel: A Study in Hamlet* (Lincoln: University of Nebraska Press, 1971), 9.
14. Ernest Jones, *Hamlet and Oedipus* (New York: Doubleday Anchor Books, 1949), 103.
15. Alexander, *Poison*, 10–11.
16. James Shapiro, *Contested Will: Who Wrote Shakespeare?* (New York: Simon & Schuster, 2010), 160–162.
17. Sigmund Freud, "Some Psychical Consequences of the Anatomical Distinction Between the Sexes," in *The Standard Edition of the Complete Psychological Works of Sigmund Freud*, vol. 19, James Strachey, Ed. and trans. (London: The Hogarth Press, 1925/1961), 241–258.

12

A MIRROR IN THE QUEEN'S CLOSET

The Good Enough Mother

After he stabs Polonius hidden behind a tapestry in his mother's bedroom, there is between Hamlet and Gertrude a struggle so elemental, so primitive it can only be a clash of primal love and hate, a contest of desire and death. Neither of them is ever the same afterward.

Hamlet	Now Mother, what's the matter?
Gertrude	Hamlet, thou hast thy father much offended.
Hamlet	Mother, you have my father much offended.
Gertrude	Come, come—you answer with an idle* tongue.
Hamlet	Go, go—you question with a wicked tongue.
Gertrude	Why—how now Hamlet — Have you forgot me?
Hamlet	No by the rood not so, You are the Queen, your husband's brother's wife, And would it were not so, you are my mother.
Gertrude	Nay, then I'll set those to you that can speak.
Hamlet	Come, come and sit you down, you shall not budge. You go not till I set you up a glass* Where you may see the inmost part of you.
Gertrude	What wilt thou do? Thou wilt not murder me? Help, help—ho!

III.iv.8 TLN 2385–2402

* insolent

* mirror

She asks whether he has forgot her, meaning her rank and his filial obligation. But on an atavistic level, she sees in her son's eyes a look that says she's a stranger.

Has he literally forgot her? Yes, the mother she is, not the mother she was in his infancy. He brings to the present an old parental image and, as is typical of the "maternal transference," he resurrects the coping mechanisms used to defend against feelings about the parent back then. He defends himself with grandiosity, primitive disdain, paranoid projection, and splitting. In Soliloquy 5 Hamlet was steeling himself against killing his mother; here Gertrude actually fears for her life, perhaps not without reason.

Scholars argue about tragic recognition in *Hamlet*, whether *The Mousetrap* is the Aristotelian turning point in this tragedy, or Hamlet's choosing not to kill the praying King, or whether it is the murder of Polonius. But if irreversible dawning of tragic knowledge at its deepest is the criterion, the ultimate crisis of *Hamlet* is the contest of erotic love and mother love that follows the fatal thrust of Hamlet's dagger.

Gertrude O me, what hast thou done?
Hamlet Nay—I know not—is it the King?
Gertrude O what a rash and bloody deed is this!
Hamlet A bloody deed almost as bad, good Mother,
As kill a king and marry with his brother.
Gertrude As kill a king?
Hamlet Aye, lady, it was my word. *[looking down]*
Thou wretched, rash, intruding fool—farewell.
I took thee for thy better.

III.iv.25 TLN 2406–2414

Hamlet has just left Claudius at prayer, rationally he must know the King is not the lump behind the arras. But when Hamlet steps into his mother's bedroom, he enters the unconscious, and there time is out of joint, past is prologue, and space obeys the laws not of physics but of wish and fear: Hamlet's in a nightmare. He hopes it's Claudius, and he fears it.

Here again, the distorting power of transference. When Hamlet asks whether it's the King, there's perhaps another reason. Suppose Freud was right, the Prince unconsciously wanted to supplant his father, the old king? What if he had an Oedipus complex that until now made him hesitate to attack the usurper? In any case, he's overcome his supposed procrastination with a thrust some see as not just fatal to Polonius but also to Freud's favorite theory.

This is a recognition scene for the audience too: From her lack of response to *The Mousetrap*, we doubted Gertrude was Claudius's accessory. Now, she is so uncomprehending of his accusation "kill a king" that Hamlet must believe her innocent of murder. The only sin Hamlet can now set against her is that she's happy in her marriage. His claim on the sympathies of the audience loosens a bit, but now we know Hamlet better than we did. He's capable of decisive action. He's not morally averse to private revenge. He harbors murder in his soul as much as any person. And we're reminded that though he's melancholy by temperament, the choleric can flash forth. So much for Hamlet the delicate intellectual. We never really knew Hamlet before, and now we see that much of the contradiction in him is a function of the plot he finds himself in.[1]

Except his misogyny. That was always there. The only parental object representations he carries in his mind are King Hamlet, the Queen, and Yorick. But this scene isn't just the elaboration of hatred of the female, it's a resolution of the infantile conflict Hamlet's always had with her. In his vast unconscious, the Prince stands for the universal. An attempt to destroy the primal mother is, according to Mrs. Klein, always the defining developmental crisis in the infant's life. For Hamlet, his development is incomplete until the end of this scene.

Hamlet	Leave wringing of your hands! Peace, sit you down And let me wring your heart —
Gertrude	What have I done that thou darest wag thy tongue In noise so rude against me?
Hamlet	Such an act that . . . makes marriage vows As false as dicers' oaths.*
Gertrude	Aye me—what act?

III.iv.34 TLN 2416–2435
* gamblers' IOUs

What act indeed! She's replaced his perfect father with a lesser man. Hamlet claims it degrades her and defiles his memory, but Freud and Jones say it's a blow falling on an old bruise: He was jealous of his father and repressed it—concealing it from himself with jealousy of his uncle.

The craft of the poet is dense here, in the theme of *seeing* as danger, of *blindness* as temporary safety, of *mirroring* as a way of resolving paradox. Hamlet's and Gertrude's lines reflect each other repeatedly. The audience is not thinking consciously about these sensory images but absorbs them on a gut level. Academics like to point to the figurative clusters of *eyes* and *ears* and *skin* for sense metaphors overloading this scene. And themes of disease, defect, death, and decay as they run through the play. These subliminal cues are so rich and subtle that scholars puzzle over why the playmaker lavished so much care on them. Especially baffling is the question of how an Elizabethan audience could have grasped such complexity on a first exposure to the play—or even a second. When scholars write about the intellectual vastness of *Hamlet*, there's a hushed tone as if describing a miracle.[2]

He thinks he has not forgot. Hamlet thinks he knows his mother better than she knows herself. He aims to hold a glass up to her soul, but actually, they mirror each other. She fears he'll murder her; his infantile wish *is* to kill her. Hamlet throws his mother down on her bed and forces her to look at his mourning locket containing a miniature of King Hamlet, side by side with her pendant bearing the coronation portrait of Claudius.

Hamlet	Look here upon this picture—and on this — See what a grace was seated on his brow,

The front of Jove himself . . . to threaten and command,
A combination and a form indeed
Where every god did seem to set his seal
To give the world assurance of a man —
This was your husband.

III.iv.53 TLN 2437–2447

The old king wouldn't recognize himself, Hamlet has so mythologized him. All normal human smut is displaced to the brother. The ego defense of *splitting* explains such mental contortions; here it's Hamlet's refusal to remember King Hamlet was human—he tries to keep his father's image split off from contamination. And, as in the Vicious Mole speech, there's irony as he accuses Claudius of faults very much his own.

Hamlet Here is your husband like a mildewed ear*
Blasting his wholesome brother . . . what judgment
Would step from this—to this? . . . What devil was it
That thus hath cozened you at hood-man blind?
Eyes without feeling, feeling without sight,
Ears without hands or eyes, smelling sans all
. . . but a sickly part—O shame, where is thy blush?

III.iv.64 TLN 2448–2456+4

* a healthy ear of corn blighted with smut

What devil fooled her at blind man's bluff? Her sensuality. Where's her involuntary blush of shame, proof of sincere contrition—and not coincidentally a response like erotic flushing?[3]

Splitting is a primitive defense against paranoia. The line between splitting and obsessional doubt is blurry, but psychoanalysis considers splitting more pathological than neurotic indecision: The neurotic can hold in mind both sides of the ambivalence, at least cognitively, while narcissistic and borderline individuals are aware of one state and its associated feelings but unaware of its opposite—which is mentally present but in a separate mental compartment. The ambivalence can switch instantly, with amnesia for the previous mental state, resulting in confused contradictory outbursts.

Freud suggests the Prince may feel insecure in his ability to love, hence the unconscious choice of doubt as a theme in his poem to Ophelia. And *doubt* also meant *suspect*, as when Hamlet says "I doubt some foul play" in his father's death. So "never doubt I love" is also a warning, "Never suspect I love, don't think I love." Freud usually sees Hamlet as a hysteric because of his sexual disgust, but sometimes he sees Hamlet as obsessive because of his vacillation. Object relations are pathological when an individual is unable to experience ambivalence but can only use splitting. It's unclear in the Nunnery scene whether Hamlet is doubting or splitting when he professes love for Ophelia, then retracts it the next breath. But Hamlet's paranoia toward women isn't healed until the climax of this scene.[4]

Hamlet has no basis for seeing his mother as corrupt. The "incestuous" marriage was approved by the court. Without consanguinity, "incest" is a technicality, not unequivocally condemned even in scripture. His mother's love for Claudius is genuine and Hamlet is only constructing it in his own mind as lustful. Even without the Ghost's speech, he needs to see Claudius as "adulterate," or filthy. He can only think Gertrude's love as some vile combination of stupidity and lust. It can't be the charming foolishness of romance. His image of their marriage bed is all too vivid; it's to him Freud's "primal scene" of parental intercourse.[5]

Hamlet You cannot call it love at your age. . . . Rebellious hell,
If thou canst mutiny in a matron's bones,
. . . let virtue be as wax and proclaim no shame
When the compulsive ardor gives the charge —
Gertrude O Hamlet, speak no more!
Thou turnst mine eyes into my very soul
And there I see such black and grained spots
As will leave there their tinct.*
These words like daggers enter in mine ears.
No more, sweet Hamlet.

III.iv.68 TLN 2452–2474

* stain

As Ophelia had earlier, Gertrude begs him to stop—in the same way with the same tone women have always used. And in ancient fashion to defend herself from worse, she makes herself believe his accusations. Surrender and identification with the abuser are protective. Feeling, believing, and enacting the other person's quasi-delusional beliefs is "projective identification." Hamlet needs to see her as hateful, so Gertrude defensively believes she deserves hatred.[6]

In Freud's case studies, mothers are one-dimensional receptacles for babies, nursing, weaning, toileting—a pram rolling through stages of infantile sexual development—oral, anal, genital. Nothing in Freud is from the mother's point of view. His mothers have one trait, there's no reason to have strong feelings about them. Similarly, Hamlet's mother was largely disdained by scholars through the mid-twentieth century. Then appeared re-appraisals of Gertrude pointing out how critics had missed her strength and wisdom.[7]

Carolyn Heilbrun is the pioneer rehabilitating her. She systematically works her way through Professor Bradley, Granville-Barker, and Dover Wilson, refuting them point by point until she comes to the Closet scene. Then an odd thing happens. She takes at face value Gertrude's lust. She does a critical analysis of the poetry and then inexplicably undermines her paradigm shifting work by *accepting* the apology for lust.

Hamlet is certain Gertrude is lustful, but the lust is in him. As targets of sexualized manic excitement, his mother and Ophelia both call his craziness "ecstasy." Commentators say the word means mere madness, but the Elizabethans took it to mean sexual excitement, as we do. Both Ophelia and Gertrude smell the sexual violence beneath Hamlet's righteousness. Rape is only kept from consciousness by splitting. He's irresistibly drawn to their sexuality—and disgusted by it. He will not be stopped. Claudius is a "murderer and a villain . . . A cutpurse of the empire" who stole the crown, "a king of shreds and patches!" A third time we hear the Queen's anguished cry, "No more!"

Enter the Ghost. Does it come, Hamlet asks, "your tardy son to chide?" Is it here to sharpen Hamlet's "almost blunted purpose?" Suddenly it points to the anguished Gertrude. "O, step between her and her fighting soul . . . Speak to her, Hamlet." But she can't see the Ghost.

Gertrude This is the very coinage of your brain,
This bodiless creation ecstasy is very cunning in.
Hamlet Ecstasy! It is not madness.
Lay not that flattering unction to your soul
That not your trespass but my madness speaks.
Confess . . . repent . . . avoid what's to come,
And . . . forgive me this my virtue:
For in the fatness of these pursy times
Virtue itself of Vice must pardon beg.
Gertrude O Hamlet, thou hast cleft my heart in twain.
Hamlet O throw away the worser part of it
And live the purer with the other half.
Good night, but go not to mine uncle's bed.
Assume a virtue if you have it not. Refrain tonight.
III.iv.137 TLN 2520–2544

Refrain tonight. She absorbs his accusations and contains them. Promising to take confession, she survives. And, his old terror about the unshriven death balmed and soothed, he relaxes.

Heilbrun sees Gertrude through the eyes of Hamlet and the academy. Across the critical history of *Hamlet* there's remarkable blindness to Gertrude's actual words, lustful *nowhere in the play*. Her son, as he admits, has a mind foul as Vulcan's forge. Heilbrun's conclusion is that Gertrude's tragic flaw, in the Aristotelian sense, is lust. The film history of *Hamlet* is a fast-forward replay of the same error. Most depict her as having a sexual drive that is excessive or perverse. Of the available versions, there are two main directorial approaches to Gertrude's femininity, whore or madonna. Olivier directs her as inappropriately seductive, almost a mistress to the Prince (as that actress had in real life been to Olivier). Absent text, Zeffirelli inserts pantomime to show the Queen cynically using sex to control her son. Richardson's is lascivious at every opportunity, so his Closet scene lapses into farce, with two fine actors reciting great poetry rolling on the floor blubbering in each other's arms. Other versions—Kline's, Gielgud's, Peter Brook's, Bennett's—don't depict the Queen as weak or stupid, but in these she's not really a woman.[8]

That leaves the Gertrudes of directors Branagh, Doran, and Almereyda—complex, three dimensional, strong, sympathetic—women who enjoy being women. Doran's Gertrude is a handsome, sincere woman who's found love in middle age. Her son's not so much a divided man as a hysterical boy delaying because he can't focus. David Tennant's Hamlet is cognitively disorganized throughout the scene and emerges more unhinged than before; and his Gertrude takes in her son's mania, twice screaming bursts of hysterical laughter. She reflects her son in a bedroom of mirrors and—strong woman though she is—she shatters. Doran's is a valid interpretation but there's no character growth following the appearance of the Ghost, no tragic recognition, no remorse.

Almereyda's Hamlet is an alienated late adolescent with a major depression. He does change and grow in the scene but many psychiatrists would hospitalize him. Ethan Hawke is an excellent Hamlet, a high-risk patient, hopeless, intermittently suicidal, an obvious danger to himself and others. His mother is wedded to an attractive Claudius, a strong woman deep in love. But Hawke's anger toward their majesties is more existential than oedipal. His disgust with Gertrude is real, though his Nunnery scene is puzzling in retrospect as he doesn't show any transferential sexual nausea toward Ophelia.

Kenneth Branagh directs Julie Christie's Gertrude perfectly. Not a word of text is left out but the scene never drags; it's a specimen performance of the mother-son interaction. Hamlet's negative maternal transference explained his horrific treatment of Ophelia—and more evidence confirms it. Here, as in the Nunnery scene and at *The Mousetrap*, his accusations show Hamlet fighting yearning and rage toward women, with supercilious sexualized contempt. Much of what the Prince "sees" is projected. For Hamlet, masculine identity is fashioned from identifications with male ideals and by disowning "female" traits by extrusion of passive longings. In Branagh's Closet scene we catch glimpses of Hamlet's disowned identification with his mother and his conflict over female parts of himself. He's split between virgin and whore, he says so himself.[9]

Hamlet's dynamic unconscious is exposed at switch points in the dialogue showing splitting of mental pictures of self and mother: She's bad, he's good. Then he's bad and she's worse. Then they're both bad and need forgiveness. The big switch in the scene, of course, comes when the Ghost interposes between them. Hamlet makes escalating attacks on Claudius, each more vicious than the last. Finally, he attacks the King's humanity in a pornographic depiction of foreplay as Hamlet vividly pictures it. (He'd intuited *Mouse* is Claudius's name for Gertrude in bed, hence *The Mousetrap* title.) In each attack Gertrude begs him to stop. On her third plea, the Ghost appears. Hamlet obeys, stepping between her and her fighting soul, asking most tenderly, "How is it with you, Lady?" The interruption of Hamlet's quasi-rape has oedipal implications, and as played here, after the peak of the assault, there ensues an emotional detumescence.

Hamlet Refrain tonight. That monster custom, who all sense
Doth eat, of habits devil, is angel yet in this
. . . to the use of actions fair and good.*
Refrain tonight
And that shall lend a kind of easiness
To the next abstinence . . .
For use almost can change the stamp of nature.
Once more, good night,
And when you are desirous to be blest,
I'll blessing beg of you.

III.iv.160 TLN 2544–2548
* custom, the force of devilish habits,
can be bent to angelic ones

His mother has survived. After the emotional climax, he starts to have self reflection, some insight into his grandiosity. There's even a bit of self mockery in "Forgive me this my virtue." Preachy, but his insight into lust addiction seems personal and timeless, his repentance genuine. He's serious now, capable of empathy. He too will ask forgiveness.

Hamlet reminds his mother that he's supposed to go to England with friends he will "trust as adders fanged." He plans to hoist them with their own bombs and "blow them at the moon." Now the situation is reversed between him and the King. He had Claudius on the defensive after *The Moustrap*, now the King has the upper hand. Looking down at the body of Polonius, he knows he will pay. These are the wages of disillusionment, hard won experience. The split in his psyche is coming together, he's sad now—but whole. Branagh plays this decrescendo with mother and son at some physical remove, not looking at each other. Nuanced silences show them processing the crisis they've come through. And across their faces flicker premonitions of a deeper silence to come.

Not discussed in the psychoanalytic literature is whether one can have a "transference" to a primary object. If Hamlet displaces his expectations of his mother onto Ophelia, that's transference. But what's it called if he projects his image of his mother in childhood onto Gertrude as she is now? Is that transference? This is a question psychoanalysis seems never to have asked, but Shakespeare misses nothing. He answers *yes*, and it's the heart of the Closet scene and the source of Hamlet's cryptic remark in the graveyard, *Get thee to Milady's chamber*. Before this scene, Hamlet sees her as she was. Sad now, not enraged, he sees her as she is.

Not just Kleinian object relations theory but also self psychology shows the scene as pivotal; it sees the individual's main task as the development of a cohesive self. Unempathic parenting leaves behind fault lines that rupture under stress to become a fragmented self. When the child is used as a selfobject, as the *parent's* "mother," the child is parentified. A child used as the selfobject of a parent is vulnerable to fragmentation. Hyman Muslin comes to this same formulation describing Hamlet's fragmentation into a "self of despair" under stress; he sees Hamlet's use of Gertrude as a healing selfobject to repair himself, just as we are arguing.[10]

Hamlet heals himself by eavesdropping on himself. Overhearing him hearing himself, we see a public self we might call The Dane, and a more private self, Sweet Hamlet, his mother's son. The switch points that interest us in the Closet scene are moments of splitting when Hamlet goes from The Dane to Sweet Hamlet, and back again. This scene is differently nuanced with different directors. The lines are the same, yet Olivier, Doran, Almereyda, Richardson, and Branagh all differ in their interpretations. But if you had to point to their commonality, it's that The Dane is trying to destroy Gertrude as she pleads with him, trying to evoke Sweet Hamlet. But the proof of the healing of Hamlet's fragmented self is how Hamlet acts when Gertrude survives his attacks: He calms down, and for the rest of the play, Hamlet and his mother are a political unit. The first thing she does with Claudius after this scene is to lie for Hamlet. The two of them, Queen and Prince, are hereafter tacitly *contra mundum*.

The Ghost, always somewhere hovering in Hamlet's conscience, at the end of this scene is no more and goes unmentioned the *rest of the play*. Hamlet has won his oedipal battle; the Prince has captured the Queen; but because of her reflexive loyalty, as when she defends Claudius from Laertes, the King doesn't realize he's lost her.[11]

Donald Winnicott understands the attempt to destroy the mother. His theories of development depend on attempted murder as part of the normal process. But the child's mental health depends on the mother surviving, then the infant gets to keep her as an inner object. Mother as a looking glass is apt here since *Hamlet* is replete with reflected images. Both Almereyda and Doran make Gertrude's closet literally a room full of mirrors which—inevitably—Hamlet shatters and, as the scene winds down, mother and son sit surrounded by broken pieces.[12]

Hamlet . . . For this same lord *[looking down]*
I do repent—but heaven hath pleased it so
To punish me with this, and this with me. . . .
I will bestow him and will answer well
The death I gave him. So, again, good night.
I must be cruel only to be kind.
Thus bad begins, and worse remains behind —
One word more, good lady: *[he turns back to her]*
. . . I essentially am not in madness
But mad in craft—'twere good you let* him know.
Gertrude Be thou assured, if words be made of breath
And breath of life, I have no life to breathe
What thou hast said to me.

III.iv.172 TLN 2548–2575
* not allow

And Gertrude keeps Hamlet's secret for the rest of her life.

In object relations psychology, the mother's face as reflector is needed during the infant's progression from a narcissistic world, where everything *is* the infant, to a world where there is distinction between the infant and the world. The nursing mother, of course, is looking at the baby. How she appears to the baby at this moment is related to who she sees there. The baby starts by seeing the mother's face, and this is how the mother gives back to the baby the baby's self. Over time this is the seed around which the person forms. Feeling real is more than just existing, it's being one's true self. Normally, the individual comes not only to relate as a self but also has a true self into which to repair for rest and refueling. The "good enough mother" (in Winnicott's most famous phrase) doesn't challenge the fantasied omnipotence of the baby. The infant needs to feel at first as if the baby created the object. Later, when inevitable frustrations arise, the baby tries to destroy the object. Baby magically creates the object, then baby enjoys and loves the object. Then the baby hates and tries to destroy the object. But the object survives. As a result, the real object exists outside, and an object representation exists inside the baby. Even if the external object disappears, the baby can find the object because now the baby has a capacity to symbolize objects with replacement images.

But what happens when there isn't good enough mothering? The baby doesn't see himself or herself in the mother's face. The baby is perceiving, not interacting. If the mother's face isn't reflective as an emotional mirror, it's not something to be looked *into* but something merely to be looked at. *Let her paint an inch thick, to this favor she must come.*

> Some babies, tantalized by this type of relative maternal failure, study the variable maternal visage in an attempt to predict the mother's mood, just exactly as we all study the weather. The baby quickly learns to make a forecast: "Just now it is safe to forget the mother's mood and be spontaneous, but any minute the mother's face will become fixed or her mood will dominate, and my own personal needs must then be withdrawn otherwise my central self may suffer insult."[13]

Object relations theories of infant development seem at first bizarre, but multiple case histories argue for something real in them. Case after case details the descent of such patients into madness during the treatment. Then over months or years of analysis, with luck and skill, the patients ascend again. These "transference psychoses" feel like the madness of the Closet scene, and Hamlet stands for anyone who has personally questioned the nature of sanity.[14]

In psychoanalyzing patients who never got good enough mothering, there can be no workable "transference neurosis" to analyze because there's not enough intact ego to neutralize anxiety over primal rage ("id impulses"). Rather there develops

> a pseudo-self which is a collection of innumerable reactions to a succession of failures of adaptation [and] whenever the environment fails in its task of

> making active adaptation, it . . . interrupts the continuity of being, that very thing which would have formed itself into the ego of the differentiating human being.[15]

A true self containing the "id impulses" is cloaked in, and protected by, a false self made up of those maternal failures and external demands from the environment.

Then there evolves the true self that is enfolded in and protected by the false self. It may have much the shape of the true self but it "develops a pattern corresponding to the pattern of environmental failure" by the mother. This compromise preserves a "continuity of being" but the "hidden true self suffers an impoverishment." The false self has achieved a deceptive false integrity, and in "the favorable case the false self develops a fixed maternal attitude towards the true self and is permanently in a state of holding the true self as a mother holds a baby." The problem, though, with even the best false self is that it cannot feel. A good enough analytic framework allows the patient's true self, which lies beneath the protective false self, to begin to experience hope. Then the true self can begin to take the risks involved in object relating. If this is done well enough, the false self eventually hands itself over to the psychotherapist.

Psychoanalyzing sicker patients was a research laboratory for object relations theorists. The influence of Winnicott is greater than anyone except Freud. He had an ineffable ability to think like an infant. Just as Freud thought unconscious conflicts become reborn within the analytic situation as a transference neurosis, Winnicott believed that an analogous "transference psychosis" needed to develop in very ill individuals. The term describes a transient psychotic episode lasting from hours to months, with the delusional system attaching itself only to the transference and interfering very little with the patient's life outside therapy.[16]

Not uncommon are reports on patients who develop a "delusional transference" in the course of which the patient literally mistakes the therapist for a parent. A neurotic patient can recognize the therapist as a real person who temporarily feels like the parents as they actually were, or as they were experienced, in childhood. According to Margaret Little, the transference is delusional when "there is no such 'stand-in' or 'as-if' quality about it. To such a patient the analyst is, in an absolute way, with the quality of 'authenticity,' both the idealized parents deified and diabolized." The success of the analysis

> depends upon breaking up the delusional transference. To do this reality must be presented undeniably and inescapably, so that contact with it cannot be refused, and in such ways that the patient does not have to use either inference or deductive thinking. It might be compared with the waking from a dream of a tiny child, but someone must be there to help the waking.[17]

She was known for uncanny intuition about object relations; and late in her life Margaret Little ascribed her recovery from her own severe illness to her analysis with Winnicott. She was grateful he allowed her to regress to a full blown psychotic transference from which she was then carefully brought back to reality. Donald Winnicott was the one who helped the waking.

Productions often present Hamlet as changed on return from the sea voyage, but as Branagh's version makes clear, the change really starts here with the rapprochement of mother and child. In several films, Hamlet emerges from this scene more antic or narcissistic than ever. But at the end of the Branagh version, Hamlet is no longer splitting. (The exception is his execrable treatment of the schoolfellows, but there are reasons for it.) The result is a sadder—and ironic and rueful—Prince of Denmark. Branagh's reading is tender and thoughtful: Hamlet has come into possession of his poetry. He's no longer terrified of death. He identifies with Yorick, his childhood parent, as he darkly jokes—and grieves—over the body of Polonius.

Hamlet This man shall set me packing,
I'll lug the guts into the neighbor room.
Mother, good night indeed. This counselor
Is now most still, most secret, and most grave,
Who was in life a foolish prating knave.
Come sir, to draw toward an end with you.
Good night, Mother.

III.iv.212 TLN 2578–2584

To fit the obsessive side of Hamlet's character and ratchet up suspense, this scene uses a device recycled from the Nunnery scene. Hamlet twice bids his mother good night and starts to leave but comes back. Hearing the rhyming couplet Elizabethan drama uses to signal the end of a scene, the audience unconsciously takes a breath, and holds it, but Hamlet returns. Finally on the third couplet they take a breath and—*Good night, Mother*—the audience can exhale at last.

Notes

1. A.C. Bradley, *Shakespearean Tragedy: Lectures on Hamlet, Othello, King Lear, Macbeth*, ed. 2 (New York: Macmillan, 1919).
2. William Empson. *Seven Types of Ambiguity* (1930, revised 1947, reprint; New York: New Directions, 1966).
   He believes Shakespeare wrote way beyond the grasp of his audience to entertain his fellow actors in the Lord Chamberlain's Men.
3. Erving Goffman, "Embarrassment and Social Organization," *American Journal of Sociology* 62 (1956): 264–271.
   Darwin was quick to note a false accusation is as likely to cause a blush as a true one.
4. Donald W. Winnicott, "The Use of an Object and Relating Through Identifications," *International Journal of Psycho-Analysis* 50 (1969): 711–716.
5. Stanley Cavell, "Hamlet's Burden of Proof," in *Disowning Knowledge in Seven Plays of Shakespeare*, ed. 2 (Cambridge: Cambridge University Press, 1987), 179–191.
6. Harold Searles, "The Schizophrenic's Vulnerability to the Therapist's Unconscious Processes," in *Collected Papers on Schizophrenia and Related Subjects* (New York: International Universities Press, 1965), 192–215.

Melanie Klein believed projective identification is a forerunner of empathy as well as an infantile defense: It's the mother's job to absorb such projections (as "introjects") and metabolize them so the infant can progress from the "paranoid" to the "depressive position." In Searles's work the transfer is called introjection. Gertrude is here functioning as a good enough mother by empathically metabolizing Hamlet's projections.

7. Carolyn Heilbrun, "The Character of Hamlet's Mother," *Shakespeare Quarterly* 8 (1957): 201–206.

   Harley Granville-Barker, *Prefaces to Shakespeare* (London: Sidgewick & Jackson, 1936), 285.

   He hates Gertrude as a "shallow, amiable, lymphatic creature" who was cunning enough to deceive her husband, an empty woman clinging to youth—but with no textual support.
8. Peter S. Donaldson, "Olivier, Hamlet, and Freud," in *Shakespeare on Film*, Robert Shaughnessy, ed. (New York: St. Martin's Press, 1998), 103–125.
9. David Leverenz, "The Woman in Hamlet: An Interpersonal View," in *Representing Shakespeare: New Psychoanalytic Essays*, Murray M. Schwartz and Coppélia Kahn, Eds. (Baltimore: The Johns University Press, 1980), 110–128.
10. Hyman L. Muslin, "Hamlet: The Self of Despair," *Progress in Self Psychology* 7 (1991): 201–218.

    Mainstream dynamic psychiatry has appropriated selfobject for the functions of the good enough mother. The vocabulary of psychodynamic psychology has shifted. Nowadays one can attend a case conference in training centers and not hear the word transference at all in the way ego psychologists once used it. When discussed, it's in terms of Kohut's idealizing transference ("There's someone I can look up to"), twinship transference ("I'm not alone, there's somebody just like me"), and mirroring transference ("Someone understand me perfectly"). Two decades ago, transference in Freud's sense was one of the most used technical terms in such discussions. Now, Klein's projective identification is used to denote the defensive functions of transference, while Stolorow's enactment substitutes for transference-countertransference responses.
11. Gertrude's defection from husband to son is how the play was performed in Shakespeare's lifetime. In the First Quarto's Scene 14, Horatio comes to tell the Queen that Hamlet sent Horatio a letter telling how Claudius had plotted his execution. The Queen says, "Then I perceive there's a treason in his looks/ That seemed to sugar o'er his villainy."
12. Mother and child as mirrors was a favorite trope of Shakespeare, as in Sonnet 3.

    Thou art thy mother's glass, and she in thee
    Calls back the lovely April of her prime;
    So thou through windows of thine age shalt see,
    Despite of wrinkles, this thy golden time.
13. Donald W. Winnicott, "Mirror-role of Mother and Family in Child Development," in *Playing and Reality* (New York: Basic Books, 1967), 111–118.
14. Donald W. Winnicott, "The Beginnings of a Formulation of an Appreciation and Criticism of Klein's Envy Statement," in *D.W. Winnicott: Psycho-Analytic Explorations*, Clare Winnicott, Ray Shepherd, and Madeline Davis, Eds. (1989; reprint, Cambridge: Harvard University Press, 1992), 447–457.

    Winnicott disagreed with Klein on the "death instinct" and felt "envy" was too complex an emotion for the newborn. But he did agree with Klein's notion of a progression from primitive destructive aggression—passing through gradual disillusionment and acquisition of reality-testing—to the "depressive position" (which he re-names "the capacity for concern").
15. Donald W. Winnicott, "On Transference," in *Essential Papers on Transference*, Aaron H. Esman, Ed. (New York: New York University Press, 1990), 246–251, 247.
16. Harold F. Searles, "Transference Psychosis in the Psychotherapy of Chronic Schizophrenia," *International Journal of Psycho-Analysis* 44 (1963): 249–281.
17. Margaret I. Little, "On Delusional Transference (Transference Psychosis)," International *Journal of Psycho-Analysis* 39 (1958): 134–138.

13

THE PRINCE AND HIS BROTHERS

War, Murder, and Manhood

After Claudius banishes him, the Prince meets Fortinbras's army marching to Poland to fight over a tiny strip of land. He's amazed they'd squander so much blood and gold for so little. Surveying thousands of soldiers, he's literally at a crossroad. Half the play after *To be or not to be* he has another soliloquy on the divine plan. He was asking then whether he was paralyzed by intellect. Now he questions honor—is he the equal of his brother prince?

Hamlet Examples gross as earth exhort me —
Witness this army of such mass and charge,
Led by a delicate and tender prince
Whose spirit with divine ambition puffed
Makes mouths at the invisible event
Exposing what is mortal and unsure
To all that Fortune, death and danger dare —
Even for an eggshell.

IV.iv.47 TLN 2743+40–47

All that death and danger dare. The seething irony of the Seventh Soliloquy, is it directed at a world Hamlet detests? Or at himself?

Hamlet Rightly to be great
Is not to stir without great argument,
But greatly to find quarrel in a straw
When honor's at the stake. How stand I then —
That have a father killed, a mother stained,
Excitements of my reason and my blood
And let all sleep—while to my shame I see

The imminent death of twenty thousand men
That for a fantasy and trick of fame
Go to their graves like beds, fight for a plot
Whereon the numbers cannot try the cause,
Which is not tomb enough and continent
To hide the slain?* O from this time forth,
My thoughts be bloody or be nothing worth.

IV.iv.54 TLN 2743+47–60

* a graveyard not big enough to hold all the dead

To be great is to fight over tiny things standing for honor. This is the perverse cost of manhood—the inverse relation between the prize and the glory winning it—the smaller the prize, the greater the glory. Evolution rewards unimpeachable displays of fitness, especially when the price is high. The peacock's tail is purchased at the price of vulnerability to predators, but this expensive symbol is paying for the survival of its genes by advertising superior mating. And war may be the costliest plumage of all. Hamlet resolves to be stupid and "honorable" like Fortinbras: His thoughts shall be bloody—or they'll be worth nothing.

In English Renaissance drama, *Hamlet* is a hybrid of ancient and modern tragedy. The Ghost is classical and Christian, Greek and Roman. But heroism is problematic to the humanistic morality Hamlet is developing. Part of the thrill of *Hamlet* comes from the scream for revenge deep in the throat of humankind. A countervailing element is the moral sense that evolved with reciprocal altruism. Between lies "free will" which the Renaissance was starting to question. When it suits the drama, the pagan and the Christian clash—right through the last scene when classical soldier Hamlet achieves revenge, then becomes the moral hero forbidding his friend's pagan suicide.[1]

None of the soliloquies is truer to nature of the Prince than the Seventh, but the Folio dropped it. Still, it finds its way back into productions. It's in Gielgud's film, and Branagh's. Nowhere in the play are lines more stirring. The Hamlet of Soliloquy 7 is no longer sicklied over with thought. Our last image of him before his banishment must *be bloody or nothing worth.*

It's shocking really, Hamlet's cruelty to Gertrude and Ophelia. Along with misogyny there's genital focus of sexual excitement, a specific anatomical target, the *nothing* that lies between a maid's legs and *country matters*, referring to her *queinte.* But there's nothing sexual when Hamlet bullies the schoolfellows or Polonius. And while Hamlet is obsessed with the sexuality of Claudius, it's not genital in a human way, it's more like a worm, not an erect penis but mushy puffy fingers fumbling at Gertrude's nape.[2]

Then consider the men we're calling *Hamlet's brothers*—Horatio, Fortinbras, Laertes, and the gravedigger. The objection will of course be made that Hamlet and Fortinbras never meet, Hamlet and the gravedigger are social class opposites, and Hamlet and Laertes kill each other. But these are the men Hamlet identifies with as men. Hamlet's brothers are exempt from his genital cruelty, his disdainful neutering, and his nauseated fascination with the royal bed. In developing a male identity the Prince has a problem. The oedipal father he might identify with is too distant, too detached for the son to be conflicted about in a normal way. Psychoanalysis and the academy agree, Hamlet's idealization must be a defense against aggression, evidence for Freud's Oedipus complex.[3]

Janet Adelman spots the double meaning in Hamlet's question, "How stand I then/ That have a father killed, a mother stained?" Only a little grammatical shuffling is needed to catch the oedipal victory: *How stand I then, that have killed a father and have stained a mother?* If so, he's like Claudius, who "incorporates the deepest and most buried part of Hamlet's own personality." The Prince is ferociously dis-identifying with his mother, associated now with darkness. "The structure of *Hamlet* is marked by the struggle . . . to free the masculine identity of both father and son from its origin in the contaminated maternal body." Hamlet is consistently more focused on Gertrude; *The Mousetrap* "localizes its pervasive boundary panic in Hamlet's relationship with his mother, whose contaminated body initially serves him as the metaphor for the fallen world that has sullied him."[4]

Adelman says the embodied danger is toxic midnight weeds, a "union" in the chalice, the hidden unction on Laertes's foil—"the dangerous female powers of the night" feared by men back to Mother Eve. By the time we meet him, Hamlet has inside only the introjected whore-mother whom the death of his father uncovered. She thinks Hamlet had already lost Gertrude in infancy. Hamlet is trying "to remake his mother . . . in the image of the Virgin Mother who could guarantee his father's purity, and his own, repairing the boundaries of his selfhood." *The Mousetrap* doesn't make sense unless you understand it as a trap for Gertrude. The inner play "is in fact designed to catch the conscience of the queen: its challenge is always to her loving posture, its accusations [flow] naturally from this attempt to catch her conscience."

Masculine identity in Shakespeare follows a standard trajectory. On the way to mature attachments the hero must sever his connection with his mother, a primal figure who's dangerous to leave; it's a temptation to regress to primitive oneness with the mother. The danger to the boy is not castration by the father but engulfment by the mother, a task that must be accomplished first, extrusion of the mother, before identification with the father. Such models help explain sexual violence toward women. The hero of the history plays is bonded with men in warrior intimacy as he attacks other men (which is his nature) and as he seeks the spoils of war (symbolized as female). Coppélia Kahn reviews battle scenes in which Shakespeare's heroes gasp out magnificent poetry and die in each other's arms after farewell kisses on the wounds and lips of the warrior comrade.[5]

Graphic rape imagery runs through the prelude to battle as the history hero arouses his men. Analogies between fortresses and women, and between penetrating walls and rape, emerge as the hero urges his men to emulate their fathers in a collective erection as battering rams, stiffening sinews, setting their teeth, holding their breath. Kahn says love is felt between these men as blissful pregenital merger, and genital sexuality is enacted in collective violence against women. The poetry in these dramatic enactments neutralizes overt sadism; and sometimes it fails to do so, when England thrusts and the hero literally threatens the French with sexual violence against sweethearts, wives, and mothers.

Freud's theories about the origin of law, culture, and religion are set out in *Totem and Taboo* and *Civilization and Its Discontents*: He thinks civilizing social inventions had their origin in a single prehistoric act, the "primal murder" of the archetypal father by the "patriarchal horde." They then became the "primal horde," a group of men who both exulted and mourned at a "totem meal" cannibalistic in form, which comes down to us in the communion of Christians. Individual control is exerted by the superego directing the ego after consultation with the "ego ideal." Control at every level is connected to shame and guilt, two emotions Freud mostly lumped together. He says "the sense of guilt [is] the most important problem in the development of civilization [because] the price we pay for our advance in civilization is a loss of happiness through a heightening of the sense of guilt." And Freud's own footnote to this page is "Thus conscience does make cowards of us all."[6]

Inherent in any civilization is a vague restlessness, a sense of some desire unsatisfied. And, he adds, a "quite peculiar relationship—as yet completely unexplained" between guilt and self consciousness *per se* as evidenced by the different presentations of guilt in various states of self awareness. This results in subjective experiences ranging from sharp remorse to diffuse discontent. To explain this relationship between guilt and consciousness, Freud alludes to the two meanings of *conscience* as Hamlet uses it, consciousness as a *state of awareness* of self in the world versus the *moral sense*. Freud implies a circularity between *conscience* and *consciousness*: The moral sense creates emotions that call attention to the mind they occur in. And, in turn, the self develops awareness of those emotions. Freud says guilt is nothing but a "variety of anxiety [that] coincides completely with *fear of the super-ego*." In this it's like consciousness and exhibits "the same extraordinary variations. . . . The sense of guilt produced by civilization remains to a large extent unconscious or appears as a sort of malaise." As with "Criminals from a Sense of Guilt," emotion is experienced but the wish is repressed. The superego, observing the ego, creates a consciousness of self. Guilt emerges as a layer of self awareness and keeps civilizations in line—at the price of general malaise. But on the individual level, hurting people is fun, fantasy encrypts desire, and symbols circumvent guilt.[7]

In "A Child Is Being Beaten" Freud described the masturbation fantasies of school children. He observed a pattern, a "characteristic detail of the content of the phantasy came to light: 'A small child is being beaten on its naked bottom.'" This gave an erotic thrill "and had its issue in an act of pleasurable autoerotic satisfaction. It might therefore be expected that the sight of another child being beaten at school would also be a source of similar enjoyment." But the sight of actual beatings was so repugnant that "it was always a condition of the more sophisticated phantasies of later years that the punishment should do the children no serious injury." Freud's patients needed "being beaten" not to be real but it needed to seem real. The fantasy was most compelling when it stood at the right distance between being in control and being controlled by the narrative, between being the subject and being its object. This presence of a wish and its opposite is the locus of play in children and of fantasy in everyone. It allowed the child to experience anal sadomasochistic thrills without harm; not only was the beating unconsciously experienced as being sexually acted upon by the parent, which was exciting, but the fact of punishment expiated the guilt that accompanied illicit pleasure.[8]

Freud differentiates neurotic symptoms (like hysterical numbness) from perversions (such as a wish to be urinated on). In neurotic symptoms, libido is converted into bodily phenomena that stand for and fulfill the desire symbolically. There's little sexual awareness because the symptom masks it. But in perversions the desire gets re-channeled toward a fetish object that's consciously sexually exciting. Arousal by a perversion becomes an end in itself, its orgasms preferred over "normal" sexual relations. In the perversions, an individual's developmental progress through Freud's psychosexual stages detours into fetishistic play; but in neurosis, development is "fixated" in the anal or phallic stage to produce obsessive or hysterical symptoms. Repression and neurotic symptoms are associated with guilt, while fetishistic and addictive relationships are associated with delayed shame (split off from consciousness as the perversion is performed). The "child being beaten" fantasy is preliminary to Freud's sociological theories about collective perversions—war and murder, rape and conquest.

Freud revisionist Jacques Lacan says that any object of desire is at the deepest level always incestuous, so desire can only approach its object in disguise. The "unconscious is structured as a language," so its hidden wishes are revealed by deep reading surface texts and deconstructing their symbolic grammar. Repressed psychic contents return as symptoms of inhibition and doing-undoing. Lacan concludes that oedipal desire, the wish that can never be satisfied, is the major driver of the plot of *Hamlet*.[9]

Lacan rightly connects rottenness in the state of Denmark to interrupted mourning. In *Hamlet* the rites and rituals are cut short, hugger-mugger, secret—the old King's, Polonius's, and Ophelia's. But he exaggerates when he says "all anybody talks about in the whole play" is mourning—Hamlet's done mourning his father, once and for all, on the exit of the Ghost from Gertrude's closet by the middle of the play. He's reconciled with the shade of his father; he no longer delays but pursues his destiny with all practical speed. And it's not true that Gertrude remains loyal to Claudius as Lacan claims: Almost immediately after Hamlet has dragged away the body of Polonius, Gertrude tells Claudius that Hamlet killed the "unseen good old man" in a frenzy. "O heavy deed!" Claudius says, using the royal *we*, "It had been so with us had we been there." Gertrude is shocked silent at this lack of sorrow for his loyal counselor, and in the next moment she lies. Hamlet is still mad, she says, but "weeps for what is done." Hamlet did not weep. Like the captured queen at chess, Gertrude is now useless in the King's game. One of the best pieces of texturing in the long third quarter of the play is Claudius's dawning awareness that Gertrude is slipping away.[10]

Lacan says mourning can never come to completion because the object is unattainable; it can't be acknowledged because it's incestuous. And it's not just in Denmark that time is out of joint, it's that way in Hamlet's unconscious too. He can't make himself kill because Claudius is not the man Hamlet is after, Lacan says. Hamlet can't grieve and move forward for the same reason he can't kill the King. Claudius stands for Hamlet's father, and he's paralyzed because Claudius has done what he unconsciously wished, forcing a hidden identification with Claudius. The Prince would be killing himself.

The formulation is plausible but incomplete. Lacan in obediently following Freud misses the same thing Freud missed. If this is an "oedipal victory" Hamlet doesn't suffer the paralyzing guilt Freud says he must pay for the patricidal impulse. At the end of the process he doesn't end up symptomatic. When he has justice on his side and proof of Claudius's duplicity, the letter to England Hamlet holds in his possession, he dispatches Claudius with alacrity. Lacan misses this. Tagging after Freud, he's always on the lookout for repression but doesn't distinguish repression from splitting. So he doesn't catch the crucial difference between behaviors that represent the indirect emergence into consciousness of *repressed* material, on the one hand, versus the sudden direct eruption of material that is dissociated or *split* off from consciousness. It's the difference between symbolized behaviors versus crude acting out of impulse. Lacking the concept of splitting, as distinct from repression, Lacan ended up concocting an arcane theory he christened "the discourse of the Other"—and even his most avid fans concede this contraption is less applicable to treating patients than to literary criticism.[11]

Repression and splitting have surface similarity, but in repression some mental contents are out of direct access. In splitting, two mental compartments are dissociated while remaining fully accessible—only not simultaneously. Two ideas and their associated affects, love and hate generally, are partitioned, so that when in one mental state, the person is amnesic for the other. But the two states reverse in a flash. Splitting leads to semiautomatic behaviors from emotions that are poorly neutralized and ideas that are only crudely symbolized. Splitting is intense, jerky, psychologically expensive, and unmodulated. Hamlet's relationships with women are characterized by splitting, as seen in the Nunnery scene and the Closet scene.

As he got older Freud lost interest in splitting, shame, and preoedipal conflicts. He instead deepened his theories on repression, guilt, and the Oedipus complex. He came to see all culture as bottomed on guilt, the experience of which is defended by taboos—the universal ones being incest and patricide, which he saw as the central transgressions of *Hamlet*.[12]

The relationships with women of male heroes in Shakespeare are, compared to male-male bonds, infrequent, imbalanced, and dangerous. Coppélia Kahn says that the Ghost "is so powerful in his injured majesty that it seems ungracious to remember that he is also a cuckold [and so long as Hamlet] can blame a woman's frailty for the indignity his father suffers, as the conventions of cuckoldry enable him to do, that image can be saved." *Conventions of cuckoldry* say you can blame the woman to rescue honor. The homosexual aspect of cuckoldry was well understood before Freud, and one of his hunches about the etiology of paranoia had to do with the symbolism of being approached from behind by another man. Khan says the Ghost

> depicts Claudius as a phallic serpent who poured poison into his victim's ear, an action that strongly suggests sexual penetration. The king . . . is in the feminine position of being penetrated by the man who has already penetrated his wife.

The Ghost rationalizes weakness by construing cuckoldry as political rather than personal—saving the royal bed from being a "couch for luxury and damned incest"—but like any defense, it comes at a price. Hamlet, as justiciar for his father, lowers that dignity by getting ensnared in the cuckoldry obsession.[13]

An Elizabethan warrior living under a queen regnant was able to accommodate some split in gender and power; if manhood was already battle-proved, there could be acceptance of a feminine side. Underneath a public rejection of emotion, tears, and "weakness," there was allowed inner femininity, if the surface holds strong. The Hamlet that rejects feminine doubting is kept separate from the Hamlet that submits to his soul as mistress in sealing Horatio as his own. Some scholars bristle at the suggestion that this style of talk is homoerotic, insisting Elizabethan men often spoke or wrote to each other in such fashion as a convention. Others jump on any man-man affection as proof of homosexuality. Either way, the schematic doesn't fit Renaissance culture. Gender typical traits are not exclusively masculine or feminine. During the duel with Laertes, Hamlet will explicitly say Laertes is only flirting. Hamlet and his brothers are free to express tender feelings for each other that, within certain conventions, use heterosexual courtship as a metaphor. But it's not something to get exercised about—so Hamlet is baffled when during the duel Laertes takes umbrage at his typical warrior badinage.

It's when people are uncomfortable with sexuality that sharp gender divisions must be made. This is seen in the type of man psychoanalysis calls the "phallic narcissist." He's instantly recognizable as the *miles gloriosus*, the braggart soldier that goes all the way back to Roman comedy. But this stock character is no laughing matter. He's the dependent little boy who's grown into a powerful body without commensurate restraint. Audiences easily understood him in ancient Greek theater. Phallic narcissists tend toward jealousy, a thin skin, and a paranoid stance long understood as reaction against passive longings for a father.

As Laertes rages over the death of his father, he regresses to a phallic narcissistic stage. Hamlet slips into this when he tries to out-grieve Laertes at Ophelia's grave, so it's Hamlet's regressive competitiveness that makes him also fall for Claudius's plot. The King tells Laertes about the French bravo, Lamord—*the death*—whom Hamlet supposedly envies. This draws Hamlet into a rigged scrimmage—he's the bait for Laertes, and Laertes is the bait for Hamlet. These young men, only sons bereft of fathers, not yet free to command, are a perfect dramatic set up. And Elizabethans would have known this was all going to end in a sword fight.

Nigel Alexander says that what ever else productions of *Hamlet* may achieve, in order to succeed, "they must produce a difficult and exciting stage fight." If the duel doesn't work the play doesn't work. This duel combines three forms of armed combat known to Tudor jurists: First, war, where it's a fight between champions of opposed armies (Hamlet for the old king, Laertes for the King). Second, trial by combat (for Hamlet's murdering Polonius). And third, an affair of honor. These codes represented the least among evils—combat of champions being less bloody than war (for example, old King Hamlet and the King of Norway); trial by combat substituting divine for human judgment; and the duel outright being l ess socially problematic than a vendetta going through generations. Elizabethans would have sensed all three undercurrents. "The war between Denmark and Norway which flickers restlessly off-stage in *Hamlet* threatened to become just such a cycle of revenge." And the Tudor succession is also flickering in the back-ground.[14]

At Elsinore, the Queen is avoiding poor Ophelia. She's loath to see the girl since her sick soul sees disaster everywhere. "So full of artless jealousy is guilt/ It spills itself in fearing to be spilt."

King O Gertrude, Gertrude,
When sorrows come, they come not single spies
But in battalions . . . poor Ophelia . . .
Divided from herself and her fair judgment
. . . her brother is in secret come from France . . .
With pestilent speeches of his father's death.

IV.v.77 TLN 2814–2828

When the doors burst open, Claudius faces Laertes and asks whether he means to kill both friend and foe. Laertes says only enemies. Hearing footsteps, he turns. It's his sister, obviously insane. Ophelia, hallucinating, thinks Laertes is Hamlet and bitterly reproaches him with flowers.[15]

Ophelia There's rosemary, that's for remembrance —
Pray you, Love, remember —
And there's pansies, that's for thoughts.
There's fennel for you, and columbines.
There's rue for you, And here's some for me —
You must wear your rue with a difference.
There's a daisy—I would give you some violets,
But they withered all when my father died —
They say he made a good end.

IV.v.174 TLN 2927–2937

After she's taken away, the King condoles Laertes and turns him to revenge: Whoever killed Polonius, on him "let the great axe fall." They plot, knowing

Hamlet is too noble himself to suspect and won't inspect the weapons, Laertes can choose an unblunted foil to stab Hamlet.

Laertes And for that purpose I'll anoint my sword.
I bought an unction of a mountebank
So mortal that . . . no cataplasm*
Under the moon can save the thing from death
That is but scratched withal. I'll touch my point
With this . . . that if I gall him slightly . . . it may be death.
IV.vii.140 TLN 3131–3139
* from a huckster an ointment so poisonous that no antidote exists

The Queen enters and describes Ophelia's death. Laertes and the King believe it without question—as audiences always do and have always done for centuries.[16]

Queen One woe doth tread upon another's heel,
So fast they follow. Your sister's drowned, Laertes.
There is a willow grows aslant the brook
That shows his hoary leaves in the glassy stream.
There with fantastic garlands did she come,
Of crow-flowers, nettles, daisies, and long purples. . . .
There, on the pendant boughs her coronet weeds
Clambering to hang, an envious sliver broke,
When down her weedy trophies and herself
Fell in the weeping brook. Her clothes spread wide
And mermaid-like awhile they bore her up,
Which time she chanted snatches of old tunes
As one incapable of her own distress —
. . . But long it could not be
Till that her garments heavy with their drink
Pulled the poor wretch from her melodious lay
To muddy death.
Laertes Alas, then she is drowned.
Queen Drowned, drowned.
Laertes Too much of water hast thou, poor Ophelia,
And therefore I forbid my tears. . . .
IV.vii.63 TLN 3155–3179

But his unstoppable—and feminine—tears force him to leave the room.

Divided from her fair judgment. One cause of her madness is gendered, Ophelia's powerlessness in the world of men. This mirrors Hamlet's two kinds of madness, one of which is also gendered: Along with his antic disposition, he's afflicted with a stereotypical male insanity, the embrace of heroic ideals and the impulse to go marching to war.

After Hamlet has his verbal duel with the gravedigger and his meditation on the skull of Yorick, a cortege approaches and Hamlet and Horatio hide among the gravestones. As they watch, the Queen strews flowers in the open grave, "Sweets to the sweet." Hamlet can't believe it: "What? The fair Ophelia?"

Laertes	Hold off the earth awhile	*[leaps in the grave]*
	Till I have caught her once more in mine arms.	
Hamlet	What is he whose grief . . . conjures the wandering stars?	
	This is I, Hamlet the Dane! Though I am not rash,	
	Yet have I in me something dangerous. . . . Hold off thy hand.	
	I loved Ophelia! Forty thousand brothers	
	Could not with all their quantity of love	
	Make up my sum.	

V.i.249 TLN 3443–3468

The stage business of two men fighting over a woman, literally, is found only in the Folio but it's never omitted in performance. Amid the hysteria, Hamlet is shocked at Laertes's rage. "What is the reason that you use me thus?/ I loved you ever." He mutters a fatalistic proverb and stalks off. Gertrude calls his bizarre behavior "momentary madness" and says that, after Hamlet recovers, he'll be peaceful as the female dove with her hatchlings—one of dozens of gender crossovers scattered through the play.

After the women are disposed of dramatically, the last quarter of the play spins the interlocking stories of Hamlet's brothers, those he holds as equals. There are similarities in how Hamlet talks to Horatio ("my dear soul. . . . hath sealed thee for herself") and Laertes ("I loved you ever"). There's affectionate irony in how he speaks of Fortinbras and in his comical but desperate jousting with the gravedigger. His attitude assumes equality in a fundamental sense—if not in birth, equality in manhood.

Horatio is obviously first among them, this astonishingly one-dimensional character. Hamlet's best friend is so artfully drawn that audiences always take him as real, like a prop or costume, and never wonder about his history. He's both a utilitarian dramatic entity (nothing but a character, the point of view of T.S. Eliot) and a real person (to Professor Bradley). Somehow the playwright gets the audience to ignore him. Why, for instance, doesn't Horatio go with Hamlet to England? Only in the final scene does he become more than one dimensional, as he takes on Hamlet's characteristic syntax and diction, speaking for him in death.

Halverson makes the droll observation that no actor ever made a name for himself playing Horatio. There are no famous stage Horatios, but he has half again as many lines as Ophelia—and key speeches. Some of his lines are barely playable ("Never believe it / I am more an antique Roman than a Dane"), so Halverson locates the power of Horatio's role in its ambiguity. Horatio is an old and intimate friend *and* a barely remembered acquaintance ("Horatio? Or I do mistake myself"). He's both encyclopedic in Danish history and unfamiliar with the drinking customs of Denmark. He's a fellow student and old enough to have witnessed old Hamlet's fight with Norway.

Halverson nails the simultaneous strangeness and familiarity of the best friend. Although it's not so clear to us, it would have been instantly obvious to Elizabethans. Hamlet early addresses him with the formal second person pronoun; Horatio is to him "you" well into the play—only in the Passion's Slave speech does he become "thou." Hamlet addresses the first player as "thou" from his first entrance and calls Guildenstern "thou" from the beginning—switching to the more formal "you" when he grows suspicious of the schoolfellows. Horatio dominates the opening and the closing scenes and does it without seeming to act either as actor or as person. His morally disinterested attitude makes him the witness whose testimony we trust. His loyalty is such a given that Claudius doesn't think to suborn him.[17]

Horatio also is a case study in psychological personality through characterization. Bert States says Horatio is a dramatic confidant who functions like the soliloquies, allowing Hamlet to think out loud. He has to be a good listener, curious—but not someone who will uncover too much too quickly. He sidesteps both psychoanalysis and postmodernism by not asking, Are dramatic characters "real," do they teach us anything about actual human beings? Such questions miss a basic continuum in human identity States says—between dreams and fiction, between myth and culture, between dramatic character and personality psychology —false dichotomies all.[18]

Alethea Hayter decried the amputation of dramatic character from "real life" when midcentury critics tried to annul psychological literary character analysis and focus only on the text. She quotes John Dover Wilson, "Horatio is not a person in actual life or a character in a novel but a piece of dramatic structure"—only to throw back in his teeth the words of his colleague, C.S. Lewis "insisting that 'the affection we feel for the Prince, and through him, for Horatio, is like a friendship in real life'." She reproaches Dover Wilson, "For the rest of us not scholars but ordinary members of the audience, the doctrine is more than hard—it is impossible."[19]

Like a friendship in real life. The scientific basis for the observation is the neuropsychological *theory of mind*, an innate function of the human brain evolved to facilitate group process. It's our instinct to ascribe to all people, some animals, and even some inanimate objects *desires, beliefs, and intentions* of their own. We reflexively endow the behavior of others with humanity in order to predict and simplify social interactions. Hayter is correct about our attribution of character-*istics* to Horatio: We evolved to do it, we can't *not* do it.

In Peter Alexander's *Hamlet: Father and Son*, there are no entries indexed for Ophelia or Gertrude, no important female scholars cited. His book embodies its own unconscious ironies, ignoring the feminine. He says Hamlet is not destroyed by a tragic flaw but rather is undone *by his virtues*. His thesis, a throwback to the Romantics, is that *the Prince achieves wholeness by means of fragmentation*: Artistic unity is achieved through opposites. He sees emotional catharsis as an end in itself and debunks the idea that Shakespeare was a pushful novice writing for bumpkins, that his audiences were too crude to spot contradictions of plot and character. The play's wholeness comes from that very inconsistency, he says, in appreciating "the care Shakespeare has taken in picturing for us the appearance of the Ghost; he was not content that the spectators should see it with their own eyes; they see it also through the eyes of the other characters." Think of it, he says, Shakespeare brought a believable ghost up from the darkness to walk about the Globe's stage "in the full light of the early afternoon" but he made it still a creature of darkness. This illusion is realized by poetry supporting the plot and the plot eliciting contradiction in characters. The Ghost is classical, heroic; the Prince intellectual, modern—contrasts present from scene one. And the "Ghost is not there merely for the thrill of it. . . . He is a moral agent in the drama, an individual in his own artistic right."

It's this contrast of properties that gives depth. When contradictory ideas are struck together, what's created is something three-dimensional born of its own internal inconsistency. Shakespeare has layered on top of the stratum of revenge a stratum of forgiveness—and does it to pose the question, *Why is it that a man's virtues help to destroy him*? Alexander cites Freud, who

> discovered that there are dreams that do not seem to offer a wish-fulfilment. Men fight over again in sleep the desperate encounters from which they may have come away maimed and wounded. Here, to adopt . . . Freud's doctrine in its relation to art, the mind seems in such terrible dreams to be embracing its own pain for some vital purpose . . . in tragedy also the mind confronts pain for some vital purpose. . . . just as in fearful dreams the suffering patient seems to be struggling to gain a mastery impossible in mere passive experience.[20]

The mind embraces its own pain for some vital purpose. Characterization is about complexity, but whether holding Yorick's skull or confronting the Ghost, "Hamlet is one and the same being," and all through the play, Shakespeare uses multiplicity to find a fundamental unity.

The grand finale of manhood and murder is Hamlet's killing the schoolfellows "not shriving-time allowed." Samuel Johnson felt the vow to kill Claudius's soul as well as his body was the play's darkest moment. But it's more a rationalization than a plan to exact immortal vengeance. How do we explain their deaths? Hamlet could have done otherwise. What makes this Renaissance genius—someone who's actually growing morally—what makes him without necessity kill his oldest friends? It's sound dramaturgy. To have Rosencrantz and Guildenstern die along with others Hamlet has touched and doomed is a nice knot at the end of a string of ironies, symmetrical, pathetic, cathartic. But does it make sense?

On the ship for England Hamlet is sleep deprived and dissociated, melancholic, lonely without his best friend, traumatized. Signing their death warrant must give him release, an explosion of displaced rage. He becomes a phallic narcissist, a creature of blood lust and appetite. The schoolfellows are reminders of his university days, so it makes sense that Hamlet regresses to adolescent impulse with them. His act makes sense too, identifying with Fortinbras's idea of honor—Hamlet feels dishonored by them. And more, it's his identification with the aggressor, the Prince is performing the same act in the same way as the King.

In "A Child Is Being Beaten" Freud links anal eroticism and perversion—it's not only a masochistic wish, it's also a defense against the wish to do the beating. Perhaps this helps explain Hamlet's unnecessary and perverse act. Does it amount to perversion? If it is, it could function like those self-restorative acts which reconstruct the fragmented self, *I kill, therefore I am*. It's certainly not a Freudian slip, sliding through the repressive barrier. It's baldly intentional. It's not a neurotic symptom, not inhibition, not compulsive repetition. It's not communication of conflict symbolized in the body, a conversion. But as a perversion, it wouldn't need to overcome the defense of repression; perversions are enabled by splitting off the act from the shame attached to it. Splitting fractures the self, and suddenly the dark contents of the soul pour out.

Stanley Cavell thinks certain images late in the play may explain earlier dramatic questions. His "deferred representation" is like the return of the repressed. Overdetermination is the rule that governs both representation and repression: Is Hamlet's act trying to tell us something, is he repeating the past in order *not* to remember it? Is Shakespeare creating this lapse to explain some dramatic action? When we first meet him, Hamlet wishes his solid flesh would melt. Is the murder of his schoolmates an echo of his wish to die, perchance to dream—suicide by proxy?[21]

We get help from Freud's "Criminals from a Sense of Guilt." Such people's crimes are done *because* they were forbidden, because doing them gives mental relief. Is Hamlet "suffering from an oppressive feeling of guilt" so that after he killed the schoolfellows, his "sense of guilt was at least attached to something"? If we substitute *shame* for *guilt* here (and we know Hamlet's shame), the answer is yes. And we do see him relieved afterward, almost post orgasmic.

But ultimately the Prince's evil act has a multiplicity of causes. It's as complex as any problem in the play. None completely explain Hamlet's murder of his friends. Again, perhaps mystery is the point. The best explanation comes from Hamlet himself: It chances in this particular man that there's a vicious mole of nature in him, and the murder of Rosencrantz and Guildenstern is his own little dram of evil. Hamlet does it just for the hell of it.

Notes

1. Reuben A. Brower, "Hamlet Hero," in *Hero & Saint: Shakespeare and the Graeco-Roman Heroic Tradition* (New York: Oxford University Press, 1971), 277–316.
2. David Wilbern, "Shakespeare's Nothing," in *Representing Shakespeare: New Psychoanalytic Essays*, Murray M. Schwartz and Coppélia Kahn, Eds. (Baltimore: The Johns Hopkins University Press, 1980), 244–263.
3. Avi Erlich, *Hamlet's Absent Father* (Princeton: Princeton University Press, 1977). Dan Jacobson, "Hamlet's Other Selves," *International Review of Psycho-Analysis* 16 (1989): 265–272.

Jacobson sees Horatio, Fortinbras, and Laertes as mirrors for Hamlet's self understanding, but "Hamlet's brothers" are not only mirrors but equals as men. In the taxonomy here, the pirate captain would be a brother; the Ghost and the player king, though male, are but spectral visitors.

4. Janet Adelman, "Man and Wife Is One Flesh: *Hamlet* and the Confrontation with the Maternal Body," in *Shakespeare's Middle Tragedies: A Collection of Critical Essays*, David Young, Ed. (Englewood Cliffs: Prentice-Hall, 1993), 29–55, 48, 50–51.
5. Coppélia Kahn, *Man's Estate: Masculine Identity in Shakespeare* (Berkeley: University of California Press, 1981).
6. Sigmund Freud, "Totem and Taboo," in *The Standard Edition of the Complete Psychological Works of Sigmund Freud*, vol. 8, James Strachey, Ed. and trans. (London: The Hogarth Press, 1913/1955), 1–255.
7. Sigmund Freud, "Civilization and its Discontents," in *The Standard Edition of the Complete Psychological Works of Sigmund Freud*, vol. 21, James Strachey, Ed. and trans. (London: The Hogarth Press, 1929/1961), 59–146, 134–135.
8. Sigmund Freud, "'A Child Is Being Beaten,' A Contribution to the Study of the Origin of Sexual Perversions," in *The Standard Edition of the Complete Psychological Works of Sigmund Freud*, vol. 17, James Strachey, Ed. and trans. (London: The Hogarth Press, 1919/1955), 177–204, 180–181.
9. Jacques Lacan, "Desire and the Interpretation of Desire in *Hamlet*," in *Literature and Psychoanalysis: The Question of Reading: Otherwise* [sic], Shoshana Felman, Ed. (Baltimore: The Johns Hopkins University Press, 1982), 11–52.
10. In Q1 Horatio tells the Queen that Hamlet sent him a letter saying Claudius plotted Hamlet's execution. The Queen doesn't seem surprised, but she asks what became of Gilderstone and Rossencraft? Horatio tells her about Hamlet's switching letters and "by great chance" having his father's seal, "So all was done without discovery." She tells Horatio she'll play along with Claudius "for a time."
11. Stefan Polatinsky and Derek Hook, "On the Ghostly Father: Lacan on Hamlet," *Psychoanalytic Review* 95 (2008): 359–385.
    Adam Phillips, "To Be or Knot to Be," review of Simon Critchley and Jamieson Webster, *The Hamlet Doctrine, London Review of Books* 35 (2013), 11–12.
12. Savvas Savvopoulos, Sotiris Manolopoulos, and Stavroula Beratis, "Repression and Splitting in the Psychoanalytic Process," *International Journal of Psychoanalysis* 92 (2011): 75–96.
13. Coppélia Kahn, *Man's Estate: Masculine Identity in Shakespeare* (Berkeley: University of California Press, 1981),133, 135.
14. Nigel Alexander, *Poison, Play, and Duel: A Study in Hamlet* (Lincoln: University of Nebraska Press, 1971), 2, 184.
15. From the beginning, flowers were her emblem, and Laertes's warning about the tender buds of spring went unheeded. Flowers are hers in the end too, strewn on her grave. The text has it in prose but here it's rendered in verse to mirror Hamlet's "numbers."
16. How could the Queen have seen what she describes? If one must have an explanation, say a merciful Gertrude is cushioning Laertes's feelings by weaving this beautiful poem. Or perhaps Gertrude herself is drowning.
17. John Halverson, "The Importance of Horatio," *Hamlet Studies* 16 (1994): 57–70.
18. Bert O. States, *Hamlet and the Concept of Character* (Baltimore: The Johns Hopkins University Press, 1992), 173, xxiv.
19. Alethea Hayter, *Horatio's Version* (1972; reprint, London: Faber and Faber, 2010), 7.
20. Peter Alexander, *Hamlet: Father and Son* (Oxford: Clarendon Press, 1955), 27–30, 74–75.
21. Stanley Cavell, *Must We Mean What We Say?* (New York: Charles Scribner's Sons, 1969).

14

"READINESS IS ALL. LET BE."

Disillusion and the Strength To Bear It

In the most important paper of his latter years, "Analysis, Terminable and Interminable," Freud admitted the limitations of psychoanalysis. He called it an "impossible profession," like teaching or public service in which one is bound to have disappointing results. Freud is disillusioned by the difficulty of neutralizing the negative transference; there are analyses that simply cannot be brought to a conclusion. There's a demonic element in humanity psychoanalysis is powerless to overcome: No matter how much positive libido exists, an "independently emerging tendency to conflict" can defeat it, a negativity whose source is some "element of free aggressiveness." This mysterious dark force is independent of the ego. It acts irrespective of libido, the life force.[1]

Mainstream psychoanalysis has trouble taking seriously Freud's return to the death instinct. Sometimes it's ascribed to age and his cancer or his horror of the Nazis. While praising his honesty, the orthodox reaction is to wonder why Freud is "paradoxically reactivating antiquated ideas." But paradox doesn't scare Freud. Writing in 1937 he knows such ideas are hard to accept, so he was "all the more pleased" to discover them anticipated by the Greek polymath Empedocles, who saw the cosmos as a perfect balance between *philia* and *neikos*, coequal forces of order and chaos, of love and strife. His tone lightens.[2]

As with Hamlet in the graveyard, the awe of death paradoxically seems to lift Freud up. Not only have his theories evolved, but this valediction is more confident, more intimate. It's reminiscent of Hamlet's Fall of a Sparrow speech. Both are saying, "Let be." Each has gone through periods of intense activity and productivity and creativity. And each—after brushes with paranoia and destructive narcissism—has reached the mental quiet that follows disillusionment.

The day Hamlet arrives back in Denmark, he and Horatio enter a graveyard where a gravedigger sings of love and death. Hamlet's struck by his light-heartedness at such a job. Horatio says long experience has given the gravedigger equanimity.

Hamlet is caught by various skulls at their feet, who they might have been—a lawyer? Or "my Lady Worm's" skull, now fit for nothing but rolling at the goal in a game of lawn bowls. Hamlet announces that he "will speak to this fellow."

But he has met his match. "Whose grave's this, sir?" Hamlet asks. The gravedigger responds, "Mine, sir," and the two are off on a fast-paced verbal duel. Hamlet asks what man it is dug for. The gravemaker says it's for no man. "What woman, then?" Hamlet asks. "For none, neither." Eventually, he finds out: For one "that was a woman, sir, but rest her soul, she's dead." The match ends with Hamlet bested and, well aware of the irony, he grumbles to Horatio how uppity the peasants are getting. He takes this opportunity to catch up on the news in Denmark. The gravedigger—perfectly deadpan—tells about young Hamlet, "mad and sent into England." Hamlet asks why England, and the gravedigger says it was because he was mad. In England he will either recover his wits or it will not matter, "There the men are as mad as he."

After pausing for the audience's laugh, the gravedigger says, "Here's a skull now" that has lain in the earth 23 years, this is "Yorick's skull, the king's jester." Hamlet, holding up the skull in amazement, recalls his happy childhood with the clown. "Alas, poor Yorick, I knew him, Horatio." Horatio tries to deflect him from morbid thoughts, but Hamlet seems to relax, grow easy in his mind thinking on the great leveler, common to kings and peasants alike.

It's all foreshadowed the day after Ophelia's burial when a subdued Hamlet tells Horatio how he escaped. Aboard ship for England, he found Claudius's letter to the English king. He broke the seal and found "an exact command" that immediately, "not to stay the grinding of the axe" his head should be struck off. He sat down and wrote in his official handwriting a new warrant. "He should those bearers put to sudden death/ Not shriving time allowed."

Reading it, Horatio says, "Why—what a king is this!" Hamlet begins to justify killing Claudius as Horatio realizes the schoolfellows were unaware of the contents of the letter they carried. He's stunned at Hamlet's sending their friends to the unprepared death the King planned for him. He asks how the substitute death warrant was sealed. Even in that, heaven was guiding events; Hamlet had his father's signet ring modeled on the Danish seal, and with it he impressed the wax. Horatio falls silent, picturing the schoolfellows like soft wax, their deaths sealed.

Hamlet Our indiscretion sometime serves us well
When our deep plots do pall. And that should teach us
There's a divinity that shapes our ends,
Rough-hew them how we will.

V.ii.8 TLN 3507–3510

After a long pause Horatio says, "So Guildenstern and Rosencrantz go to it." Hamlet shrugs. "They are not near my conscience," and he takes Claudius's original letter and slips it into his doublet. He is in possession of hard evidence at last. Justice is on his side.

In *Hamlet* scholarship, the tide turned from questions about the character's motives to the question of the meaning of the play. Scholars compared it to Greek drama in its function as religious practice and praised the vastness of its architectonic structure. The play asks questions so profound that to individualistic tragedy must be added *Hamlet* as a kind of secular worship service. Hamlet-as-Pilgrim descending into revenge and rising upward under the canopy of "heaven ordinant" culminated in the academy's final verdict: What the play is about is the ultimate mystery, the meaning of human existence.

As the play unfolds, there is more reference to Providence rising above Nature and Fortune as authors of destiny. Hamlet's been going back and forth between pagan conceptions of causality and a Christian view. Fortune and Nature were overlapping causes of human misfortune. On the arrival of the schoolfellows, Hamlet was mocking Fortune. Returned from the sea, he's starting to accept good and ill with equal thanks. Fortune is perverse but Hamlet is finding Providence, though chastening and inscrutable, a comforting idea. He goes from rage and shame to disillusionment, to the ability to tolerate sadness and ambivalence. As he moves toward acceptance, he gains a capacity to connect with others as people, not just narcissistic reflections. By the end of the Closet scene, he has healed the split in his psyche by integrating the split image of his mother. Now, he's capable of full individual particularized object relatedness.

Melanie Klein's version of original sin is ontological hatred of the mother by the infant—hatred that is not reactive but pure primal destructiveness. It begins with the newborn as a primordial ooze of rage and consuming love. To protect the mother, the infant conceptually splits her into good and bad and "directs his feelings of gratification and love towards the 'good breast,' and his destructive impulses and feelings of persecution towards what he feels to be frustrating, i.e., the 'bad breast,' " so that love and hate as well as the good and bad aspects of the mother "are largely kept apart from one another. The infant's security is based on turning the good object into an ideal one."

Klein's ideas seem bizarre at first, but image of the infant loving the "good breast" and feeling persecuted by "the bad breast" is Klein's trope for the terrifying world of the helpless newborn, who uses splitting to defend itself against danger. "These processes—that is to say splitting, denial, omnipotence and idealization—are prevalent during the first three or four months of life, which I termed the 'paranoid schizoid position.' "[3]

Klein thought the newborn alternately loves and hates the mother, depending on the experience of the moment, good or bad. This black-and-white stage is the "paranoid position," in which all infants are ruthless splitters. Then comes a stage of introjection of the mother as a whole person and development of empathy toward her, along with the development of a capacity for guilt. From this ambivalence, the infant acquires a sense of the mother's having painful feelings too and feels guilty about aggression toward her. (Klein uses *depressive* idiosyncratically; to her it's not a pathological state only, but also the name for the sad and empathic stage of development Winnicott calls a "capacity for concern.")

Klein's developmental progression from the "paranoid position" to the "depressive position" nicely fits the philosophical tone of people who make the journey late in development:

Hamlet He that killed my king and whored my mother,
Popped in between the election and my hopes —
Is't not perfect conscience to quit him with this arm?*
Horatio It must be shortly known to him from England
What is the issue of the business there.
Hamlet It will be short.
The interim's mine. And a man's life's no more
Than to say—*one.*

V.ii.64 TLN 3568–3579
* since he came between me and the crown,
isn't it justice to kill him

Quit him with this arm is with a thrusting gesture: Hamlet is asking the rhetorical question whether it's his duty to kill Claudius. Horatio's pointed non-answer turns it into a real question and makes Hamlet think. Within this speech, Hamlet's tone changes. His internal clock appears to slow down, almost to stop. Time collapses into—*one.*

This passage (here much abridged) is usually played start to finish with Hamlet in a rage, but it's more effective if there's an evolution in attitude. Hamlet is stunned at Ophelia's death, and somewhere inside he's questioning the morality of revenge.

Hamlet But I am very sorry, good Horatio,
That to Laertes I forgot myself,
For by the image of my cause I see
The portraiture of his.

V.ii.74 TLN 3579–3582

The regret is for his disgusted behavior over Laertes's ostentatious grief. But the regret is abrupt and the about-face on Laertes is difficult to pull off in performance. The actor playing Hamlet must make it real; he has to credibly go from revenge to compassion in a few lines. And the actor playing silent Horatio has to foster in the audience a belief in Hamlet's change of heart.

British psychoanalyst Harry Guntrip was a follower of Mrs. Klein. He chose object relations pioneer W.R.D. Fairbairn as his first training analyst and even more famous Donald Winnicott as his second analyst. Before he died Guntrip wrote a recollection of his analyses with these two towering figures. His memoir captures their theories but, more, it illustrates how disillusionment figures into the termination of a psychoanalysis.[4]

Guntrip became a psychoanalyst in order to cure his own inability to feel *real*, as he put it, which he attributed to "total amnesia for a severe trauma at the age of three and a half years, over the death of a younger brother" Percy. Guntrip's attempt to recover the direct memory of a dead 2-year-old boy in his mother's lap weaves through the story from beginning to end. For his analysis Guntrip chooses Fairbairn because he was a leading expert on deprived children. But soon he and Fairbairn are wrangling over whether Guntrip has an Oedipus complex. Fairbairn feels it's key to the pathology, Guntrip feels Fairbairn is blinded by his own Oedipus with Freud. This analysis runs to a 1,000 hours over 10 years. As Fairbairn grows aged and infirm, Guntrip feels he's made the analyst into the dying Percy, and Guntrip can neither heal nor abandon him. Worse, he can't tell Fairbairn he's sure the strain will literally kill the analyst. At some point he starts to crave an analysis with Winnicott, increasingly prominent and also famous for the treatment of deprived children. Guntrip eventually says goodbye to Fairbairn, but it doesn't read like a real termination.

By now we know all about Guntrip's mother's rage and depression during his childhood. In her old age she confessed to him that when her sister died, she was terribly alone and "tried keeping a dog" but she had to give it up. The reason was, she said, she "couldn't stop beating it." This part of his mother Guntrip knows all too well, but he never acknowledges any identification with her rage and sadism. The analysis with Winnicott is much shorter, about 150 hours. But from the first session, Winnicott comes across as so calm, warm, and strong that it almost doesn't matter what interpretations he makes.

In vivid quotations, Guntrip captures Winnicott's voice, so this second analysis feels alive. Even in the first session Winnicott assures him that Guntrip did have a bit of time with a good enough mother at some point. Winnicott supposedly says that Guntrip's presence helps him too—a huge relief to Guntrip, who begins to feel he is not so bad after all; he extrapolates that he is a "good enough mother" to himself too. (If you have trouble following Winnicott, it does not matter. His patients seem to have had no difficulty.)

There is, however, one resistance. The single idea of Winnicott that Guntrip will not accept—and which Winnicott presents several times—is that Guntrip is not fully aware of his "own primitive sadism, the baby's ruthlessness and cruelty" as Winnicott puts it. Unmentioned by Guntrip is that Winnicott never digs for the negative maternal transference—but it seems to the reader that Winnicott is content to leave all Guntrip's rage projected onto Fairbairn.

One day early in 1971 Guntrip gets word Winnicott has died. That night he has a dream of his mother, in black, immobilized, ignoring him. This inaugurates 2 months of evocative dreams finally culminating in his recovering at last the visual and affective memory of the dead brother Percy he has been searching for most of his life. And with it he has found his true self. Guntrip died in February of 1975, 4 years later.

Three subplots relevant to transference, disillusion, and termination weave through the Guntrip story: First, he had the persistent fantasy that his rage could literally kill Fairbairn. He actually thought he saved Fairbairn's life by terminating. Second, Guntrip never really terminated with Winnicott. But his death triggered

Guntrip's final missing piece of psychoanalysis—suggesting Guntrip believed the same of Winnicott as he had Fairbairn: Guntrip's rage would kill Winnicott, that Guntrip had to wait until after Winnicott was safely dead of natural causes. Then Guntrip could finally remember his dead brother Percy and activate and resolve the deadly negative transference. Third, none of these three giants in the history of psychoanalysis truly was able—or even wished—to terminate analysis.

All psychoanalyses terminate badly, otherwise they never end at all. The "termination" of a psychoanalysis is a big deal. Nobody is ever perfected, no analysis is ever complete, but termination is exalted in the literature as the cure of cures. Freud was frank about how seldom his cases terminated, and he never devised a protocol for the process. Only a fraction "terminate" in the strict sense of the word, with the analyst agreeing the patient is ready, symptoms in remission, transference neurosis interpreted. Despite much ado about cure, the patient's disposition to transference is never extinguished. Often, it's a process more like exhaustion. Or triggered by externals in the life of the patient—job, finances, illness, death. The analyst is not a disinterested party in a financial sense, so there's always more to analyze. The typical treatment bumps along to a disillusioned halt with patient and analyst sadder but wiser—or worse, an "as if" termination when two people in denial congratulate themselves they've done it right.

Janet Malcolm ends her mordant profile of the New York psychoanalytic scene with the observation that patients have to terminate, but not analysts, in virtue of the mere fact of their becoming analysts. They identify themselves with their own analysts, which defends against grieving. If termination is facing the inevitability of death, then "analysts never grow up and never have to die." They remain "Peter Pans, indefinitely staving off adulthood and extinction in the Never-Never Land of analytic practice." So "the literature of termination is vague, unfocussed, trivial, off the point, evasive, and uncomprehending."[5]

Malcolm's own termination is told in two different versions. Comparing texts side by side shows how the last two paragraphs of her book silently amend her original piece in the *New Yorker Magazine*. It had ended "We shook hands as we always did. I felt tears welling in my eyes, and didn't look to see if there were any in his."[6]

Her later version is without tears and even a bit dismissive toward the analyst. But it perfectly parallels the post-termination working-through process. Malcolm is more removed, more neutral toward the analyst in the rewrite months later, when she emphasizes his limitations and downplays his appeal. So she exemplifies how successful terminations turn—toward reality. To end a perfect analysis with a cured patient is not really the grail that psychoanalysis used to claims. Disillusion sets in, entropy prevails. Perhaps the better idea is that a good psychoanalysis doesn't win by "working-through" termination, but it loses gracefully, admitting its own interminability. *Let be.*

A case study in therapeutic disillusionment—an old man and a 4-year-old girl: He's got end stage heart disease, she's terrified of a dark witch inside her. She's fighting for sanity, hatred is eating her up. The man is Donald Winnicott. The girl is Gabrielle, her pet name is the Piggle. The story of their analysis, sixteen on-demand sessions ending when she was five, was published after Winnicott's death.[7]

Even when readers don't completely follow the story, they're struck by Winnicott's "holding environment," his intuitiveness, and the Piggle's courage as she's trying to recover her "good enough mother." The patient was firstborn to Oxbridge intellectuals, the mother rather cold and rigid but the father quite maternal and warm. She was well until a baby sister was born after she was a year old. At that time she developed nightmares and a too-grown up way of acting and speaking, a high pitched stilted false voice. The parents told Winnicott about her symptoms, about "the black baba," a "babacar," and "black mummy," all apparently a part of her internal persecutory world—the evil baby, the evil mother, and the container for both.

"I'm too shy," she says at the first meeting as she is following Winnicott into the office. He thinks to himself that shyness shows a sense of self, the beginning of a formed ego, an appreciation of the inner world versus the outer world. He sits cross legged on the floor and turns to what will be their transitional object for the session. "Already I had made friends with the teddy-bear who was sitting on the floor by the desk." And he means it, he was already in the transitional space. "Bring teddy over here, I want to show him the toys." Winnicott is impressed with the Piggle's precocity but worries that it is premature ego development. Her little sister came just before she was ready for "simple ambivalence." He is thinking that to cope she either had to become too grown up or become a bad baby herself—or both, with a split in her ego.[8]

This session and several following it are explorations of her guilt over the "black baba" which seems to be a fusion of her hate, the new baby, and herself. It travels in a "babacar" that belongs to the hateful "black mummy," a thinly disguised version of her own mother. Winnicott effortlessly engages with the Piggle and embodies early on the mirroring function of the mother. He is reflecting back to her that she's not *identical* with her hatred. He's interposing himself in the splitting defense between her positive transference and her hatred. This moves her through the primitive anxiety that was constricting her into a false self.

Midway in the analysis, she wants to send a thank you present to a woman that used to work for the family, someone that Piggle was fond of, and who left their home. Winnicott says in what must be one of the more cryptic footnotes in the history of psychoanalysis, *Gratitude implies acceptance of separateness, of the reality principle, a fruit of disillusionment.* Being grateful implies an acknowledgment of dependency; fusion of love and hate, attainment of ambivalence and gratitude mark a step toward empathy for others, a "sense of concern." It also signals the child has developed sufficiently to experience guilt and shame—and to use sad feelings to make reparation. To apologize.

Winnicott always said he pitied people who are "merely sane." He proves himself to be beyond sane here, as his own health gets worse. After his heart attack, Piggle mentions the long trip into London to see him and strings many toys together to make a long train. "The long distance has to do with the time between now and your last visit, and Gabrielle is taking a long time to find out if I am alive." She tries to defend against anxiety, asking, "When will your birthday be? I want to give you some presents." He parries, "What about my death day?" She says something about how long a gift takes to get to its destination. "If I were dead it would take longer still," he keeps the pressure on. Then she finally does allow herself to feel, "You would not open it because you would be dead. It's terrible."

The theme of shyness comes full circle in their last session. They are sitting reading and he says, "So the Winnicott you invented was all yours and he's now finished with, and no one else can ever have him." They read some more and he caps off the treatment. "I know when you are really shy, and that is when you want to tell me that you love me." And she smiled and nodded. She had passed through disillusion to reality and acceptance, through hate to gratitude and concern. With that comes the ability to make restitution, to make a true heartfelt apology.[9]

The courtier Osric brings a message. The King requests Hamlet duel Laertes. The King—says Osric fanning himself with his feathered hat—is betting on Hamlet with short odds since Laertes is a ranked fencer. Hamlet wants to reconcile with Laertes, but all this filigree is too much.

Hamlet	Sir, his definement suffers no perdition in you, though I know to divide him inventorially would dazzle the arithmetic of memory . . . his semblable is his mirror. . . .
Osric	Your lordship speaks most infallibly. . . . You are not ignorant of what excellence Laertes is at his weapon?
Hamlet	I dare not confess that, lest I should compare with him in excellence. But to know a man well were to know himself. . . . if it please his majesty. . . . Let the foils be brought. The gentleman willing and the King hold his purpose, I will win for him if I can. If not, I'll gain nothing but my shame.

V.ii.113 TLN 361.0+6–3642

Even in flights of magniloquence, Hamlet emulates the stoics. Asked whether he knows what excellence Laertes is, he demurs: To know Laertes he would have to equal him, and Hamlet refuses to presume. He's accepted Claudius's wager. Fortune has him in her toils. He has a premonition, but he hears the voice of Providence. Horatio has no illusion this is a fair fight.

Horatio	You will lose, my lord.
Hamlet	I do not think so. Since he went into France I have been in continual practice. . . . But thou wouldst not think how ill all's here about my heart. But it is no matter.
Horatio	I will forestall their repair hither and say you are not fit.

Hamlet Not a whit. We defy augury. There's a special providence in the fall of a sparrow. If it be now, 'tis not to come. If it be not to come, it will be now. If it be not now, yet it will come. The readiness is all, since no man of aught he leaves knows what is't to leave betimes.* Let be.

V.ii.209 TLN 3658–3673+1

* dying prematurely, no man knows what future pain he leaves behind

The stage beyond the mourning inherent in the depressive position is acceptance of blame. Selfless apology shows the individual can rise above narcissistic aims. It signals attainment of true object relatedness. Hamlet's apology to Laertes seems dishonest and cowardly to many. Is he hiding behind a madness that he only simulated? How does he intend the apology, is it some awkward insanity defense?

Hamlet Give me your pardon, sir. I have done you wrong.
But pardon it as you are a gentleman. This presence
knows . . . how I am punished. . . . With a sore distraction.
What I have done . . . I here proclaim was madness.
Was it Hamlet wronged Laertes? Never Hamlet.
If Hamlet from himself be taken away
And, when he's not himself, does wrong Laertes,
Then Hamlet does it not. . . . Who does it then?
His madness. . . . Hamlet it is . . . that is wronged.
Let my disclaiming from a purposed evil
Free me so far in your most generous thoughts
That I have shot my arrow o'er the house
And hurt my brother.

V.ii.226 TLN 3678–3696

But analysis of all three texts of the play—and film versions of the scene correctly played—shows the apology is exactly right: Hamlet is able to empathize with Laertes. In his image, as he says, Hamlet sees the reflection of his own. Laertes is human to him, and Hamlet too has become human. He wasn't before, that was his real madness, a state of dead and icy narcissism.

So arrives in due course the paradigmatic duel in all drama, the shuffled weapons, the poisoned cup, the corpse littered stage. When silence falls, it's for Horatio to tie up the loose ends. He bows to the new Danish king and the court, *who look pale and tremble*—us, of course. He walks out on the thrust stage where late the sweet Prince stood and turns to the house.

Horatio What is it you would see?
If aught of woe or wonder, cease your search. . . .
And let me speak to the yet unknowing world

> Of carnal, bloody and unnatural acts,
> Of accidental judgments, casual slaughters,
> Of deaths put on by cunning and for no cause —
> And in this upshot, purposes mistook,
> Fallen on the inventors' heads —
> Of that I shall have also cause to speak,
> And from his mouth whose voice will draw no more. . . .
> *V.ii.362* TLN 3855–3889

Through a strange psychic cannibalism we take in the people that are important to us. This "identification with the lost object" is everywhere. Freud felt that beloved others are "precipitated" inside us through our longing for them. Following Freud, Klein and Winnicott added the essential ingredients of death and destruction: The original maternal object could survive outside us—then be taken back inside—only after we tried with all our might to destroy that object. Shakespeare well understood identification, and he ends his play with it.

Standing amid the blood and corpses, the rapiers and cups, the overturned furniture moments after Death has passed by, Horatio becomes three dimensional. Instead of a dramatic prop, he becomes the voice of the hero. Death all around him, and changed by seizing the cup of his own eternity, Horatio takes on the diction and cadence of the Prince. With *woe or wonder* he reprises the antitheses that bind together the whole play. With *see . . . speak . . . hear* Horatio places the final punctuation on the themes of eye, mouth, and ear—and the voice of Hamlet that will draw breath no more. An *upshot* is the final tie-breaking arrow in archery, and this is it—*carnal, cunning, casual* Death with *no cause*—a careless shot over the house that hurt a brother. Horatio is now the voice of Hamlet, with its familiar alliteration and assonance, those doubled phrases, that signature repetition.

In the final chapter we terminate with *Hamlet* and Freud by analyzing the Ghost, the play's most complex character after Hamlet. It's a termination that also disposes of Freud's Oedipus complex. Hamlet indeed does hesitate in the first half of the play, for motives only partly conscious, so hidden "double business" does lead to delay. But not exactly for the reasons Freud thought.

Notes

1. Sigmund Freud, "Analysis, Terminable and Interminable," in *The Standard Edition of the Complete Psychological Works of Sigmund Freud*, vol. 23, James Strachey, ed. and trans. (London: The Hogarth Press, 1937/1964), 216–253.
2. Harold P. Blum, "Analysis Terminable and Interminable: A Half Century Retrospective," *International Journal of Psycho-Analysis* 68 (1987): 37–47.
3. Melanie Klein, "The Origins of Transference," *International Journal of Psycho-Analysis* 33 (1952): 433–438.
4. Harry Guntrip, "My Experience of Analysis with Fairbairn and Winnicott (How Complete a Result Does Psycho-Analysis Achieve?)," *International Review of Psycho-Analysis* 2 (1975): 145–156.

5. Janet Malcolm, *The Impossible Profession* (New York: Jason Aronson, 1981), 155.
6. Janet Malcolm, "Profiles, Aaron Green" *New Yorker*, November 24, 1980, 55–133; December 1, 1980, 54–152.
7. Donald W. Winnicott, *The Piggle: An Account of the Psychoanalytic Treatment of a Little Girl* (Madison: International Universities Press, 1977).
8. Winnicott, *Piggle*, 9, 17, 96.
9. Ibid, 124, 189, 198.

15

THE FINAL CURTAIN

The Ghost and the Death Instinct

Fortinbras, the new Danish king, greets the ultimate antagonist. He surveys a stage littered with corpses and salutes, one prince to another.

> O proud Death,
> What feast is toward in thine eternal cell
> That thou so many princes at a shot
> So bloodily hast struck?
>
> *V.ii.365* TLN 3857–3860

The image of Death is medieval, phallic, warlike, bloody. But for Freud in "The Theme of the Three Caskets," Death is a pagan goddess. From Lear's daughters to Portia's boxes, from gold, silver and lead to the sun, the moon and the earth, Freud meditates on the "sacred nature of the number three." Absent in this charming paper of Freud are ideas that offended his critics—infantile sexuality, bisexuality, and penis envy. But Freud never ignores incest: Shakespeare's plays represent the three relationships a man has with woman—the mother, the mate, and Mother Earth. It's "in vain that an old man yearns for the love of woman as he had it first from his mother; the third of the Fates alone, the silent Goddess of Death, will take him into her arms."[1]

Freud not only saw sex and death in *Hamlet* but the inevitable struggle between fathers and sons. To him it was no accident that *Hamlet* coincided with John Shakespeare's approaching death, and he thought it stirred in William a universal oedipal ambivalence. Freud's notion that the play reveals something about the playwright and his father must be read with severe skepticism. Still, it's plausible. John Shakespeare was a glover who worked tanned animal skins; a tanner would have had a social station not much above a butcher's, but Shakespeare's father climbed higher. He rose to the level of mayor in Stratford. While later he had fallen to skipping church, possibly to avoid the debt collector, toward the end of his life the father was lofted by the status of his famous son. Before he died his son applied for a family coat of arms and was eventually elevated to "gentleman" status. So whatever climbing John might have begun, William continued—but surely not without a sense of the ironies involved.

Lines in *Hamlet* evoke the pursuit of John and William of the Shakespeare coat of arms. The gravedigger jokes about the biblical Adam as a gentleman, and the first ever to bear arms, by which he means not heraldic insignia but the upper extremities. Hamlet jokes with Horatio about the social-climbing peasant being right on the heels of the courtier. But most suggestive, a passage on death and the tanner:

Hamlet	How long will a man lie in the earth ere he rot?
Gravedigger	Faith. If he be not rotten before he die—as we have many pocky* corpses nowadays that will scarce hold the laying in—he will last you some eight year or nine year. A tanner will last you nine year.
Hamlet	Why he more than another?
Gravedigger	Why, sir, his hide is so tanned with his trade that he will keep out water a great while. And your water is a sore decayer of your whoreson dead body.

V.i.164 TLN 3353–3361

* syphilitic

Freud thought oedipal motifs in *Hamlet* reflected the playwright's relationship with his son as well. The play follows by 4 years the death of Hamnet Shakespeare (1585–1596). Noting the identity of names, Freud felt there would be guilt in the father over the normal oedipal rivalry, which would need to be worked through after the son's death. Freud suggests the play was what psychoanalysis would come to call grief work. It's work to process guilt toward the dead. Hope for artistic immortality runs all through Shakespeare, as does continuity in the child one leaves behind. But in 1600, Hamnet is dead, and William as he writes knows the name Shakespeare stops with him. Now the coat of arms is mere vanity of vanities.

Hamlet	Horatio . . . dost thou think Alexander looked of this fashion i'th' earth? To what base uses we may return? Why may not imagination trace the noble dust of Alexander till he find it stopping a bunghole? . . . Alexander died. Alexander was buried. Alexander returneth into dust. Of earth we make loam. And why, of that loam whereto he was converted, might they not stop a beer barrel?

Imperious Cæsar, dead and turned to clay,
Might stop a hole, to keep the wind away.

V.i.195 TLN 3382–3401

Hamnet Shakespeare died in 1596, the year William applied for a coat of arms. If you pull out a magnifying glass and look at a clear photograph of Shakespeare's last will and testament, you see "Hamnet Sadler" as one of the witnesses. Hamnet Sadler stood as godfather to his namesake, Hamnet Shakespeare. In addition to the witness signature, Hamnet Sadler is named in an interlinear insertion in the body of the testament, on the previous page as "Hamlett Sadler." In this addition, Shakespeare left *Hamlett* Sadler money for a memorial ring. This suggests *Hamlet* and *Hamnet* were pronounced the same, since the insertion was made by someone writing from dictation. If you pronounce *Hamlet* and *Hamnet* aloud, you barely hear a difference; the medial *en* and *el* sound identical. And Elizabethans pronounced the *el* and the *en* the same after a median *em*, for example *chimney* and *chimbley*.[2]

Scholars don't credit Freud with the Hamnet-*Hamlet* connection as grief work, but think for a moment about Shakespeare physically writing the play. Try to imagine what it feels like to write over and over your son's name, hundreds of times. By flickering candle, the shadow of the lost object falls upon the page as the pen races across it, line after line.

Earlier we compared the narcissistic shame of the Ghost and the unconscious shame of "prisoners of childhood." There is a related concept, *destructive narcissism*. This selfish ruthlessness is interwoven with a controversial idea Freud called the "death instinct." In 1920 Freud introduced his theory of dialectically opposed life and death instincts. In this view the death instinct bubbles up from the deepest part of the psyche, and from the beginning of life is directed outward against the world. He thought hate evolved before love, so primordial aggression was the starting point for development. But the death instinct, he said, was not seen in its pure form since it soon fused with the life instinct. The death instinct could only be detected indirectly from the destruction it caused.[3]

Freud never perfected his concept of life and death instincts, but he would occasionally use the metaphor to explain "moral masochism" and the "negative therapeutic reaction" in unanalyzable patients. His pessimism about its power to destroy analysis deepened as he aged; he concluded it was beyond the reach of the analyst's interpretations in the analytic process: Only if the death instinct emerged as overt negative transference hatred toward the analyst was there hope of analyzing it. But the dragon had to come out of the cave of its own accord before the analyst could engage it.

The concept of a death instinct passed from view as ego psychology refined itself. Psychoanalysis always yearned for scientific respectability, and the idea of a grim reaper inside the psyche smacked of superstition. The concept faded, except from the fertile mind of Melanie Klein. She insisted on aggression as the primary drive in the earliest stage of infancy, her "paranoid position," and she emphasized the role of primitive murderous envy as a normal part of child development. She described the result when this primal rage is blocked: It thwarts healthy development of the newborn from the "paranoid position" into the "depressive position" of the toddler. She worried about primal rage. If it reemerged in the transference, it could destroy a psychoanalysis.

The few psychoanalytic papers that exist on the death instinct owe a debt to Mrs. Klein; they tend to be based on clinical observations of patients for whom *identification with death* is a coping mechanism. Herbert Rosenfeld starts with Freud's fusion of the two instincts, life and death. But he finds that, in destructive narcissism *contra* Freud, the life instinct doesn't tame the death instinct; the death instinct takes over the life instinct. The life and death instincts remain split, in different parts of the psyche, each unaware of the other. The raw death instinct creates a *grandiose self image.* Once the death instinct has triumphed, the ego is immune to the conscience. Any threat to self-idealization becomes the enemy; an arrogant grandiose self is engorged by the autoerotic thrill of superiority. Aggression gets erotized, not neutralized, and its raw energies are converted into perversions.[4]

Fetishes, addictions, and perversions are not only ends in themselves but also serve as coping behaviors. In normal development, psychosexual experiences (foreplay, fantasies, enactments) act as psychic organizers: The intense physical and affective charge of an orgasm is like a memory hook that a part of the self is hung on for safekeeping. And just as sexual experiences function as psychic glue in normal development, so do they aid repair of the self in damaged individuals who suffered neglect by parents. One theory of perversions (now called *paraphilias*) is that the individual is trying to fix a broken self image. The attempted "repair" is done by engaging in an intense, forbidden act which has a reparative personal symbolic meaning. The hidden fantasy is that these intensely felt acts triumphantly restore the existence of the self: Unconsciously the sadomasochistic fetishist is fantasizing, *I rape and murder—therefore I am*!

Rosenfeld spent a good part of his career trying to psychoanalyze destructive narcissists. He describes the pit of despair they go down into as they're in daily relationship with the analyst; his observations ring true to experienced clinicians. Such ruthless individuals have hidden under their pride and cruelty a psychotic self. They are stuck in Klein's paranoid-schizoid position, and the paranoid death wish gets focused on the analyst in the transference. Freud lost hope of analyzing the negative transference in such individuals, but Rosenfeld describes stages of developmental repair in the destructive narcissist in psychoanalysis: Over time there is an increase in sadistic rituals in search of self-soothing; flights from psychic pain by means of self-numbing addictive behaviors; acute hypochondriacal terrors of impending death; flight into a delusional notion of death as a Nirvana-like state; and suicidal fantasies or suicide itself. But with luck and persistence these can sometimes be worked through.

Destructive narcissists are analyzable but, like Freud, Rosenfeld eventually concludes it's not possible to analyze the pure death instinct in a clinical situation. The only hope, he feels, is for the patient to allow some part of the libido that's a hostage to death to become attached the analyst. This evokes Freud's definition of psychoanalysis as "a cure through love" and asks again the ancient question, *Is love stronger than death*?

In Soliloquy 6 Hamlet refused to kill Claudius until he could destroy his soul—justice because King Hamlet was poisoned while sleeping, taken unprepared and sent to Purgatory. This foreshadows Hamlet's revenge on Rosencrantz and Guildenstern when he learns Claudius arranged for him his father's fate, to be taken unaware in his sins "fresh as May."

Hamlet I found, Horatio,
A royal knavery—an exact command
No, not to stay the grinding of the axe,
My head should be struck off.
. . . I sat me down, devised a new commission . . .
That—on the view and knowing of these contents —
He should the bearers put to sudden death,
Not shriving time allowed.
Horatio So Guildenstern and Rosencrantz go to it?
Hamlet They are not near my conscience.

V.ii.18 TLN 3518–3562

Not to stay the grinding of the axe and *Not shriving time allowed* mirror each other. Horatio says nothing, but he may be sensing how this story ends.

Ambassador The sight is dismal,
And our affairs from England come too late
. . . To tell him his commandment is fulfilled,
That Rosencrantz and Guildenstern are dead.

V.ii.367 TLN 3861–3865

Hamlet's dying request is that Horatio tell all the events great and small motivating him. Certainly Horatio won't mention the Ghost but how much, one wonders, will he disclose of Hamlet's vicious murder of the schoolfellows?

None. He won't forget how Hamlet faced the Ghost alone, how he alone was the object of its macabre attentions. He'll remember Hamlet's horror of the unprepared death, fearing not so much Purgatory as hell. Horatio will understand and he will forgive. But as he comes to find out, the deaths of Rosencrantz and Guildenstern are doubly ironic: In the end Hamlet too dies unshriven.[5]

Psychoanalytic literature on the death instinct is almost nonexistent, but Stephen Rush studied patients who are "At One with Death." He feels much of the work on destructive narcissism, from Freud to the present, is missing one important idea: The literature may be graphic about the narcissist's nightmares, suicidal impulses, sadomasochistic enactments, cruelty unto death—but psychoanalysis tells the story from the wrong point of view, from the internal victim's point of view. This makes sense, since it is the victim that gets the analysis. Yet what needs to happen, Rush says, is the analyst must make contact with a split-off part of the destructive narcissist's self that hides behind and tortures the other part of the self.

One of Freud's early ideas is *identification with the aggressor* as seen in normal development when people take into themselves qualities of people they love and fear. He described how the little boy is afraid of the power of the father while loving and admiring him. By becoming like the father, the son both improves his behavior and relationship with the father, and feels more powerful himself. Rush describes identification with the aggressor, death.

> The psyche may seize death, which is like a ravening beast at its throat, and make it its own, a part of the self. In the absence of a protecting sensuous mother . . . the most vital force around appears to be that which is inflicting the distress. . . . The destructiveness may come from a person, an illness, a circumstance, or an accident. . . . The power of the destructiveness becomes idealized and re-created. The destroyer is then an internal object.[6]

Mastering trauma means actually becoming master through identification. Destructive narcissism becomes a two-person affair, a relationship between the self and a *sadistic internal figure* built on the idealization of power. There is "an intervening creation of an idealized internal object, created from the experience of the horror, with whom the individual feels identified."

The idea is that, in creating the death instinct concept, Freud found a psychodynamic equivalent of the second law of thermodynamics, that the universe is proceeding inexorably toward destruction. With humankind, the knowledge of death, "the tendency of life to yield to gravity and come to a stop, reverberates in the psyche, producing movement toward disintegration." These intimations of mortality become "the spark to ignite mankind's destructiveness." Hopefully, though, with the metaphor of the death instinct, evil can be faced as humankind's tragic destiny.

> Some live with a lethal nemesis, a dopplegänger who is at one with death. . . . The idea of a destructive desire in one's own mind that secretly seeks to harm the mind itself might seem bizarre, were there not such an overwhelming abundance of evidence. . . . on the world stage . . . how readily masses of people can be recruited to enact extremes of destructiveness.[7]

At one with death. In most psychoanalyses, the victim of the sadistic introject is supported, pitied, and even treated—but *as victim.* "Too often, only half the narcissistic pair is analyzed." What needs to happen is for the analyst to dig away at the dependency of the sadistic introject, since even it has a "yearning for the breast." Always kept in mind is the dual nature of the object of analysis, the grandiose sadistic internal object *plus* its internal victim. Bit by bit, the patient's grandiosity is exchanged for satisfaction of the reawakening need for love.

One must summon to the battle with the death instinct all that the psychoanalyst has ever personally known of hatred; the analyst's own tormenting internal objects have to be acknowledged so there's no unconscious collusion to deny murderous rage. But analysis fails if there is too little life instinct. So Freud, Klein, Rosenfeld, and now Rush, are all saying the patient can be analyzed only if there is libido that can make contact with the analyst despite the death instinct. Destructive aggression as a defense against inner terror is treatable in psychoanalysis. But killing just for the hell of it is another matter. They all seem to draw a line beyond which are the unanalyzable people that have only death instinct and no love at all—sometimes called evil "malignant narcissists" in contrast with mere "destructive narcissists."

Destructive narcissists are like the Hamlet described by Wilson Knight in "The Embassy of Death." Knight's Hamlet contaminates the court of Denmark with his death fetish and eventually poisons it. Knight sees Hamlet as a man suborned by hell, so all he touches dies. His arguments are masterful—and disturbing if you like Hamlet. Wilson Knight coldly hates him.[8]

The atmosphere of *Hamlet* is a conflict between health and disease. Knight sees the court as a celebration of life over death. Denmark is not rotten, it's just fertile, like a barnyard. The other characters embody humanity in all its mixtures. Even Claudius's murder of his brother is merely human, in contrast to inhuman Hamlet, who is

> pale with the consciousness of death. . . . the only discordant element, the only hindrance to happiness, health, and prosperity: a living death. . . . Hamlet's soul is sick. The symptoms are, horror at the fact of death and an equal detestation of life, a sense of uncleanliness and evil in the things of nature; a disgust at the physical body of man; bitterness, cynicism, hate.[9]

The burden of remembering which the Ghost places on Hamlet is fundamentally devilish. "If the spirit had been kind, it would have prayed that Hamlet might forget." But his memory is too perfect, his brain too cold, his intellect too sharp. He is a superman among men, one who has an unclean, cynical connection with death. When he says, " 'The spirit that I have seen/ May be the devil,' it was. It was the devil of the knowledge of death, which possesses Hamlet and drives him from misery and pain to increasing bitterness, cynicism, murder, and madness."

Knight's literary ideas attract psychoanalytic notice. In a hybrid of Kohut's self psychology and existential philosophy, the idea of a hero in love with death fits perfectly the narcissistic coping mechanism of splitting. We saw that the exploitation of the child as a parent's transitional object or selfobject does two things. It stimulates the child's grandiosity. And it devalues the child by making it into a thing. The child (having a split self) then repeats the same pattern by parsing the world into idealized and devalued images. This splitting characterizes Hamlet's investment in death. As his father is idealized and his mother debased—and neither realistically seen—his world and self are polarized. This same mechanism is used on death, so that "just as Hamlet fails in his confrontation with the reality of father, mother, and self, so too does he fail in his confrontation with the reality of death." His parents have "conspired with their child to deny and evade the facticity of death.

And in denying death they have denied too that with which it is inextricably bound, the facticity of life."[10]

So Hamlet is in love with death, but it is a "death" he created and romanticized through splitting. The lack of reality in his contact with death keeps him from reality in his contact with life. This would explain Hamlet's behavior in the graveyard, where he's truly baffled at Laertes's rage and concerned more with the formalities of mourning than the fact of Ophelia's death.

Wilson Knight wrote a sequel revising his analysis of Hamlet's character; in the interim, he'd studied Nietzsche. He describes *Hamlet* as a kind of inverse morality play, parodied by Hamlet's play within a play, which is "satiric and Jonsonian; his philosophy death ridden . . . his sex disgust Swiftian." Hamlet's "left divided, all but insane, spasmodic. More: he is ill-mannered which as we shall see, is perhaps worse." In "*Hamlet* Reconsidered" Knight takes note of Hamlet's growth over the course of the play and sees him as a Christ figure that strove for, but didn't make it to, redemption. He's receptive to *both and* interpretations—suicide or revenge, being or nonbeing, mind or heart, life or death, good or evil, pagan or Christian—Knight comes to terms with the antinomies: For any character, speech, or problem, "Probably all these meanings are somehow contained." But, still, for Knight, Hamlet remains ugly.[11]

Knight's cold eye on Hamlet relieved a cloying sweetness throughout the critical history of the play. It's one of a small handful of negative reactions—Salvador de Madariaga, T.S. Eliot, and D.H. Lawrence being notable others (with Samuel Johnson occupying a category all his own). But Wilson Knight had a subtler sense of the play than most; and he was a well respected scholar of Shakespeare, able to stand up to John Dover Wilson and others who tried to explain away Hamlet's bad character. But Wilson Knight's best insight is on Hamlet's abominable treatment of Ophelia. She represents his last chance for life and love, and Hamlet destroys her. By doing so, Hamlet loses his only chance to escape soul death, he loses his salvation—romantic love. Knight's perspective allows a unique interpretation—and a nice solution—for one of the stickier *Hamlet* problems: His bursting into Ophelia's chamber. If he's faking madness to get her to spread disinformation to the court, then Hamlet is viciously deceiving her and ruthlessly setting her up for monstrous cruelty. But Knight says Hamlet comes to Ophelia sincerely and for reasons of his own. At this point it's a couple of weeks since he saw the Ghost. Ophelia has obeyed her father and repelled Hamlet's advances. The director of a production generally has two notions to work from, Hamlet's faking or not faking madness. And a film maker has two ways to present it, from Ophelia's point of view as written—or cinematically. In Zeffirelli's film and in Olivier's, the encounter is depicted directly onscreen, and in both, Hamlet's only pretending madness.

The other possibility, a sincere Hamlet, is seen in Almereyda's film. Here, the encounter is depicted not narrated. Hamlet is wounded and grieving and lovesick, and altogether believable. In Branagh, Gielgud, and Richardson, the encounter is narrated by Ophelia as Shakespeare wrote it, and you must decide by hearing her—and picturing him—whether Hamlet is manipulating. Or is he crazed and desperate for something from her? Or perhaps, in some measure, both?

Wilson Knight argues that he is not play acting, this is real Hamlet. Elsewhere in the play, Hamlet's species of "madness" is not mute and disorganized like this, it's sharp wit, used like a rapier. This behavior described by Ophelia is incoherent, *unlike his behavior anywhere else in the play. With one exception*—just after Hamlet has seen the Ghost. In Knight's reading, Hamlet knows Ophelia is his last hope. The image of the Ghost has been festering in his soul for weeks while Ophelia refused to see him.

So in his state of fearing the Ghost and longing for Ophelia, he can't stand it and bursts into her chamber. Hamlet is not so much antic or mad as he is *possessed*. A devil is wrestling with the angel of life inside him. For weeks he's been watching his love, his life, his soul fade away. Ophelia is his only chance. Looking at her now and trying to memorize her image—looking into her eyes, holding her wrist, nodding to himself—he feels his soul pulled another direction; he feels the grip of the Ghost's command, *Remember*! And as Hamlet looks back at her, unable to stop himself, he is slowly pulled from the room.

Where does destructive narcissism leave off and just plain evil begin? What defines the barely analyzable souls Rosenfeld and Rush tried to understand, what distinguishes them from the evil narcissists Freud felt were beyond help? And what of the particular men Hamlet describes that have a "vicious mole of nature"? Are these separate categories? Are destructive narcissists partly inhuman—or are they just us under different circumstances? Superimpose two questions: *Is evil nothing more or less than the pure death instinct—unalloyed with love, libido, and life*? And a second question, *Is the Ghost a devil or is it the spirit of Hamlet's father*? Is the Ghost a depiction of an evil malignant narcissist? Or is it a destructive narcissist with some chance of salvation? In grappling with evil and the riddle of the Ghost, we come to realize they're in some sense the same question asked different ways. If we answer one, we answer the other.

Shakespeare's was a historical moment that marked the passing of a medieval sense of self and the birth of an early modern self. Polonius's advice to Laertes grows out of the medieval "conscience." Hamlet's soliloquies mark the beginning of modern consciousness. By 1599 when Shakespeare was rewriting *Hamlet* he'd developed a keen sense of his audience. Folk philosophy was good enough for theater, better than sophisticated theology, so Shakespeare began to form the idea of a new Ghost. People love ghost stories, and he knew every person in the audience had multiple expectations. He needed a ghost that had something for everybody. Even him, because he himself would be playing the Ghost.[12]

Now what kind of ghost? A Catholic ghost? That type of ghost comes to confess and scourge itself and beg prayers of the living. A purgatorial ghost is already a saved soul, how ever tormented. But a saved Christian cannot call for private revenge. Protestants insist all ghosts are demons, and there's no Purgatory in Elizabeth's church. Supernatural beings aren't the residua of human beings that once lived, they're astral spirits or simulacra of humans, but they never lived, *they were never human*. But the Protestant God does permit demons to come and trick the unwary, the careless, into tests of virtue where you might lose your soul. Horatio and Marcellus are frantic to stop Hamlet following the Ghost, but he pushes them aside.

Hamlet Why, what should be the fear?
I do not set my life at a pin's fee.
And for my soul—what can it do to that,
Being a thing immortal as itself?

I.iv.64 TLN 653–656

The Elizabethan audience gasps. They know what a demon "can do to that." There was a kind of accepted catechism in Latin, by a scholar like Horatio for counter-tricking the demon to make it reveal its ghastly aims. A good Christian—humble, prayerful, faithful—would be able to tell human from inhuman, perceive evil, defeat demons. Hamlet is proud and impulsive. He's nearly crazed and hasn't the cool head and pure heart it takes to dicker with the devil.

What about ghosts in folklore? They might be lovers betrayed, returning to punish infidelity. Another would be familiar to the audience, the ghost as omen, seen before assassination, natural calamity, or war. This is the Ghost when it first appears to the soldiers. What about classical notions of the afterlife? In the pagan scheme, a ghost fits with Senecan revenge tragedy acting within a tradition of private revenge. This works well in Shakespeare's reworked *Hamlet* because Hamlet goes back and forth between pagan and Christian sensibilities all through the play. The classical ghost is from a pagan afterlife, the underworld familiar to university students; they know which frame of reference Hamlet is in at any given moment: In his classical mode, he refers to Fortune—in his Christian mode, he speaks of Providence.

So Shakespeare creating his Ghost is using all these types. By raising questions about the Ghost, *Hamlet* forces the audience to experience doubt. Critics and psychoanalysts must try to reduce doubt, but what if uncertainty is the point, what if leaving the question open is the keystone in the arch of dramaturgy? Hamlet, like all of us facing death, "parses every affirmation by the grammar of doubt."[13]

Doubt becomes a whole sub-school in *Hamlet* studies. If he wants his Ghost to be a Senecan ghost calling for private revenge, he will have it—but he also gives the Ghost some spirit of justice, calling for public revenge in pay for Claudius's usurpation. The Ghost in *Hamlet* is all these—a vademecum ghost, Catholic-purgatorial in origin, Protestant-demonic in form, and a great thrill for the groundlings and the gentry.

Finally, and most powerfully, Shakespeare wrote a Ghost that is the perfect jilted lover, lifelike in its self-absorption, self-pity, and penchant for stalking. While few in the audience would have first hand experience with starry portents or public revenge, most could recall the lash of sexual jealousy. And would identify with the Ghost's feelings of uxorious protectiveness, alternating with savage hatred.

Ghost Let not the royal bed of Denmark be
A couch for luxury and damned incest.

> But—howsoever thou pursues this act —
> Taint not thy mind, nor let thy soul contrive
> Against thy mother aught. Leave her to heaven
> And to those thorns that in her bosom lodge
> To prick and sting her. Fare thee well at once.
> . . . Adieu, adieu, Hamlet. Remember me.
>
> *I.v.82* TLN 767–776

The Ghost displays the same sexual cruelty that Hamlet shows toward Gertrude and Ophelia. The prick is for hurting the woman, a serpent to sting but not to pleasure her. The Ghost rages, yet the son is supposed to protect the mother.

One last aspect of this Ghost remains, and that is its liturgical roots. At the time of Shakespeare's birth there were people alive who had seen the morality play *Everyman*, and it lived on in folklore and cultural memory: God sends his servant Death to fetch every man. *Everyman, stand still. Whither art thou going thus gaily? Hast thou thy Maker forgot?* Everyman wails, *O Death, thou comest when I had thee least in mind.* He faces the unprepared death suffered by King Hamlet and feared by Hamlet. Terrified but thinking fast, he negotiates a delay in the summons—long enough for Everyman to whip and scourge himself penitentially so that he goes to Purgatory and not to hell.

Elizabethan drama grew out of medieval religious plays, and Nighan says that "it does not demean the play to view it as a sophisticated morality play exploring the mystery of a Divine Providence that allows evil to flourish . . . for a greater good." He sees in the visitations of the Ghost the snares of a malevolent demon which echoes the great Tempter of the morality plays. And, indeed, the Ghost leads Hamlet into peril of his soul. It's not from a pagan hell but from the Christian one, a demon sent by God to test Hamlet's faith by trying to damn his soul.[14]

Another argument for the tempter Ghost is Eleanor Prosser's study of revenge tragedy. But hers is not sent by heaven (which she would consider heretical), hers is from hell. For her the play is about an evil spirit taking gradual possession of Hamlet and leading him along into damnation. Temptations undermine his moral struggle and encourage pride and false certainty. His moral dilemma "resolved" in the end, Hamlet drifts inexorably down to evil. She claims the Ghost's second appearance serves "only one purpose: not to lead Gertrude to Heaven but to leave her to Hell." Noting the Ghost keeps itself invisible to the Queen, Prosser reasons that if it had shown itself to her, she would know Hamlet is sane, not mad. Also, if the Ghost showed itself, Gertrude would learn facts about Claudius and have the option to know the truth, if she had the courage to face it. This Ghost cannot, Prosser says, be a spirit of Grace, since Christian love would compel it to materialize. It would have to show itself to her to give the option for salvation and ultimately preserve the one person she loves most, Hamlet.[15]

Prosser's erudition is impressive, her theology impeccable, her fairness exemplary. But, like flinty-eyed Wilson Knight, she wins few friends among sentimental Hamlet lovers. Her view is that the play's purpose is to help the audience struggle with the agonizing complexity of moral dilemmas. On the moral obligation of Hamlet to refuse the Ghost's command, she is severe, "the command to murder is as malign as we sense it to be, and Hamlet himself is responsible for his descent into savagery." Her brilliant theological and literary research notwithstanding, we will ultimately come to a different conclusion about the true nature of the Ghost.

Freud uses the Ghost to illustrate the phenomenon of "the uncanny." His word for it translates as *unhomely*, but it equally encompasses the homely, the familiar. It's this antinomy, this dual nature, that's key to the uncanny. It's only the familiar that *can* be uncanny. In as much as strange things can be terrifying, still they lack that creepy feeling that occurs when the familiar suddenly becomes alien. The skin crawls and "each particular hair" stands on end.

Themes of the return of the dead are fertile ground for the uncanny but they don't always produce it; many uncanny things have nothing to do with death. "The souls in Dante's *Inferno*, or the supernatural apparitions in . . . *Hamlet*, *Macbeth*, or *Julius Caesar*, may be gloomy and terrible enough, but they are no more really uncanny than Homer's jovial world of gods." Freud says the uncanny only happens when something *secretly familiar* undergoes repression and then returns.

> An uncanny effect is . . . produced when the distinction between imagination and reality is effaced, as when something that we have hitherto regarded as imaginary appears before us in reality, or when a symbol takes over the full function of the thing it symbolizes.[16]

Primitive mental operations underlie the uncanny: Infantile fears and wishes, when the familiar becomes uncanny by disclosing previously disowned sexual and aggressive impulses beneath. And, the uncanny can emerge from old discarded cultural superstitions when they suddenly seem to become real. Magical belief in the omnipotence of thoughts, the lethality of wishes, and the ability of the dead to walk again are productive of the uncanny. These turn out to be similar to primitive impulses repressed into the individual unconscious.

Freud is dead wrong about the Ghost not being uncanny. It is—Shakespeare made the Ghost both familiar and unfamiliar. The audience seeing a multi-purpose ghost can relate to one or more of its cultural ancestors. It's familiar *qua* ghost. And the audience can identify with Hamlet in his first encounter with the Ghost when he sees a familiar figure turn strange. A king in full armor speaks, not with the deep voice of authority and command but in the whiny, shrill, strangled voice of terror and shame. Later, in Gertrude's closet, Hamlet sees the strange become familiar. The Ghost assumes the image of Hamlet's father in his familiar nightgown. It repeats its familiar command. Then it becomes strange again in its eerie departure—not like a king's royal leave-taking, but abrupt, furtive, weak. Even if the Ghost were not manifestly uncanny, the audience would still believe it is to Hamlet because that's how he acts. We see his gooseflesh, his "knotted and combined locks" standing on end.

The uncanny happens "when a symbol takes over the full function of the thing it symbolizes," when it becomes concrete and all too real. The Ghost encompasses the whole mystery that it stands for: *What is death, and what happens after*?

	Enter Ghost [in his night-gown: Q1]
Hamlet	Save me and hover o'er me with your wings, You heavenly guards—What would your gracious figure?
Gertrude	Alas he's mad.
Hamlet	Do you not come your tardy son to chide, That lapsed in time and passion lets go by The important acting of your dread command? O say!
Ghost	Do not forget, this visitation Is but to whet thy almost blunted purpose — But look—amazement on thy mother sits! O step between her and her fighting soul — Speak to her, Hamlet.
Hamlet	How is it with you lady?
Gertrude	Alas how is't with you That you do bend your eye on vacancy And with the incorporeal air do hold discourse?
Hamlet	. . . On him, on him, look you how pale he glares! Do you see nothing there?
Gertrude	Nothing at all. . . .
Hamlet	Nor did you nothing hear?
Gertrude	No—nothing but ourselves.
Hamlet	Why look you there—look how it steals away, My father in his habit as he lived. Look where he goes, even now out at the portal!

III.iv.83 TLN 2482–2519

With the final appearance of the Ghost, Hamlet does at last have an unambiguous command to obey, and he does "step between her and her fighting soul." William Flesch spots the real source of the homely from which this scene's uncanny emerges—the familiar nuclear family where

> in Gertrude's room . . . the eeriness of this moment comes from the strangeness of the reconstituted family relationship. The play's last, impotent generosity is to make possible the parent-child relationship that had been lacking until this moment—to make it possible even as it becomes impossible.[17]

Gertrude's horror at her son hallucinating magnifies his horror realizing she can't see the Ghost. Flesch says this is the only scene in all of Shakespeare with the oedipal triangle alone onstage together—what might be the most paradigmatic scene of all in the family romance—but with the mother terrified, the child possibly insane, and the father dead. Familiar becoming un-*familiar*, but *in the family*, Freud's basic recipe for the uncanny.

Through four centuries, the nature of the Ghost has been more problematic than any character except Hamlet. The others, Gertrude, Claudius, Polonius, Laertes, Ophelia, all grow and change through the play, all deepen in complexity. But they are two dimensional. The Ghost is the one other three-dimensional character besides Hamlet. Shaw called the Ghost's part "one of the wonders of the play" and said Shakespeare "would not trust anyone else with it, and played it himself" for that reason.[18]

The plausibility of the first act of the play depends on the Ghost's being a complex character. Its revelations get the audience's attention, but something else gives the Ghost dramatic force. Hamlet and the audience already suspected Claudius; Hamlet already hated the marriage and hasty succession; Hamlet already was disgusted with Gertrude; and Hamlet already was obsessed with death. Even without "foul and most unnatural murder" and "forged process of my death," jealousy is sufficient to carry the motivation of revenge. The Ghost's exhortation for Hamlet to avenge his father's murder is followed by a more emotional charge concerning Gertrude. Even if we remove from the script the hundred words relevant to the murder, we still find the Ghost compelling. Its bitterness over an unprepared death, jealousy, disgust with Claudius all make emotional sense. Hamlet doesn't follow the Ghost's commands because he hears Claudius is a murderer. He does it because emotion is contagious. He was already jealous.

What is it, really, that makes the Ghost so powerful? It must have something to do with Shakespeare's craft in fashioning a character that has so few lines, so little time onstage—yet spans every dimension, including *the question of what it is to be human*. Second guessing the Ghost is one of the four or five major preoccupations of *Hamlet* studies. Scholars have tried to imagine themselves in Shakespeare's audience to answer questions of what actual Elizabethans would know or not know, feel or not feel. But practical critics retort, Shakespeare *intended* his audience to assume this is in fact the spirit of his father, Shakespeare *intended* his audience to believe Hamlet should avenge his father's death, and they should *want* him to do just that.

And truly, through the centuries, haven't audiences done exactly that? Haven't they mostly started off believing the Ghost is Hamlet's father, mostly accepted at the outset that Hamlet should avenge his father, and mostly cheered Hamlet on in his efforts? Early on they hear the Ghost characterize murder as "most foul, as in the best it is." But they don't consciously register the phrase "as in the best it is," to mean *murder, even for the best reason, is still a sin.* That realization develops gradually, so *Hamlet* evolves into a morality play. This is *the central reason for Hamlet's procrastination*: Deep in his heart he knows revenge is a sin.

Over the whole of *Hamlet*, doubt about the identity of the Ghost and the justice of revenge must wax and wane in the audience. On a subliminal level, the audience is feeling, *I believed it was his father, now I'm not so sure.* And then, *I thought the issue of revenge was simple, but apparently it's more complex*. Doubts commingle and increase up until the second and final coming of the Ghost. This event is climactic not only because the action accelerates and emotions peak, but it's a climax in the Aristotelian sense. Elements of the plot now are irreversibly changed. This is the last time the Ghost is ever seen. It's loomed over the whole play and suddenly it vanishes. From here on—mid-play—nobody mentions the Ghost. Not once.

Why did the Ghost appear precisely at this moment? The Ghost and Hamlet take for granted he needs a push to get on with revenge. Like a guilty child, Hamlet's contrite for having "lapsed in time and passion." The Ghost agrees before Hamlet can even complete his confession. It's come to sharpen Hamlet's "almost blunted purpose." Again before it can complete the thought, the Ghost interrupts itself and involuntarily cries out for Gertrude's pain. It's here that we're finally sure the Ghost has a human soul. This pivotal moment seems so simple, so natural. The interplay of Hamlet's and the Ghost's lines show two *human souls* in agony.

When the Ghost makes its final appearance, there are changes in Hamlet's forms of address. Before, it was *thee* and *thou* for the Ghost. Now, for the first time, Hamlet uses the pronouns of respect he would have used with his father in life (. . . *your* . . . *your* . . . *your* . . .). Hamlet is now speaking to the Ghost as to a human being. The Ghost addresses Hamlet with the familiar pronoun an Elizabethan parent would use with a child (. . . *thy* . . . *thy* . . .) and they speak together as father and son. Hamlet refers to the retreating figure of the Ghost as *my father. . . . his. . . he . . . he. . . .* Hamlet finally acknowledges the Ghost to be his human father.

There's a change in Hamlet after the Ghost's final exit. Hamlet was violent, chaotic—now he is reorganized, focused. And now he does take the Ghost's words to be his father's command: He immediately tries to comfort his mother. It's uncertain whether the Ghost has come to spur Hamlet's revenge or whether it really comes to protect Gertrude. But the Ghost materializes just as Gertrude begs Hamlet for mercy a third time. It's not like Shakespeare to ask us to believe the Ghost came about revenge and at this precise moment just happened on this poisonous scene. Gertrude had been in fear of her life. The audience might doubt Hamlet would kill her, but the lovesick Ghost is taking no chances. The Ghost doesn't know much about young Hamlet, nor much cares. But lack of fatherly concern for Hamlet doesn't subtract from the Ghost's husbandly protectiveness, which seems very human.

Shakespeare has created as his Ghost a destructive narcissist. It contains a powerful death instinct, it harbors its own demon. But even in the first appearance, the Ghost suddenly protects Gertrude—*nor contrive against thy mother aught.* This unexpected flash of love is like the little gleam of libido deep in the destructive narcissist that the psychoanalysts are looking for, the starting point for a cure. If the Ghost were simply a Protestant demon—by definition a spirit that never was human—canonically it couldn't simulate the human immortal soul flawlessly. The Ghost is a patchwork of many types of Elizabethan demons, astral spirits, supernatural beings, so it has aspects of all of them when it makes dramatic sense. But dramatically or theologically it's nonsense for a pure demon to perfectly simulate a lovesick husband.

The Ghost is a case study of the destructive narcissists of Freud, Klein, Rosenfeld, and Rush. The Ghost is possessed by its own demons of envy, grandiosity, contempt—subverting, seducing, tainting, torturing—but the Ghost is also being challenged by libido, the life instinct, passionate love for Gertrude. This is not Prosser's malevolent spirit, it cannot be all bad, we cannot believe it is completely evil. This Ghost possesses a vicious mole of nature that tries to poison the whole. This is a very human Ghost, one of Shakespeare's great characters. Yes, there is evil, yes the death instinct wants to infect the son too. But a goblin born in hell cannot love, by definition. Evil is the absence of love.

But most telling, it's impossible to believe that a character without humanity could speak such magnificent poetry. Though possessed, the Ghost is quintessentially human, a solution that's satisfying on all levels—artistic, dramatic, poetic, theological, philosophical, and psychological. The character that Shakespeare wrote for himself in his time of loss of a son and impending death of a father is a dual creation of astonishing power and beauty. It is the true spirit of King Hamlet and, simultaneously, the Ghost is an ambassador of death.

So at last the fatal match. The weapons are brought, Hamlet takes the nearest, Laertes tries one or two more. Claudius says if Hamlet hits Laertes in the first exchanges, "the King shall drink to Hamlet's better breath." He'll drop a fabulous "union" or pearl into the goblet for Hamlet's honor while the cannon salute. Immediately Hamlet scores a hit, and the court murmurs excitedly. The cannon trumpets sound and the King drops the poisoned pearl into the toasting cup. He tries to hand the chalice to Hamlet, who refuses to drink yet and calls for the second bout. Hamlet makes another quick hit. Claudius tells Gertrude "our son shall win," and she excitedly seizes the poisoned chalice and raises it to toast her son. Claudius shouts, "Gertrude, do not drink!" But she ignores him and Claudius in an agonized aside says, "It is the poisoned cup. It is too late."

In the third round Hamlet jokes that Laertes is not thrusting seriously but just flirting. Laertes bristles at Hamlet's quip. Time is called, Hamlet lowers his foil and starts to turn away, but Laertes lunges and wounds him. Foul! Hamlet looks at his wound in disbelief. Realizing Laertes's weapon is unblunted, Hamlet attacks. He knocks the poisoned foil from Laertes's hand, seizes it, wounds Laertes, "They bleed on both sides," Horatio says. Laertes gasps as he falls, "I am justly killed with mine own treachery" because the "foul practice/ Hath turned itself on me." In the confusion, the Queen falls. Claudius tries to cover over what's happening, but Gertrude with her last breath says, "The drink—the drink—O my dear Hamlet—drink—poisoned."

"Hamlet, thou art slain," Laertes says and, knowing he will be dead in minutes, confesses to the court standing transfixed: He and Claudius poisoned the tip of Laertes's weapon. He says, "No medicine in the world can do thee good./ In thee there is not half an hour's life." Hamlet looks at the foil he now holds. "The point envenomed too?/ Then venom, to thy work!" Hamlet runs Claudius through. "Here thou incestuous, murderous, damned Dane." Hamlet forces wine from the poisoned cup down the King's throat. "Drink off this potion—is thy union here?"

The dying Laertes is reconciled with Hamlet, they exchange forgiveness, and Hamlet blesses him, "Heaven make thee free" from the sin of his dishonorable plot with Claudius. "I follow thee," Hamlet says, and Laertes dies. But Hamlet is weakening. "I am dead, Horatio. Wretched Queen, adieu."

So, what's the final word on the Oedipus complex? Certainly Freud never doubted it. In the last year of his life, in a valedictory mood, he circled back one last time to

> another dramatic hero, Shakespeare's procrastinator, Hamlet. . . . I venture to say that if psycho-analysis could boast of no other achievement than the discovery of the repressed Oedipus complex, that alone would give it a claim to be included among the precious new acquisitions of mankind.[19]

Jones seconds Freud but has to misread the play to do it, accusing Hamlet of oedipally neurotic blindness and, most unfairly, of "intellectual cowardice, that reluctance to dare the exploration of his inmost soul." But he can't wipe away the fact that Hamlet *doesn't hesitate* to stab Claudius when he thinks the lump behind the arras is the King.[20]

Among the precious new acquisitions of mankind? Is Hamlet acting out against his father in an oedipal way? Is there evidence of the universal rivalry of son against father that Freud thought he discerned? Yes, there is a passive-aggressive flavor to Hamlet's behavior; he could be construed as the foot-dragging son—until the second appearance of the Ghost. But after he obeys the Ghost's command to comfort Gertrude, everything Hamlet does from then on is because he chooses, not because he's recalling old King Hamlet's command. After the Ghost's exit, Hamlet completely stops remembering him. And is it because he has repressed murderous wishes toward his father and incestuous desire for his mother? No, it's because he's done fighting his father's battles. It's not just Hamlet's delay that's pertinent to oedipal aggression, it's the erasure of all traces of his father. Not only does the Ghost completely disappear from the play in the middle of the play, there's no further reference to old Hamlet *as father*. Gone is the extravagant idealization, gone the bitter grieving—never to be seen again.

What of Freud's idea that fear of castration makes the son identify with the father, his values, his prohibitions? Hamlet doesn't seem castrated. Freud's recipe for the oedipal triangle isn't just son toward mother, not just son versus father. All three points, all three sides, define the Oedipus complex. Son fights with father over mother. And while Hamlet does renounce his mother, it's not to leave her to King Hamlet. As for Claudius, Hamlet has taken Gertrude from him by the middle of the play and at the end hands her back like a discarded vessel.

After the Closet scene, even in the final catastrophe when Hamlet is getting revenge, no mention is made of old Hamlet, no dedication of the act in his memory, no explanation to the court that Hamlet is avenging him. And when Hamlet kills Claudius, where does he send him? "Follow my mother." The smooth arc of remembering and avenging King Hamlet is left hanging, castrated and incomplete. The audience should also be subliminally aware of an afterimage: The Ghost had full armor and a heavy broadsword, Hamlet has won with a whippy little foil and a poisoned cup. As Garber points out, swords and cups are ancient symbols for male and female, leaving Hamlet identified with his mother.

So the verdict on Hamlet's Oedipus complex? Freud's favorite theory is too simple to capture the ambiguity, fluidity, and nuance in Hamlet's dynamic unconscious. It's plausible as one of the reasons Hamlet delays—and, then, only in the first half of the play. There are grossly incestuous aspects of Hamlet's posture toward Gertrude. And transference to Ophelia. And there are male-male competitive issues between Hamlet and other men—Claudius, Polonius, the gravemaker—along with Laertes and Fortinbras, young men also bent on avenging their fathers. But the Prince loves a contest for its own sake. Hamlet struggles against them for dominance in every sense, not just over a woman. And words are his favorite weapons. What's more, Hamlet seals his personal victory in the end when he passes his father's crown—and Claudius's—to Fortinbras, son of old King Hamlet's mortal enemy. Hamlet has for a few moments the Danish empire in his gift, and he bestows it on his brother prince.

Hamlet Had I but time . . . O I could tell you —
But let it be. Horatio, I am dead,
Thou livest—report me and my causes right. . . .
Horatio Never believe it,
I am more an antique Roman than a Dane —
Here's yet some liquor left.
Hamlet As thou art a man,
Give me the cup, let go, by heaven—I'll have it.
O good Horatio, what a wounded name,
Things standing thus unknown, shall I leave behind me!
If thou did'st ever hold me in thy heart,
Absent thee from felicity awhile,
And in this harsh world, draw thy breath in pain
To tell my story—what warlike noise is this? *[march off]*
Osric Young Fortinbras, with conquest come from Poland.
Hamlet O I die, Horatio,
The potent poison quite o'er-crows my spirit.
I cannot live to hear the news from England
But I do prophesy the election lights
On Fortinbras. He has my dying voice,
So tell him — *[breaks off]*
The rest is silence.
Horatio Now cracks a noble heart. Good night, sweet Prince,
And flights of angels sing thee to thy rest.

V.ii.336 TLN 3820–3850

Is death stronger than love? The question from the undiscovered country remains unanswered. Here at the end, the only love that still lives on is the love of Horatio for the Prince. And even then, we wonder how long it will survive, how long the new king will suffer the continued existence of so honest a man as Horatio. As Fortinbras foreshadows, *Go. Bid the soldiers shoot.*

So with the final firing of the guns, Shakespeare has a termination of his own. With the close of *Hamlet* at the end the sixteenth century, Shakespeare moves beyond the medieval concept of personhood, he prepares for the end of the reign of Elizabeth Tudor, and he marks the birth of modern humanism. And, not incidentally, he prepares western culture for the theories of a different kind of genius three centuries later.

Notes

1. Sigmund Freud, "The Theme of the Three Caskets," in *The Standard Edition of the Complete Psychological Works of Sigmund Freud*, vol. 12, James Strachey, Ed. and trans. (London: The Hogarth Press, 1913/1958), 289–301.
2. Eric Sams, "Hamlet or Hamnet: That is the Question," *Hamlet Studies* 17 (1995): 94–98.
3. Sigmund Freud, "Beyond the Pleasure Principle," in *The Standard Edition of the Complete Psychological Works of Sigmund Freud*, vol. 18, James Strachey, Ed. and trans. (London: The Hogarth Press, 1920/1955), 1–64.
4. Herbert Rosenfeld, "A Clinical Approach to the Psychoanalytic Theory of the Life and Death Instincts: An Investigation into the Aggressive Aspects of Narcissism," *International Journal of Psycho-Analysis* 52 (1971): 169–178.
5. Stephen Greenblatt, *Hamlet in Purgatory* (Princeton, Princeton University Press, 2001).
6. Stephen Rush, "At One with Death: Destructive Narcissism," *Psychoanalytic Quarterly* 69 (2000): 711–740, 714–715.
7. Ibid, 738–739.
8. G. Wilson Knight, "The Embassy of Death: An Essay on *Hamlet*," in *The Wheel of Fire: Interpretations of Shakespearian Tragedy*, ed. 3, (1930/1949; reprint, London: Routledge, 2001), 17–49.
9. Ibid, 24, 35, 43.
10. John Russell, *Hamlet and Narcissus* (Newark: University of Delaware Press, 1995), 48.
11. G. Wilson Knight, "*Hamlet* Reconsidered" in *The Wheel of Fire: Interpretations of Shakespearian Tragedy*, ed. 3, (1930/1949; reprint, London: Routledge, 2001), 338–366.
12. Phoebe S. Spinrad, "The Fall of the Sparrow and the Map of Hamlet's Mind," *Modern Philology* 102 (2005): 453–477.
13. Harry Levin, *The Question of Hamlet* (New York: Viking Press, 1959), 43.
14. Raymond Nighan, *Hamlet and the Daemons: An Inquiry into the Nature of the Ghost and its Mission*. http://67.104.146.36/english/hamlet-new/foreworddone/introduction.html, accessed July 22, 2011.
15. Eleanor Prosser, *Hamlet and Revenge*, ed. 2 (Stanford: Stanford University Press, 1971), 200, 248.
16. Sigmund Freud, "The 'Uncanny,'" in *The Standard Edition of the Complete Psychological Works of Sigmund Freud*, vol. 17, James Strachey, Ed. and trans. (London: The Hogarth Press, 1919/1955), 219–252, 244.
17. William Flesch, *Generosity and the Limits of Authority: Shakespeare, Herbert, Milton* (Ithaca: Cornell University Press, 1992), 167.
18. George Bernard Shaw, "Hamlet," *The Saturday Review*, October 2, 1897, reprinted in *Shaw on Shakespeare*, Edwin Wilson, Ed. (New York: E.P. Dutton, 1961), 85–92.

19. Sigmund Freud, "An Outline of Psycho-Analysis: Psychoanalytic Work," in *The Standard Edition of the Complete Psychological Works of Sigmund Freud*, vol. 23, James Strachey, Ed. and trans. (London: The Hogarth Press, 1938/1964), 190–193.
20. Ernest Jones, *Hamlet and Oedipus* (New York: Doubleday Anchor Books, 1949), 113. K.R. Eissler, *Discourse on Hamlet and HAMLET: A Psychoanalytic Inquiry* (New York: International Universities Press, 1971).

A NOTE ON TEXTS AND SOURCES

Quotations of Freud are from *The Standard Edition of the Complete Psychological Works of Sigmund Freud*, translated and edited by James Strachey, London, Hogarth Press, 1955–1974. For *Hamlet* I've used Israel Gollancz and several other editions, especially Arden, Harold Jenkins for the 1604/1605 Second Quarto (Q2) and Ann Thompson and Neil Taylor for the 1603 "bad" First Quarto (Q1) and the First Folio of 1623 (F).

The *Enfolded Hamlet* of Bernice W. Kliman, 1996, has been indispensible (www.HamletWorks.org). In her conflation of Q2 and F, each line in the play is numbered by a system of consecutive "through line numbers" (TLNs) 1–3907. What's presented here as the text of *Hamlet* is an amalgam. Depending on what seems most accessible to the ear of a modern theater audience, *textual choices have been made on a line-by-line and word-by-word basis from a melded text* of Q2 and F.

I emphasize this because readers familiar with standard editions of the play may think I'm misquoting; but what's presented here is a mosaic constructed from the two texts intentionally edited to support a particular critical interpretation. It's argumentative but, so far as I can tell, it's what Shakespeare meant. In one instance I may drop a line or word from Q2, in another, a line or part of a line from F, in yet another, a line—or several—found in both. Omissions within a line are typically marked with ellipses. The First Quarto of 1603 has been used to resolve conflicts, usually in favor of playability. Through Line Numbers at the foot of passages quoted are keyed to Kliman's *Enfolded Hamlet* as well as traditional act/scene/line notation.

This version of *Hamlet* is a bit idiosyncratic, but there's method in it when read (especially aloud) with adjacent discussions. Above all, *Hamlet* should make sense as entertainment. Any *Hamlet* text ultimately comes from one of the three original published versions—1603, 1604, and 1623—or a conflation. They differ significantly. While there's no "correct" version, there seem to be dozens of flawed ones. Over the centuries, hundreds of interpretations have been debated by critics and editors. A reading of any line in the play is open to dispute. Any rendering of the plot is also subject to question. The version here is an alloy that envisions staging *Hamlet* for a modern audience. Spelling is updated to US English, and the punctuation of each line has been reinterpreted to square with my reading of the play. All ellipses are mine but any emphases within quotations are those of the original texts throughout.

One disclaimer: As a general hospital psychiatrist I'm not a professional academic Shakespeare scholar nor an institute-based psychoanalyst with candidate trainees, so I have to apologize for shorting both those specialized groups who need and deserve deeper review of their respective fields over the past decade or two. But for this book, the background is mainly what I consider the golden age of Shakespeare studies, Bradley to Bloom but generally stopping short of the work of new historicists and postmodernists and their successors. *Hamlet* is a long play and this is a long book; not everything in the two world literatures can be covered. Roughly coterminous with my "Shakespeare scholars of the golden age," the body of psychoanalytic theory cited here extends from Freud through Jacques Lacan but stops before neuro-psychoanalysis and critical advances in the neurosciences popularized by Mark Solms and others. Nor regrettably does it extend to the later postmodernists and their welcome and creative refashioning of philosophy and literature for today's academy (for which I especially recommend MIT's "Short Circuits" and Bloomsbury's "Arden Shakespeare and Theory" series).

The Droeshout portrait, photo Robert Zinck, 2013, is by permission of the Houghton Library from the Chauncey copy of the Folio of 1623 (f STC 22273). The Freud portrait is from the original negative, mounted and blind stamped *Max Halberstadt, Hamburg* circa 1921, by permission of the Library of Congress. The cover design/frontispiece are after Brendan K. Bathrick, *Telos* 153 (Winter 2010), adaptation by permission of Telos Press Publishing.

SELECTED FILMS OF *HAMLET*

Michael Almereyda (director, screen adaptation), Ethan Hawke. *Hamlet*. 113 minutes. New York: Miramax, 2000.

Kenneth Branagh (director, title role). *Hamlet*. 242 minutes. Culver City, CA: Castle Rock/Columbia, 1996.

Peter Brook (director, adaptation), Adrian Lester. *The Tragedy of Hamlet*. 132 minutes. Paris: ARTE France, 2001.

Gregory Doran (director), David Tennant. *Hamlet*. 182 minutes. London: BBC Home Entertainment, 2009.

John Gielgud (director), Richard Burton. *Hamlet*. 191 minutes. Burbank: Theatrofilm/ Warner Brothers, 1964.

Kevin Kline, Kirk Browning (directors). *Hamlet*. 173 minutes. New York: MMI Image Entertainment, Educational Broadcasting Corporation, 1990.

Laurence Olivier (director, title role, screenplay), Alan Dent (screenplay). *Hamlet*. 153 minutes. London: Two Cities Films, 1948.

Tony Richardson (director), Nicol Williamson. *Hamlet*. 114 minutes. Culver City: Filmways 1967/ Columbia, 1997.

Franco Zeffirelli (director, screenplay), Cristopher DeVore (screenplay), Mel Gibson. *Hamlet*. 135 minutes. Burbank: Warner Brothers, 1990.

INDEX